BUSINESS PLANS TO MANAGE DAY-TO-DAY OPERATIONS

WILEY SMALL BUSINESS EDITIONS

BUSINESS PLANS TO MANAGE DAY-TO-DAY OPERATIONS

Real-life Results for Small Business Owners and Operators

Christopher R. Malburg

John Wiley & Sons, Inc.

New York • Chichester • Brisbane • Toronto • Singapore

This book is dedicated to Marilyn. She's the one who truly believes, "why plan—it only gets in the way of what would have happened anyway!"

In recognition of the importance of preserving what has been written, it is a policy of John Wiley & Sons, Inc., to have books of enduring value printed on acid-free paper, and we exert our best efforts to that end.

Copyright © 1993 By Christopher R. Malburg
Published by John Wiley & Sons, Inc.

This publication is designed to provide accurate and authoritative information in regard to the subject matter covered. It is sold with the understanding that the publisher is not engaged in rendering legal, accounting, or other professional service. If legal advice or other expert assistance is required, the services of a competent professional person should be sought. From a *Declaration of Principles jointly adopted by a Committee of the American Bar Association and a Committee of Publishers.*

Library of Congress Cataloging-in-Publication Data:

Malburg, Christopher R.
    Business plans to manage day-to-day operations : real-life results for small business owners and operators / Christopher R. Malburg.
      p. cm.
    Includes index.
    ISBN 0-471-57296-9 (cloth). — ISBN 0-471-57299-3 (paper) [—Book/Disk Sets]
    1. Small business—Planning.   2. Small business—Management.
   3. Corporate planning. I. Title.
   HD62.7.M337 1993
   658.4'012—dc20   92-34809

Printed in the United States of America

10 9 8 7 6 5 4 3 2 1

Preface

Starting in the late 1980s and continuing into the 1990s, social, political, technological, and economic upheavals have become the rule rather than the exception. Anticipating these events and having a plan of action ready when they arrive represents a vision that separates business superstars from the rest of the field.

Entrepreneurs and small business managers constantly look for a profit edge. We need to foresee and correctly respond to shifts in the business environment. The lack of adequate business planning resources and the inability to mobilize correct responses to meet demands of a changing environment can leave a company in the dust of its competition faster than any other management oversight. No segment of business feels this more than small and medium-sized companies. Yet the often slim margin of error demands fast, accurate decisions that impact the company both today and tomorrow.

Business Plans to Manage Day-to-Day Operations provides an easily understandable guide through the minefield of business planning. The fat has been trimmed, leaving only the essentials required to lead you through the maze of goal-setting techniques, tactics, operations, and financial assessments necessary to navigate your firm through a shifting environment.

Care has been taken to choose those topics that answer the most relevant questions. Each chapter has been structured to present key issues, then deal with them clearly and concisely. *Business Plans to Manage Day-to-Day Operations* omits the often garbled fluff contained in academic tomes. Instead it tells you:

- Where to start to prepare a company plan
- How to integrate goals with your business operation as it stands today
- Who should be on the planning team
- How to motivate people to achieve the plan
- How to implement the plan
- How to keep the business on track with the plan

Planning should not be treated as an academic exercise. Time, especially that of small business managers, is at a premium. You've got better things to do than dream up pie-in-the-sky strategies. I promise not to waste your energy on things that won't help you.

Instead, we'll focus on where you want the business to go *in the next year or two*, how to get there, and what methods work best to track your progress.

You'll find the techniques presented are:

- Relevant to the business issues you face each day
- Easy to implement and track
- Predictable in their results
- Aimed at providing fast solutions

I hope your planning efforts are fruitful and this book helps you accomplish your objectives.

Wishing you luck and prosperity,

Chris Malburg

Contents

Introduction

WHAT THIS BOOK WILL DO FOR YOU

Today's entrepreneurs and small business executives face a world of unforgiving foreign competition, changing technological innovation, and shifting economic priorities. *Business Plans to Manage Day-to-Day Operations* provides three essential tools to control business planning in this hostile environment:

- Identification of company goals and assessment of future impacts from outside the company (Chapter 2)
- Formulation of a blueprint to execute the plan (Chapter 3)
- Control of the plan and essential mid-course corrections (Chapter 11)

Business Plans to Manage Day-to-Day Operations illustrates solutions to the special planning needs of small and medium-sized companies. Here are some of the things you will learn:

- How to recognize those planning decisions most likely to be successful and how to avoid those that will not (Chapter 1)
- How to assign the proper personnel to the planning team (Chapter 1)
- Ways to delegate planning responsibilities and establish accountability for the plan's success (Chapter 1)
- How to identify threats to your company and formulate an action-oriented response (Chapter 2)
- Specific techniques to identify the most productive organizational structure, human resources, and financial capacities (Chapter 2)
- How to discover gaps in your company's capability to meet its goals (Chapter 4)
- How to insulate the plan from uncertainty (Chapter 4)
- How to integrate a financial forecast into your business plan (Chapter 6)
- Clear-cut methods to simulate the effects of changes in the marketplace, then devise contingency plans (Chapter 10)

WHO CAN BENEFIT FROM THIS BOOK?

Business Plans to Manage Day-to-Day Operations has been specifically written for entrepreneurs and managers of small and medium-sized businessess. The ideas and methods described are geared to help busy people who have a company to run in addition to charting its success. The chances are good that you've already been involved in preparing a business plan. You may have even been responsible for preparing the initial business plan when your company was first established.

However, planning how to spend someone else's money is much different from spending your own. Business plans used for *selling* the concept of the company during startup often fall short of anticipating what occurs later in the real world.

Business Plans to Manage Day-to-Day Operations wasn't written just for managers. Those responsible for a single department are equally important. This book provides insight into the overall planning effort. It shows how the work of *everyone* involved in the planning process must coordinate to hit a common target.

The techniques illustrated in this book not only help you do your part of the plan better, they'll help you participate more effectively in the entire planning process.

HOW TO USE THE BOOK

Business Plans to Manage Day-to-Day Operations demonstrates the planning techniques most useful to small and medium-sized businesses. Additionally, the formulas, worksheets, and checklists aim at providing a continuous format for use *after* the plan has been created. In that sense, this is a reference book of considerable usefulness now and in the future; for the novice as well as those who have been through the process before.

First read the entire book. Even if you have already done some planning, chances are that you'll discover new ideas and formats for presenting targeted goals along with ways to implement and control the plan. Perhaps you'll want to concentrate first on the chapters most relevant to your own role in the plan. If your job is to put together manufacturing projections, for example, you'll probably want to begin at Chapter 5.

Next, refer back to particular sections of the book for help on specific topics. For example, the performance ratios can be used repeatedly for periodic checks on progress within the various departments.

CHAPTER SUMMARIES

Here are brief descriptions of what you'll find in each chapter.

Chapter 1: Manage Plan Development

Chapter 1 shows how to pull the diverse parts of a business plan together so that it all makes sense. Additionally, the chapter provides a means to assign responsibility and accountability to those who create, then execute the plan. Chapter 1 tells how to ensure that:

■ Proper control over the planning process is maintained
■ Managers intent on doing things their own way (or worse, the way it was always done) don't stifle creativity
■ Operating divisions work in concert with one another to achieve targets
■ Analysis paralysis over excessively detailed planning issues is not used as an excuse for wasting time

Chapter 2: Establish Company Goals

Chapter 2 answers the questions:

■ Where do we want to go?
■ What changes must we make to get there?

This section begins the planning process. We'll zero in on company goals. These are not the amorphous, so-called *strategic imperatives* found in the Fortune 100's long-range plans. Rather, they are specific targets that small businesses must hit in order to grow and prosper in the next year or two.

Chapter 3: Blueprint for Implementation

Chapter 3 presents a series of action steps for implementation of the plan using such techniques as:

■ Identification of specific actions required to meet each goal
■ Timing for each action step
■ Expected results at each milestone
■ Assignment of responsibility for the results of each action step

- Scheduling deadlines for action steps so that little time is lost waiting for completion of preceding critical items
- Choosing milestones that have the most impact

Chapter 4: Plan for Uncertainty

Plans will be wrong. That's expected. Chapter 4 demonstrates how to build enough flexibility into your business plans so departures due to uncertainty can be absorbed without affecting the overall outcome.

Uncertainty also requires that buffers be included in the plan for events beyond our control. Chapter 4 identifies the buffers needed to insulate the plan from uncertainty. Additionally, we'll devise contingency actions in the event that uncertain variables swing outside their *range of tolerable error*.

Chapter 5: Operations

Chapter 5 details the operational plan that tells managers what must be done in their particular department to achieve short-term objectives. Emphasis is placed on such practical control points as:

- Accountability for plan execution
- Benefits of centralized or decentralized planning and control
- Details such as how to treat intercompany sales and transfer pricing

Chapter 6: Finance—How Much Do We Need and When Do We Need It?

Chapter 6 illustrates creation of the financial plan. Results flow through the firm by department and onto the prospective financial statements. Chapter 6 demonstrates how to ensure that your goals and operational targets are translated into a single common denominator by:

- Distilling the operational plan into a set of projected financial statements and supporting schedules
- Developing a mechanism to compare actual performance against the plan each month

By using the techniques presented in this chapter, each department's operating goals can be plugged into the plan and examined to see how they further the company's overall objective.

Chapter 7: Benchmarks

There's no mystery to implementing the plan in small and medium-sized businesses. It does, however, require that a series of things be done in a particular sequence and by specific deadlines. Benchmarks are the yardsticks by which we measure the progress toward goals. Chapter 7 illustrates the methods used to establish meaningful performance benchmarks that track the plan's implementation timetable.

Chapter 8: Delegate Authority and Responsibility

Only by delegating both the *authority* to make decisions and the *responsibility* for their success can a company grow. Chapter 8 identifies the most likely positions within the company's various operating departments in which to delegate authority and responsibility for plan implementation. This chapter shows how to:

■ Establish a mechanism to identify the implementation steps that should be delegated
■ Make specific people responsible for achieving certain goals
■ Monitor the use of authority

Chapter 9: Performance Incentives

Everyone works for some sort of incentive. Chapter 9 shows how to design and operate a performance incentive system for plan implementation. The objective is twofold:

■ Create a reward structure that delivers incentives for meeting plan objectives to those responsible
■ Identify progress toward meeting objectives and obtaining a reward

Chapter 10: Design a Monitoring Mechanism

Chapter 10 shows how to establish a monitoring function that highlights deviations and provides for corrective action. Issues addressed include what information should be reported, how often, and to whom. The goal is to provide enough flexibility so managers don't waste their time on things not critical to the plan's implementation.

Chapter 11: Update the Plan

Regular updates keep the plan on track. Chapter 11 shows how to identify critical areas of the plan that must be assessed frequently to be sure they are still consistent with company goals.

PART I
CREATE THE PLAN

1

Manage Plan Development

OVERVIEW

Business plans are usually developed for three reasons:

■ *Communication of what you intend to do with the company to those outside the firm (such as lenders and investors).* These are little more than sales tools to demonstrate the *feasibility* of an idea. They are compiled from mathematical models by experts and are often included in the prospectus of a securities offering. The originators of these projections have little allegiance to the ultimate success of the plan. The business projections that result are often a function of untested theory and wishful thinking. Further, there is usually little emphasis on responsibility and accountability for plan results.

We won't be overly concerned with trying to communicate our intentions to outsiders. However, the fact that you've created a viable operating plan *can* be used to help cement things like lending decisions. Indeed, the very fact that you can demonstrate successful past implementation of your business plan is usually more than most lenders or investors are ever provided.

■ *Focus on strategy.* Strategic decisions include issues such as the type of businesses in which the company wants to compete over the next decade. Strategic plans are less useful to the workaday small business executive than to the corporate mogul. It's true that strategies are important to forward-thinking, aggressive companies. These larger firms have both the management and financial resources to test different strategies and see which works best.

We won't spend excessive time on strategy formulation. It doesn't help the immediate bottom line so important to the entrepreneur and small business executive. Rather, strategic plans function as global roadmaps that chart the company's general direction over a long period of time. Small businesses can go bankrupt by then.

3

■ *Operational benchmarks.* These are much more useful for our purposes. Particular individuals are made responsible for specific results. Benchmarks provide a blueprint to get the company from point A to point B.

Entrepreneurs and the managers of small and medium-sized companies need to know the answers to prosaic questions such as:

■ How can increased sales levels for next season affect our ability to raise needed working capital?
■ What kind of investment in inventory is required to meet the additional demand our sales force intends to create?
■ How should our purchasing terms and accounts payable policy be changed to accommodate the added strain on our cash resources?

The objective is to take the company from its present position, put it in gear, and drive it toward management's targets one or two years down the road. The process is precise. We'll clearly define our goals. Responsibility for achieving milestones along the way gets placed squarely on the shoulders of specific individuals. Managers are held accountable for their performance against the plan. Indeed, those three elements of the planning process—clearly defined goals, responsibility, and accountability—are what makes this real-life approach to creating workable business plans so successful.

Management theorists might look down their noses at us, saying "You're only doing budgets." They might continue, "Anyone can hit short-term targets by practicing a *hold-management's-feet-to-the-fire style.*" "Where's the challenge," they'll finally ask. Let them.

The point is that few small business owners as well as executives of larger enterprises have any control over where they're going in the long run. Their worries center on the real-life problems facing their companies next month and at year-end. Small businesses need to identify short-term targets and draw together a team within the company that can hit the bull's-eye. The idea is that if you reach these short-term goals, those farther out over the horizon will take care of themselves. You are happy, your managers are happy, and so are your investors and lenders.

Further, these short-term successes provide a cushion allowing time to gaze into the future and formulate a grand strategy. Except by then you'll be so skilled from our short-range target practice that the longer-term strategies become just another extension of the same process. Many of the principles illustrated here can be applied to the more distant future with equal success.

PLANNING TECHNIQUES

Few people would waste the gas or the time hopping into their cars with little idea of where they wanted to go. The same holds true for running your company. When you get to work each morning, chances are you have a list (maybe mental, but still a list) of the things you need to accomplish that day. During the course of the day, you manage your time. Maybe you take minutes allocated for other things to work on particularly stubborn problems. Sometimes you skip lunch. Too often, you work late. All this is directed toward meeting the short-term goals you established early in the morning *for that day.*

This illustrates the process by which we're going to create a real-life business plan:

- You identified your targets—in this case, they were the things you wanted to accomplish that day.
- You probably delegated some of the work to others who could help you meet your goals.
- You made decisions throughout the day regarding how you were doing according to your plan. Later, we'll call this time continuum the *planning horizon.* Maybe you made mid-course corrections (remember skipping lunch?) in order to meet your goals.
- The quality of your work was evaluated each step of the way to be sure you accomplished what you wanted.

You didn't just sit down and start working at 8 A.M. (or earlier, as so many of us do). You had a plan. You knew where you were going and how you were going to get there. You prioritized the tasks. You recruited competent people to help. By the end of the day, your checklist was completed.

However, you unconsciously did some other things that greatly helped the process:

- There was a single person in charge of the whole effort who had a vested interest in seeing the plan succeed—*you!*
- Responsibility for each task was executed by someone capable of doing what was required—again, you. If you needed outside help, you got it.
- Your one-person *plan implementation team* was held accountable for meeting the deadlines and for the quality of the work—again, probably you or a few others.

Our short-term plan for the entire business is no different. Our methods employ each of these techniques. The added complexity derives from the increased number of people involved. I should also add that the inevitable variety of personalities involved in determining goals and mapping the route to meet them also increases the difficulty of the project.

Just as you wouldn't hop in the car and drive aimlessly around, neither would you run your company without an objective. Businesses, and the people who operate them, need to be guided by a central goal. Managers understand how their particular function fits into the grand scheme of things. They feel a commitment to the group's success. Peer pressure and commitment to the team's common goals are far better motivators than threats or financial incentives.

USE OF THE PLAN

We've all seen entrepreneurs and small business owners complain that their companies are *market driven*. That is, they can only react to changes in the marketplace and try to minimize the damage. Their reasoning is that they are too small to influence the much larger market. They say they are at the mercy of the multinational corporate giants against which they must compete.

However, most companies—regardless of size or competition—have the ability to manipulate their own destiny. Indeed, lack of size is often used as an excuse to avoid planning and controlling the company. When effective short-range planning techniques are used, there are several immediate spin-offs:

- The entire management team focuses and agrees on those things the company needs to do in the near future to achieve maximum profitability.
- Specific targets are established along the way *for each critical department*.
- Everyone knows how they are performing against the plan.
- Response to changes in the market or assumptions that later proved incorrect are implemented *while they still have a chance to do some good*.

If you don't believe in the importance of getting the management team focused on a common goal, hear what Stuart Sloan, chairman of Egghead Software, Inc., the nation's largest software retailer, said to me about his company's planning efforts:

> *We're just beginning now to start planning the business. The first step was getting the management team to think about*

common goals and what we need to do to become more profitable. It's not yet even the planning document that's important. At this early stage, it's the communication and teamwork *that I want to see.*

Egghead started out with just a few retail outlets, but grew very rapidly. Sloan's emphasis on his management team's communication and coordination is more indicative of a business a tenth the size of Egghead. Nevertheless, this entrepreneurial focus continues to work.

THE CONCEPT OF A PIPELINE

Think of your business plan as a manufacturing pipeline that receives raw materials and spits out a finished product. Here are the input items that go into your plan:

- Talent from your managers and employees
- Capital
- Inventories of raw materials
- Assessment of short-range market changes
- Prediction of competitive responses to your firm's actions

The planning mechanism grinds through these input items. The process involves:

- Determining your profit objectives
- Working backward from there to derive specific department goals that, when achieved, meet your profit goals
- Assessment of the company's resources, such as human and financial assets

Out of the process comes the identification of:

- Changes that must be made in property, plant, and equipment
- Adjustments in human resources (either up or down) that provide know-how needed to meet the goals
- Financial resources that must be obtained (or repaid) so that the right amount of money is available when needed by the company
- Indicators that tell the team how they are doing individually and how the company is doing as a whole

The plan displays the products or services the company sells in terms of units, sales, and revenue. The results are quantified in terms of profit and as return on the investment required.

STRUCTURE OF THE PLAN

Planning is one part of the management equation many of us have heard preached in school. The complete equation included:

- Planning
- Organizing
- Leading
- Controlling

Each of these areas are used to structure the planning process (see Table 1-1). Take a look at the manager's need to *organize* his or her department or job. The planning process goes a long way toward accomplishing that goal. The plan provides a time-frame by which to establish specific benchmarks for performance. The task of the manager is to organize his or her work around meeting those goals as they come up.

The second part of the plan structure involves *leading* those responsible for both creating the plan and executing it. Small businesses have an advantage over their larger counterparts. The smaller the company, the easier it is for everyone to see the common goals. Further, and even more important, the firm's progress toward those goals is more readily determined.

Feedback does a lot to motivate people toward action. People who receive positive reinforcement for success want more. They'll try that much harder to continue receiving praise. The acclaim may come from the planning team leader, other members of the team, or just from the self-satisfaction of watching their efforts create a positive effect. Whatever the source of feedback, the plan must be structured to provide it accurately and in a positive and timely manner.

Not only must the plan leader get the right people on the team, but he or she must influence their actions. This influence propels people to work toward meeting the plan goals. Certainly part of the influence an effective leader exerts comes from personal skills, for example, the ability to convince people that you know what you're doing and they'll be better off by following you. The other part of this motivation comes from a more formalized reward structure. Chapter 9 deals with this subject in detail.

When you structure your business plan, the incentive for performance must evolve right along with it. It's usually best if this develops in the beginning. The sooner the team reaches its peak motivation for working on the plan, the better.

The third part of the plan structure has to do with *control*. We'll assume that the planning team has been properly selected—they arrive already possessing the tools to do the job. Without the right

Table 1–1 The Planning Structure

Organize the planning team

- Select the right team members
- Delegate specific responsibilities for meeting the plan goals
- Hold the team accountable for success of the plan
- Give them the authority to do their jobs
- Establish deadlines and stick to them
- Determine performance standards and make sure everyone understands them

Lead the planning team

- Structure decision-making authority
- Team members participate in key decisions
- Ultimate authority rests with the team leader
- Communicate decisions and their results
- Identify the impact of decisions on team members' activities
- Motivate team members
- Structure feedback so it's timely and accurate

Control the plan

- Structure controls to *guide*, not chaperone
- Clearly define targets to track the progress of the plan
- Measure performance of the team and its members
- Evaluate performance
- Communicate the impact of performance to the members
- Make adjustments as needed to compensate for performance

people, the project has failed before it starts. Further, let's assume the team is motivated and takes responsibility for success of the plan. They *own* the plan. Under these conditions, control becomes a productivity enhancer.

The purpose of control is to guide the plan and the team. It's not done to make sure everyone is doing his or her job—if the team is motivated and competent, that won't be necessary. Instead, the control exerted by the team leader is used to help the members do their jobs *better*. Even more important, control is used to coordinate the many different operations of the plan that must work together. Often people concentrate so hard on their own areas of responsibility, they loose sight of the overall objective. Effective control by the leader keeps everyone on track.

Timing

As with any process, planning takes place over a period of time. Timing is one of the most important tools your business plan provides. As a manager, you want to see how the company's performance is tracking against the plan. You need to know when critical items are needed—such as capital. The only way to do that is by knowing where you are supposed to be at a given point in time.

From a control standpoint, you'll identify specific performance deadlines for each department throughout the plan. As the deadlines approach, the likelihood of success or failure can be seen. In the event that goals won't be met, there are contingency actions already provided by the plan.

Usually each department affects the success or failure of its counterparts. If a major milestone was missed by, say, the head of finance failing to secure the required line of credit, other provisions must be made. A possible solution might be lengthening purchasing terms. As long as these contingencies are implemented, the plan stays on track.

MEMBERS OF THE PLANNING TEAM

The purpose of the plan is to determine *where* your company needs to go, how it's going to get there, and what needs to be done along the way to be sure the plan stays on track. These objectives require that particular people be involved from the start.

Managers reading this book who work for large companies may wonder about the utility of a planning staff. These staff specialists are a luxury usually afforded only by larger firms. The planning staff doesn't work at making the product sold to the company's customers. Nor are they accountable for making their plan happen. Instead, they're highly paid scribes and accountants—overhead, in other words.

For small and medium-sized businesses, I don't recommend the use of a planning staff. Instead, your planning team should include those people who are responsible for hitting their department's targets and, in so doing, making the overall plan happen. Even the smallest of businesses usually assign responsibilities for:

- Sales and marketing
- Finance and accounting

- Manufacturing or providing the service to customers
- Personnel
- Purchasing

These are the areas you want represented on the planning team. The heads of these departments have all the information (or can get it if your company is somewhat larger) to help set goals. These are also the people you'll make responsible for reaching the goals.

Participative Planning

You can't jam your own will down the throats of your managers and expect to develop the sense of commitment so necessary to success. By having the right disciplines represented from the start, *the department heads* develop ownership for the plan and its success. It becomes their baby. Additionally, by keeping the planning team small, it's more manageable. Eventually, a sense of cohesion between the team members develops.

Further, the department heads are in a better position to develop the detailed *subplans* within their specialized areas that show how to achieve their part of the plan.

The planning team must be comprised of individuals who are in a position both to judge how each of their responsibilities impacts specific plan goals and to manage their use by the company.

Variables Used in Planning

Here are the major variables involved in developing a workable business plan:

Staffing
Includes both the number of people as well as their organizational level, years of experience, and potential for promotion.

Sources of Capital
The person responsible for funding the plan must be in a position to judge the *type* of financing facilities best suited to the company's capital requirements and ability for repayment. This person also needs to know how much money is needed and when.

Promotion and Marketing
The person on your planning team responsible for marketing must also have a good idea of the impact promotion has on product

demand and sales. In addition to being a major cost factor, promotion figures heavily in determining gross revenue.

Pricing

Two disciplines are often involved in pricing products and services: sales and marketing as well as manufacturing. First, the break-even point must be determined for the product. Next, all the overhead items must be added to calculate the true cost of offering the product. Required profit is added to finally determine a price. Adjustments are made to costs and profits to meet the plan's goals.

Production

This is relevant for manufacturing firms. Both the equipment used in production along with the methods and technologies employed must be represented on the planning team. Often use of a new technique may lower the manufacturing costs sufficiently that the retail price of a product can be lowered without reducing profit. This places the firm in a more competitive position.

Operations and Operating Costs

Reductions in fixed and variable operating costs are often used to take up the slack for other areas of the plan that have fallen short of their goal. Because they are so critical, the person who can determine what these costs should be for a given level of production and can influence their outcome should be included on the planning team.

INTEGRATING ACCOUNTING AND PLANNING INFORMATION

Of course, it would be ideal if the accounting system had a module into which we could put the plan numbers. Indeed, many of the new accounting systems already provide for this requirement. In fact, some of the best-selling systems come with preprogrammed comparison reports.

However, if you are happy with your present accounting system (except for this one feature), or if you don't wish to upgrade accounting systems right now, there's a way to produce this type of analytical tool without having to be a computer genius.

Here are the steps you need to take on the front end of the planning project in order to develop a convenient monitoring mechanism on the back end:

Step 1: Format the Plan Numbers

As the plan evolves to the final product that everyone agrees on, chances are that it will take the form of monthly numerical targets for each department. In many cases, these targets are dollars (revenue, for example). In other cases they are quantities (such as units shipped or reworked).

We want the plan at this initial stage to be in a format that allows us to conveniently obtain the actual performance numbers and compare apples with apples. In the case of financial targets, this should be readily presented by the computer system. For the other targets, make sure that those responsible for meeting the plan have devised a way of providing the actual monthly performance for tracking purposes.

Step 2: Available Data

Chapter 10 shows how to develop a plan-monitoring mechanism. Keep in mind when you develop your plan that you'll want to watch its progress. A component of this monitoring is data. We need a mechanism that extracts the actual performance information from your company and funnels it into your plan-monitoring mechanism. Ideally, this is done by your computer. If your accounting system doesn't have a preprogrammed facility for doing this, there's often another automated assist available.

Many accounting systems provide a facility for *translating* their accounting information into a software format compatible with some of the more popular spreadsheet programs. You're in luck if your accounting system does this. Then all you have to do is figure out what information you wish to compare against your plan. After that, set up a routine that accomplishes the *download* from accounting format to spreadsheet format.

If your planning was done on a spreadsheet, the next step is to merge the downloaded actual results from the accounting system (now also in spreadsheet format) into your plan file. Usually we have the computer do the work, employing what is known as a *macro*. A macro is a set of preprogrammed instructions that execute an entire array of commands at the touch of a button.

Step 3: Assessment of Results

Understand that development of the plan is just the beginning of the process. We're serious about attaining the planned results. We'll monitor the results each month and make mid-course corrections as needed in order to reach our ultimate goal. Over time the organization learns to anticipate the questions revolving around variances from plan. Not only are these questions answered, but corrective action is implemented at the same time. Really astute managers take a reading *during* the month, extrapolate the results, and take corrective action in time to hit their planned results *for that month*.

> ### PLANNING POINTER
>
> When downloading accounting results to a spreadsheet format, always include the account names and numbers (if necessary) as well as the column headings. This prevents having to guess which numbers belong to which line item or column. Additionally, if you have year-to-date numbers coming from the accounting system, verify that they are correct. Sometimes the commands to obtain YTD information for different years are similar. You don't need the embarrassment of comparing this year's plan to last year's actuals.

Develop your plan with assessment and correction of actual results as part of its objective from the start.

TYPES OF PLANNING

Within the realm of the short-range working plans that we're developing here, there are two varieties you should be familiar with. They are the overall company plan and the department subplan (sometimes called the departmental position plan). The results of the comprehensive company plan flow down to the department plan. The planning team should be involved in both.

Overall Company Plan

Don't mistake this with anything resembling a strategic plan. I promised we wouldn't get involved with that and we won't. However, the task of the planning team includes directing the ultimate results of the company as a whole. Often, these overall company plans have among their targeted results such things as:

- Development of a particular technology that helps in manufacturing or providing services to customers
- Development and rollout of new products or discontinuation of unprofitable ones
- Specific dollar levels for revenue and net income
- Earnings per share or return on investment

To a certain extent, the planning team must recognize the impact of anticipated changes in the outside environment. For example, in

1986, with the Tax Reform Act looming over their heads, many tax-oriented real estate limited partnerships had to find a new way to make money. Suddenly the tax advantages that made their ventures profitable for investors were wiped out. Due to the Tax Act they would no longer be able to sell their limited partnership interests.

Examples of other concerns from outside the company could be such things as disposal of toxic effluents from the plant or rezoning the manufacturing facilities. Changes of this magnitude are within the scope of the planning team when organizing the overall company plan. The team is not concerned (for these purposes, anyway) with such things as shifts in consumer preferences five years down the road. Those issues are usually beyond the scope of most small business plans. However, if you have access to that kind of information and it influences your current plan, don't ignore it.

Department Position Plan

Once the planning team has formulated the overall company plan for the next twelve (sometimes twenty-four) months each member of the team must create his or her own department plan. The objective here is to identify *exactly* how the targets are to be reached for each department. The departmental plans provide the blueprint for execution of the overall company plan.

At this level, the working relationships of different department managers become important. There must exist not only a commitment by each member to the overall plan but also a perceived obligation to the team for its success. Often the goals or performance of one department conflict with another. Sometimes the slack created by failure of one department to reach its target in time can be made up by another. Without that commitment to the overall plan *and* to the team's success, the plan can too easily derail.

Large companies with more than one division often carry this planning process down from the holding company level, to the divisions, and *then* to the various departments within each division. Such firms have representation on the planning team for each level that carries out the critical responsibilities that make the plan succeed.

If the firm is large enough, there may be a divisional planning team as well that reports to the corporate planning team. For our purposes, the techniques are the same for development of the plan.

TIMETABLES FOR COMPLETION

Control over the time taken to develop and execute a small or medium-sized company's plan is important. The smaller the business, the less time its managers have for *thinking* about expected results. The margin of error at smaller businesses is also much less than for their larger cousins. If General Motors Corporation misses its planned net income level by 25 percent, the problem is serious and some heads will likely roll. However, the company can still survive. However, for a small, thinly capitalized business that posts annual earnings of less than $1 million, a 25 percent drop-off can be devastating and possibly even fatal.

For this reason, the smaller the company, the more important its timetable for plan development and execution (see Table 1-2). As small business managers, we can't afford a mistake that, for example, causes our lenders or suppliers to question the company's ability to pay its bills.

Elements of the Planning Cycle

Business planning employs a cycle that includes:

- Identification of the company's goals and objectives over the planning horizon
- Recognition of the critical factors required to achieve the plan goals
- Distillation of these factors into detailed departmental targets
- Execution of the plan
- Evaluation of departmental and companywide results
- Course changes when necessary

For our purposes, the planning cycle should begin about three months prior to the date our planning horizon begins.

PLANNING POINTER

The planning period usually parallels the company's fiscal year. Such consistency makes the reporting and comparison of actual results against planned targets much easier.

The simple schedule in Table 1-2 illustrates the steps most companies take to develop their plan for the next twelve months. The calendar should include actual due dates for each milestone. Additionally, each member of the planning team should be encouraged to allow as few major demands on their time as possible when their contribution to the plan is due.

Table 1–2   Business Plan Schedule

Activity schedule for 12-week business plan development	
Activity	Week due
Gather information regarding:	1
■ Market	
■ Customer demand	
■ Risk factors	
■ Competition	
■ Investors'/owner's expectations	
Determine company goals.	2
Identify items critical to success plan.	3
Specify company targets that enable the business to reach its overall goals along with the time-frame for their completion.	4
Develop operational targets for departments along with the time-frame for their completion.	5
Determine capital expenditures requirements along with the time-frame in which they are to be reached.	6
Identify additional systems, equipment, and resources required to execute the plan.	7
Ascertain working capital requirements along with the time they are needed.	8
Assess financial impact of operational targets.	9
Develop financial targets along with the time-frame for their completion.	10
Identify personnel levels needed to execute the plan along with hiring/firing dates for specific positions.	10
Obtain consensus and agreement to plan by those who are held accountable for its success.	11
Determine and implement plan-monitoring mechanisms.	12

If this approach sounds more rigid than you're used to, then we've done our job. The planning process is serious. The plan gets your company from where it is today to where you want it to be sometime in the not-too-distant future. Few things are more important. Without deadlines for the various stages of plan development, it won't be taken seriously.

Nurturing, easy-going environments are fine for some types of work. However, the planning function is not one of them. Managers who fail to deliver their part of the plan not only fail the planning team, but they fail their co-workers and ultimately their employer, investors, and lenders.

AVOID ANALYSIS PARALYSIS

Development of a working business plan doesn't require huge amounts of detail. Indeed, the less detail incorporated into the plan, the better. Detailed plans tend to be overly time consuming, expensive to create, and a real pain to maintain. Part of your plan development should identify the level of detail necessary for your team to:

- Establish exactly how their particular functions figure into achieving the company's goals
- Provide milestones used to track progress against the plan

Detailed analyses and assumptions beyond those two criteria are unnecessary. Often, they only get in the way of making the plan work.

PLANNING POINTER

Remember that detail is expensive to generate. If it wasn't needed in the first place or isn't used, the cost of development can never be recovered. It's better to start out with too little detail, then develop it later if necessary.

INTERNAL PLANNING CONTROLS

Business planning, especially at smaller companies, needs tight controls. Why? Because there are so many other problems and opportunities that compete for the manager's time. Generally, the key people involved in the business plan are also the chief decision makers in the company. They (rightly) ask the question, "Why should I spend my time working on a business plan that *may* make us money over the next year or two when I can work on something else *today* that definitely makes us money?"

That kind of logic is hard to refute. Many entrepreneurs and small business managers go after the quick buck. Those are the ones that don't survive over the long haul. Without a definite direction for the company and predetermined goals to shoot for, those money-making projects today are merely plugs in the holes of a ship that eventually sinks.

Most of the topics already discussed in this chapter are methods we use for the internal control of the plan. They include:

- Participation in development of the plan
- Responsibility
- Accountability
- Fixed schedule for the plan
- Milestones of progress (often called *deliverables*)
- Monthly progress analyses
- Peer pressure from the planning team
- Incentives

If you've developed your business plan carefully, the plan itself should provide part of the internal control structure.

Plan Creation

Structure the creation of the plan using a step-by-step methodology. Members of the team that participated in plan creation aren't about to see their time wasted. That aids greatly in moving the effort along. In this sense, commitment of the team members provides an effective enforcement vehicle through peer pressure and cohesion. The objective here is twofold:

- Create a meaningful business plan that gets the firm where it needs to go
- Complete *development* of the plan within the time-frame required

Control of Plan Logic

Think about the process by which you make a decision:

- Define the problem
- Identify potential solutions
- Evaluate each possible solution in terms of:
  □ Probability of success
  □ Cost and ease of implementation
  □ Consistency with overall objectives

- Pick the best solution
- Implement the solution
- Monitor results from the decision

This probably appears like a long-winded explanation. However, if you think about it, that's what you do every time you make an important business decision. The same process is used to develop and control your business plan. The only difference with the plan is that each step is documented, the people responsible for success are held accountable, and the results are evaluated each month. Without this formality, the plan probably won't evolve either within the time frame required or in the form necessary for implementation.

PULLING THE PLAN TOGETHER

Let's build a bridge between the steps we've outlined to identify our plan of attack. This *linkage* between formulation of company goals into a plan and the end results provides the control structure necessary for success.

Goals—Make Them Measurable

The first step in bridging the chasm between the plan and its results begins with the goals your team establishes. The overriding rule here is to make sure progress toward the goals can be measured. A goal, for example, of increased profits means nothing. A better goal would be to increase net income by 12 percent over last year to a level of $2.3 million. Likewise, a goal of achieving a 4 percent market share probably helps very little for two reasons:

- Measurement of something like market share, except in certain specific circumstances, is tough to do.
- Increased market share—by itself—is not a viable goal. Indeed, increased market share may be a specific target for the sales and marketing person to reach gross revenue targets that further the company's overall goals.

Standards Provide the Bridge Between Goals and Results

Without standards—the targets each group must meet—the plan goals remain shapeless globs drifting out there on the horizon. There's little incentive to meet them. Not only must the standards be identified by some quantifiable benchmark, but they must be achieved by a specific time. Additionally, it may help to breakdown the tasks needed to achieve specific targets into their component parts.

Departmental Goals

The final link in this chain is to identify specific targets each department must meet in order to make the plan work. At small firms, these *subplans* are usually included with the overall company plan. An example of this linkage would be:

- *Company goal:* Increase net income by $10,000 for the year.
  - *Finance department:* Increase cash flow $100,000 by a specific date. Use it to reduce draw on the line of credit. This reduces interest expense and helps reach the company goal for net income.
  - *Sales department subgoal:* Reduce sales terms from 45 days to 30 days. This reduces working capital requirements, which allows the finance department to increase its cash flow.
  - *Credit and collections department:* Implement receivables tracking system. Reduce weighted average receivables aging from 52 days to 45 days. Change credit authorization requirements. Hire professional collection person.

The things that each department can do to facilitate the goal of increased net income described above carries over to still other departments besides those included in our example. Notice how we've taken a broad-based goal (but still with a definite, quantifiable, and measurable target) and reduced it to specific action steps taken to make the goal a reality. Further, each subgoal has a due date.

Now that we've figured out how to develop the plan, and its necessary ingredients and potential pitfalls, we'll begin actually creating one. Chapter 2 dives into the first step in creating an effective plan—establishing company goals.

2

Establish Company Goals

OVERVIEW

Goal-setting doesn't have to be the foggy philosophical discussion you may have experienced the last time you were involved in a strategic plan. Indeed, for small businesses, that sort of thing really isn't required for the short-term planning that we're doing here. Our focus in Chapter 2 is:

- Where do we want to go?
- What changes must we make to get there?

DESIGNING GOALS

Large companies with a modern and structured approach to planning may have as many as six different steps to reaching workable goals:

- Statement of the philosophy and mission of the company
- Formulation of a strategic plan consistent with corporate philosophy
- Company objectives and goals that help the company reach its strategic objectives
- Action plans that propel each operating unit to its goals
- Implementation, monitoring, and adjustments as the plan moves forward

For our work here, we'll bypass the philosophy, mission, and strategy. Instead, our efforts concentrate on simple tactical goals that take the firm from where it is today to an improved position *on the foreseeable horizon.*

Our objectives are:

■ Consistent with the direction in which the company wants to go
■ Compatible with the *individual goals* of the managers responsible for executing the plan
■ Feasible

The first part of these objectives, consistency with company objectives, follows the old saying:

Be careful what you wish for; you may get it.

That's another way of saying that above all, the short-term goals we set in preparing our business plan must reach the endpoint we desire. Example 2-1 is a case of a goal that missed the mark.

In Helen's case her goals weren't consistent with either the capability of her company or even where her firm really wanted to go. The overall goal should not have been to get as many orders as possible. Rather, the *short-term* goal for all four seasonal product lines should have been to maintain a specified level of profitability stated both in percentage and hard dollar figures. From that, the number of orders required, production costs, and the working capital necessary to finance the plan could have been determined. With that kind of

---

Example 2–1   Fashion Design House

Helen owned a women's clothing design and manufacturing firm. She's now gone bankrupt. During the four years she was in business her company specialized in high-end *haute couture*. A single dress could retail for between $5,000 and $10,000. Helen's goal was to generate a huge number of orders. She centered her business plan around doing the things that would accomplish this goal. Guess what—she was successful. Her firm received national press coverage. She was heralded as one of America's fastest rising fashion design stars. Several large stores placed orders for her line beyond her wildest expectations.

However, her bank refused to increase her line of credit so she could buy the required materials (fine Italian leathers requiring payment in advance from the jobber in Florence). She needed additional funding to pay her production people and to carry the receivables until her customers were finally ready to pay. The apparel industry is notorious for its slow-paying customers.

At risk of breaching her contracts and facing lawsuits, she eventually borrowed the working capital at an interest rate that cut her profit below the break-even point.

information Helen could have made informed decisions about which orders to accept and when to stop selling.

Too often entrepreneurs loose sight of the ultimate objective—to maintain the business at a specified level of profit. Without that profit level, you may as well invest the capital in T-Bills and forgo the headaches of running a company.

Make Department Goals Consistent with Overall Company Goals

The second part of our goal-setting focus—to make the goals of the responsible managers consistent with the company's objectives—isn't as easy as you might think. Everyone has his or her own agenda. What's good for the company may not necessarily be *perceived* as being good for particular employees. For example, implementation of an automated warehouse order picking system may be perceived by the warehouse manager and staff as:

- Cumbersome
- Too complicated
- Ignorant of experience the warehouse manager has gained over the years
- A threat to the manager's position and importance

Given that perception, what chance do you think such a system has of succeeding? Suddenly the reasons for installing the system in the first place—to reduce warehouse operating costs and accelerate the shipping schedule—take a backseat to ensuring the idea fails.

Management theorists call this divergence *goal incongruity*. We call it bad news for the company and its business plan. Making sure that the goals of each department, when achieved, reach the overall company goals is only half the battle. The planning team must also make each department goal consistent with those of *the individuals* in that department.

The best way to do this is through participative goal setting. Rather than force a set of objectives on a manager, it's better to have her identify the things her department needs to help the company achieve its goals. The reasons are practical as well as psychological:

- Everyone has a deeper commitment to an objective that they helped set. You may have heard the same thing as a child when your parents said, "You made your bed, now lie in it."
- Who better knows a particular department than those responsible for its operation?

Dysfunctional Goals

Even at firms where the individuals responsible for goal setting participate in the planning process, there may be a potential for dysfunctional goals. This occurs most often when the overall objective is established without the manager's participation. Suddenly he's charged with making his department cooperate. Sure, the manager gets to share in setting his own *departmental* targets. But the overall objective—and the reason for having to meet these targets in the first place—is beyond his control.

In these cases watch out for dysfunctional managers trying to beat the system. One way they do this is to report results at less than what they actually were. There are usually two reasons for this:

■ The manager can use the unreported results as a cushion in the event he doesn't reach his goal in the next operating period.
■ The manager may be afraid that the excess performance— which he and his people broke their backs trying to achieve— will become standard in the next planning period. Then they'll be faced with having to break their backs forevermore.

Certainly this perception of workers exemplifies the authoritarian view now scoffed at by modern management theorists. However, it can happen in cases where managers have goals inconsistent with either those of the overall company or their own private objectives.

HOW TO IDENTIFY GOALS

We'll deal with the process of goal recognition from two different standpoints:

■ The company as a whole
■ Individual disciplines within the company that provide its driving force

The trick is to formulate these goals so that:

■ They truly get the company where it wants to go
■ The interim results are measurable both for the whole company and for each contributing department
■ The success of one goal doesn't mean the failure of another

This last part, elimination of the so-called zero-sum game, can be the toughest. Companies that exert too much pressure on their managers to achieve their planned goals sometimes create more problems for themselves.

Consider, for example, a manager whose feet are held to the fire to meet his goals. What happens? He begins protecting himself. He wastes time documenting other departments failures that adversely impact his ability to meet his goals. Managers stop trying to help their co-workers. In retaliation, other departments start doing the same. They lose sight of the big picture and concentrate on themselves. War breaks out between departments, each competing to meet their targets at the expense of the other. If allowed to continue, the planning team may win a few minor battles, but ultimately the company loses the war.

The structure of goal setting has these points—generally done in this order:

- Establish overall company goals
- Determine critical targets within each department to reach overall company goals
- Identify criteria for progress evaluation
- Construct the reward structure for meeting goals

Members of the planning team, like everyone else, have four reasons for setting the particular goals they do:

1. Their own personal needs: They determine what these goals and the ensuing rewards will mean to *them*.
2. Personal ambitions: Often people perceive a goal as an opportunity to demonstrate their talent and further their careers.
3. Organizational needs: Both the culture and the leadership of the company influence the planning team's commitment to the goals they establish.
4. Structural influences: These are the progress-reporting and reward systems.

When combined, these four motivations determine the level of commitment each member of the planning team has to meeting the established goals.

Specific Goals

The objectives of the company as a whole as well as of the individual departments should be specific. We don't want any confusion about what level of performance was intended and when it was supposed to occur. Further, we must be able to track our progress toward that goal. Given these two requirements—precision and measurement—the best format for our goals is a quantitative one.

For example, say one of our primary goals is to provide a 15 percent annual return on invested capital to our shareholders. This number is unambiguous, easily calculated, and it has a deadline (fiscal year-end). Even more important, subgoals that get us to the main objective are equally quantifiable, traceable, and have a deadline as well.

Table 2-1 shows the difference between effective and ineffective goals.

Table 2–1 Examples of Goals

Here are some examples of effective and not-so-effective goals:

Effective goals

Pay shareholder dividends equivalent to $5.00 per share.

Raise company profit margin to 10% by year-end in the following increments:

- End of first quarter: 8.5%
- End of second quarter: 9.0%
- End of third quarter: 9.5%
- End of fourth quarter: 10.0%

Change the mix of product sales by June to emphasize the more profitable lines as follows:

- Product A: 40% of total sales
- Product B: 30% of total sales
- Product C: 20% of total sales
- Product D: 10% of total sales

Reduce average required working capital to between $1.0 million and $1.25 million during the course of the year.

Ineffective goals

Increase our market share.

Change the image of our company.

Reduce overhead expenses.

Improve the asset turnover ratio.

Notice that the ineffective goals are hazy in their objectives, not easily measured, and lack any sort of time-frame for completion. Small businesses should not concentrate on more than a few overall company goals at a time. Anything more than, say, three to five such goals tends to confuse company priorities and creates a contest for the resources needed to reach each target.

Notice also that there is a precise method—an action plan—that can be plotted in order to reach the more effective goals. This cannot be said for the ineffective goals. Planning gurus call this the *waterfall effect*. Action plans outlining the particular steps logically fall out of the overall company objectives; similar to a waterfall.

START FROM THE BEGINNING—WHERE ARE YOU NOW?

What's the first thing most of us do when we open a map? Usually, we find our present location. Next, we find where we want to go. Finally, we trace the best route to get there. Contrary to what you may have heard, *you can get there from here!*

We do the same thing with small business planning. Of course, the CEO or owner may say, "I know where we are now." Possibly; but there are some things even he may not know. Further, the people in operations may not share the same view as that of top management. Either way, divergence between perception, reality, and goals must be uncovered at the start.

We'll structure the assessment of our current position to include those areas of the business that contain the particular goals we want to meet. Essentially, the idea is that if we want to get from Point A to Point B, everyone has to agree where Point A is from the start.

Current Position Indicators

Identify the company's present location using these areas of focus:

What Business Are You In?
This might seem an elementary question. However, you'd be surprised how many people don't know their real business. For example, consider a small company that was in the payroll processing business. They thought they just did the payroll accounting, quarterly and annual payroll tax returns, and payroll check printing for their clients. However, what they really provided was a *financial processing convenience*. Their clients hired them to do something they chose not to do themselves for a variety of reasons. Given that, their

business was ripe for expansion into other financial processing services like bookkeeping and personnel administration consulting.

A second example was a petting zoo that traveled to shopping malls. The owners thought they provided an animal attraction. Their advertising focused on the new baby pygmy goats they had just acquired. Unfortunately, there was no change in their business as a result of the goats. However, the owner noticed that mothers drove up to their location in the mall parking lot, dropped off the kids, then continued on to do their shopping. A light went on—the petting zoo was really in the *child care business*. The advertising focus was changed to target the mothers' desire for their kids' safety and preoccupation. Business improved immediately.

Here are some questions to assist you in identifying what business you're really in (see Example 2-2):

- Where does most of your revenue come from?
- What market does your company serve?
- What need within that market does your company satisfy?

Markets Served

By identifying your markets, the planning team gets an idea of how they expect them to develop over the operation period. The things we want to know about the firm's current markets include:

- Are the markets growing or declining? How fast? Why?
- Is our market share growing or declining? How fast? Why?

Competitors

Never make the mistake of underestimating the competition. Your planning team should know almost as much about the competition as they do about themselves. Your current position assessment should:

Example 2–2   What Business Are You In?

What business is Travis' Downtown Pizza franchise really in?

- *Where does most of its revenue come from?* From sale of pizza.

- *What markets are served?* Businesses in the downtown area.

- *What need within that market does the company satisfy?* Delivery of fast food to people working late.

- *What business are you in?* After-hours food service catering to businesses.

- Identify the principal competitors
- Make clear why the best and worst competitors perform as they do—specify their success and failure factors
- Understand (or speculate about) the competition's goals

Customers and Markets

At least a part of your goals involve your customer base. Assessment of your current customer position shows everyone involved in the planning effort:

- Those customers with whom the company is most and least successful
- Reasons for success and failure of particular customers
- Potential dependency on a declining market segment

Products or Services

It's surprising the discussion generated by simply identifying the company's products and services. The issues we want answered in our current position assessment include:

- What products and services do we now provide?
- Of those, which are viewed as being on the upswing or downswing?
- What products and services are already scheduled to be provided during the upcoming planning period?
- What products and services does our customer base want or need?
- What products and services does the competition now offer or plan to offer?

Operations

We want to know how our operations are presently doing. The current position assessment should include:

- Facilities, fixtures, and equipment
- Capacity of technology now used to meet customer requirements
- Cost-efficiency of the present operation
- Qualifications of the present work force
- Changes in work force such as key people coming or going or expiration of a union contract
- Capital expenditures already committed for the upcoming planning period—what they will provide and their completion date

Finance

The current financial position assessment shouldn't just emphasize the balance sheet of the company. We want to know the status of the financial systems as well. This provides a clue as to what changes are needed to execute the plan. Here are the financial issues you want to include in the current position assessment:

- Status of key financial indicators, such as ratios, working capital, disposable cash, accounts receivable and payable, debt, and available credit facilities
- Capability of credit authorization procedures
- Accounts receivable processing and collections
- Management of the accounts payable system
- Adequacy of banking relationships
- Status of the system of internal accounting controls
- Any material funds inflows or outflows expected during the planning period
- Changes in the environment outside the company that could have a financial impact—such as legislative or taxation changes, possibly interest rates as well

Human Resources

People are the most valuable assets any company has. Your current position assessment should objectively evaluate those people responsible for making the plan happen. If changes are required, it's better to know before the actual planning process begins than midway through.

PRACTICALITY OF GOALS

Before we get into formulation of goals, let's stop to consider their practicality. We want to peg the company goals, as well as those of individual departments, at an attainable level. The most effective goals are *reasonably attainable*. They are just high enough to provide a reach. But they're not so far above present capabilities as to intimidate people and cause them to give up from the start. Likewise, they aren't set so low as to make people think their goal is a slam dunk and not take it seriously.

Example 2-3 is the story of how one bank mismanaged its goals.

WHERE DO YOU WANT TO GO?

We talked earlier about the need to know the firm's current position—its capabilities, standing in the market, products, competition,

Example 2–3   Reasonable Goals

There was a large international bank that allowed its divisions a certain amount of autonomy. The took pains to foster an entrepreneurial spirit in these divisions. Each division prepared its annual business plan and submitted it to the parent company.

However, when times got tough for the bank, the parent entity would review the plans, then issue "tasks" to its divisions. A task was a change in the planned objectives of a division. Within two years these tasks became more and were less realistic for the divisions.

The result: Division managers viewed the tasks as unattainable dictums set forth by people sitting in an ivory tower who didn't understand *their* business. The tasks weren't taken seriously. Division results came in at levels below the original plans even without the tasks. It didn't take long before the division managers anticipated changes the parent would make and began low-balling their plans from the start to counteract them. The result was that the changes made to division targets by the parent company actually decreased plan objectives.

financial capacity, customers, and human resources. Just like reading a map, once we know our present location, we're ready to plot out where we want to go. We'll begin with identification of the overall company objectives, then move on to the specific actions each department must take to help move the firm toward its goals.

Specify Company Objectives

These are simple, straightforward statements of where you want the company to go. The company objectives should be written out so everyone can see them. Additionally, the entire planning team should participate in determining these overall objectives. Absent that participation, the level of commitment by those on whom the plan depends for its success diminishes.

Here are four guidelines that should help you create your objectives:

1. State the desired results, *not* the activities that will produce those results. That comes later in the planning process when we create the departmental action plans that achieve our overall objectives.
2. Identify the time-frame in which the desired result is to be attained.

3. Structurally, the objective should contain an action verb and a subject, such as ". . . increase profit by _____ to a level of _____ ."
4. Make the objective clear and understandable. Avoid use of jargon and acronyms. We want people to think about the target, not about interpreting what was meant.

Measurable Objectives

All objectives should be measurable—otherwise, how could you track your progress? However, the actual objective doesn't necessarily need to be stated in terms of quantity. For example, if customer complaints have been received that your company's products are dead on arrival (DOA has been frustratingly true of some computers and their peripheral devices), your objective might be: "Reduce customer complaints of nonfunctioning products to a point equal to (or better than) the industry standard." Then name the standard.

As part of the departmental action plan, the standards that get these complaints down to the level acceptable are specified along with the time-frame. These might include such things as improvements in quality control procedures, substitute vendors, a change in packaging, or an adjustment in shipping instructions.

Scope of Overall Company Objectives

The company objectives should be global in scope. That is, they should impact the firm as a whole. One test is to ask, "To whom are these objectives important?" The answer should be, *the most important people to the firm: Shareholders, partners, lenders, management, and employees.* These people probably don't care about the accounting supervisor's objective to reduce the receivables days of sales outstanding from 45 days to 35. They do, however, care a geat deal about the end results from the accounting supervisor's action plan: Reduce the potential for a capital call because working capital requirements declined.

Growth as a Goal

The goal of growth seems to crop up in many business plans—especially those of new companies. A computation that provides an idea of how realistic goals for growth rates are is called the *growth rate index* (GRI). Table 2-2 shows how it works.

After having computed the GRI, you know that the greatest rate of growth your company is likely to realistically sustain won't be above that figure. Factors that can increase the GRI include:

- Rising sales
- Improved asset turnover

Table 2–2 Computation of Growth Rate Index

Growth rate index	
Assumptions	
Net income	$ 900,000
Add back interest expense	50,000
= Net income before interest expense but after taxes	$ 950,000
Net assets employed at beginning of year:	
Total assets	$5,000,000
− Cash	100,000
− Short-term investments	250,000
− Current liabilities except short-term debt	1,500,000
= Net assets employed at beginning of year	$3,150,000
Dividends paid	450,000
Target debt/equity ratio	60%
Target deferred taxes to equity ratio	10%
Computation	
Net income before interest expense but after taxes	$ 950,000
/ Net assets employed at beginning of year	3,150,000
× Fraction of earnings paid out as dividends:	
Dividends	450,000
Net income	1,000,000
Fraction of earnings paid out as dividends:	45%
Reciprocal	55%
= Subtotal #1	16%
Target debt/equity ratio +	60%
Target deferred taxes to equity ratio	10%
+ 1	100%
= Subtotal #2	170%
Interest expense	50,000
/ Net income before interest expense but after taxes	950,000
= Interest expense as % of NI before interest but after taxes	5.3%
Reciprocal is Subtotal #3	94.7%
Growth Rate Index:	
Subtotal #1	16.6%
× Subtotal #2	170.0
× Subtotal #3	94.7
= GRI	26.7%

- Lower dividends paid to investors
- Increased debt/equity and deferred tax/equity ratios
- Decrease in ratio of interest expense to net income

PLANNING POINTER

An effective goal using rate of growth would be:
   Achieve an annual rate of growth over the end of fiscal 199X equivalent to:
- Gross revenue: 10%
- Net income: 12%
- Discretionary cash: 15%

Return on Investment as a Goal

Every business is capitalized using someone's money. Large publicly traded corporations use a pool of investors' money in exchange for stock in the company. The stock entitles the shareholder to ownership of a piece of the company. Some companies issue bonds. The bond holders own a debt obligation owed them by the company and are guaranteed a fixed return on their investment.

Most companies—especially smaller ones such as partnerships, sole proprietorships, S-corporations, and C-corporations—have pressure on them to return a benchmark rate to their owners each year. For many companies the return on investment (ROI) is a constant in their business planning. They rarely embark on a new venture (such as a new product or service) without making certain that its projected profit level is at least as high as their target ROI.

Most owners like seeing target ROI numbers. This gives them something against which to gauge the alternative use of their money. Companies whose earnings and payouts hit a competitive level in the market for investment capital usually have little to worry about obtaining additional funding.

PLANNING POINTER

An effective goal using ROI is:
   Achieve an annual return on invested capital of 25 percent.

Profit as a Goal

Entrepreneurs and small business managers always keep their eye on the firm's profit line. Profits come in several forms:

- Gross profit—also called gross margin and measured in dollars and as a percentage of sales
- Profit before interest and taxes (commonly termed "operating income")
- Net income

For our purposes, probably the best form of profit when setting a goal is that of *net income*. To accountants, net income has a particular meaning—the bottom line. This is what is left after *everything* has been deducted from sales including taxes. The owner's profit comes out of net income. Funds required for use to expand the business also come out of net income.

PLANNING POINTER

An effective goal using profit is:
   Net income for the year is between $500,000 and $525,000.

What Have Your Noticed About These Company Goals?

First of all, each one is broad. Achievement of these goals requires that a number of things be done in each department. Secondly, each goal concerns the people at the top of the organization. Return on invested capital, for instance, impacts drill press operators less than the production plan for the upcoming month. They are responsible for the production plan, but probably aren't accountable for the return on invested capital.

Third, these goals are generally financial in nature. This reflects the small business manager's concern for the bottom line.

Out of the few companywide goals flows the rest of the plan. This is the same theory used when making the transition from strategic to tactical planning. What we've done is *downsized* our focus. Overall company goals provide the target point for the rest of the company.

Of course, you can choose other goals for your company. They don't even necessarily need to be financial in nature. However, they should all contain these qualities:

- Briefly specify exactly what performance you want the company to exhibit in the particular area.
- A plan of action for each of the departments can be easily extracted from the goal.

- Results of the goal are readily measured.
- A time for completion of the goal is specified.

DEPARTMENTAL ACTION PLANS

Once the planning team agrees on the overall goals of the company, it's time to decide how to get there. In this phase, each department formulates an action plan—a roadmap, really—of how they are going to help the company achieve its goals.

Included in these action plans are the answers to such questions as:

- Who will be our customers?
- What products and features will these customers demand?
- How will we compete against other contenders in our industry?
- Which technological innovations should we pursue and which should be left alone?
- What capabilities in our management and staff will need to be changed?
- How will political and legal changes affect our ability to achieve our goal?

Sales and Marketing

Most small and medium-sized businesses are market driven. That is, the action plan for the sales and marketing group pretty much dictates what the rest of the firm does. Products, capital expenditures, and manufacturing and shipping schedules are all dependent on the marketing strategy.

The manager must take the goals established for the company as a whole and break each one down into the parts that affect the sales and marketing effort. Sales and marketing goals often include areas such as:

- Positioning both the company and its products in the marketplace
- Advertising and other promotional efforts
- New product developments
- Identifying target customers and markets
- Market penetration and share
- Number of accounts
- Customer service
- Sales strategies
- Order entry system
- Credit approval

Sales and marketing goals are designed to effect the overall company goals. Generally sales goals appear at the top of the business plan—largely because they influence the top numbers, such as revenue.

If we take the three overall company goals established earlier of growth, return on investment, and profit, the sales and marketing subgoals could be something like this:

Increase Number of Units Sold by 7 Percent Over Last Year

This subgoal ties in directly with the company goal of a 10 percent growth rate in gross revenue.

Raise the Sales Price of Each Unit Sold by 7 Percent

This addresses part of the overall goals to increase net income by 12 percent and ROI to a level of 25 percent, and brings profits up to between $500,000 and $525,000.

Make the Credit Authorization Limits More Strict so They Reject 5 Percent More Applicants

This goal aims at the company's third growth goal of increasing disposable cash by 15 percent. If quality of the customers rises, there will be fewer delinquent accounts and payment of receivables will accelerate, thus freeing disposable cash.

Of course, some of these goals may seem mutually exclusive at first glance. Don't the laws of supply and demand require that *fewer* units be sold as the price goes up? Perhaps. However, the sales and marketing group will address that in the detailed plan it makes for accomplishing its goals. It could be they have added a new feature to the product that increases both demand and the offering price since the competition hasn't yet come out with the same thing.

The point is, sales and marketing goals must be as precise as the overall company objectives. Further, they must help move the firm closer to accomplishing its overall objectives.

PLANNING POINTER

The marketing and sales goals should immediately follow the overall company goals for most firms. Chances are the other departments need the marketing goals in order to formulate their own goals. Sales volume is a case in point. The financial and production groups need to know the sales targets and the accompanying timetable in order to plan things like purchasing and schedules of working capital borrowing.

End-product of the Marketing and Sales Goals

The goals set by the marketing and sales group should tell us several things:

■ Where it intends to go, usually stated in mathematical terms
■ When it intends to get there
■ How these goals, when achieved, help the company meet certain specific goals it has established
■ What impact these goals have on other departments

Coordination with other departments is vital. Part of that coordination requires production of a sales budget for each month over the planning horizon. This tells the other departments what they can be expecting in terms of units sold and the accompanying revenue. The sales budget may be something as simple as the one shown in Table 2-3.

From this point, the operations group can determine *when* the raw material for manufacturing needs to be ordered, how much to order, and the amount of inventory and safety stock to have on hand. Additionally, the production schedule can be put together. The operations group can also begin to formulate their objectives for the year now that they know what will be asked of them.

Table 2–3   Sample Sales Budget—First Quarter and Year-End Total

	TDO Enterprises, Inc. Sales budget for 1993			
	Month 1	Month 2	Month 3	Total
Product: Pillows				
Units sold	100	110	120	1,860
Average price	$ 10.00	$ 10.00	$ 10.00	$ 10.00
Total revenue pillows	$ 1,000	$ 1,100	$ 1,200	$ 18,600
Product: Comforters				
Units sold	300	310	320	4,260
Average price	$ 15.00	$ 15.00	$ 15.00	$ 15.00
Total revenue comforters	$ 4,500	$ 4,650	$ 4,800	$ 63,900
Product: Sheets				
Units sold	500	510	520	6,660
Average price	$ 12.50	$ 12.50	$ 12.50	$ 12.50
Total revenue sheets	$ 6,250	$ 6,375	$ 6,500	$ 83,250
Total sales budget:				
Units sold	900	930	960	12,780
Total revenue	$11,750	$12,125	$12,500	$165,750

The finance group can determine the company's cash flow using the revenue generated from this information. Additionally, the new customer profiles provided by the marketing people, combined with what the accounts receivable manager already knows about the present customers' paying habits can be used to anticipate collections for the year.

Operations

The operations group essentially figures out what targets it must meet in response to both the overall company plan and the marketing objectives already determined. These targets are synthesized into a set of operational objectives that lead to what eventually amounts to a blueprint for achieving the technical side of the company plan.

Depending on your company, operational goals may cover a variety of areas. Typical targets contained in operational goals might involve:

- Arrangement of production facilities—addition and often elimination of surplus capacity
- Manufacturing, production, or service delivery
- Product design and engineering
- Packaging
- Shipping
- Quality control—things such as rejects and rework costs
- Direct labor production standards
- Purchase price standards
- Machinery up- and downtime
- Inventory control, including items such as amount of raw materials, work in process and finished goods, safety stock, order quantities, and obsolete inventory
- Purchasing—coordination with the finance department on terms of payment
- Overall cost of manufacturing
- Union and collective bargaining agreements

Some operational departments include not only manufacturing and product delivery, but such things as personnel and the computer system(s). If so, then the goals of these departments must also be included in the operational goals.

Let's take both the sales and marketing and the overall company goals we've already derived. Using these, we'll determine some of the operational goals that might apply.

Linkage of Operational Goals with Other Goals

Earlier, we said that one of our sample company's overall goals was to increase gross revenue by 10 percent. To accomplish this the sales and marketing department was going to increase its sales volume by 7 percent. Therefore, the operations department must be able to accommodate the added production required. As a result, the first operational goal might be:

> *Construct and bring on-line a second
> production facility that increases capacity to
> the amount required.*

The operating plan provides the timetable and construction costs for this goal.

The second operational goal has to do with the overall company goal of raising net income by 12 percent and pegging profits between $500,000 and $525,000. To help accomplish these goals, operations may:

1. Reduce manufacturing costs of specific products by 10 percent by March.
2. Reduce the number of rejected units and units requiring rework by 20 percent by April.

Subgoals appearing in the actual operations plan might include a timetable for implementation of a new manufacturing method (or equipment) that increases production efficiency while keeping labor hours constant. Another subgoal might include establishing manufacturing labor standards to better control production costs.

A fourth operational goal addresses the need to increase disposable cash by 15 percent. In this case let's say the operations group has control over inventory. Therefore, our goal is:

> *Reduce average inventory on hand by 20 percent.*

The subgoals specified in the operation plan might include such targets as raw material inventory, production schedules to produce finished goods inventory, establishment of an economic order quantity system, reduction of units in the safety stock, and installation of a just-in-time raw materials inventory system. Each of these goals reduces the operations department's tendency to suck up working capital that could either be better employed elsewhere in the company or not used at all.

Finance

In its strictest sense, the finance group has little control over actually achieving the company's goals. However, there's a lot it can do to assist other departments in achieving their goals. Much of this comes from reporting. Additionally, if borrowing, investment, or cash management are included among the company's goals, the finance group can directly influence their attainment.

Some of the areas where the finance group may establish its goals include:

■ Acceleration of cash inflow
■ Accounts receivable
■ Accounts payable
■ Cash management system
■ Financial reporting
■ Capital expenditures
■ Financing and borrowing
■ Investment of excess cash
■ Internal accounting controls

Linkage of Financial Goals With Other Goals

Your CPAs should tell you (if they haven't already) that it's wrong to think of your accountant as just a bean counter. An innovative and aggressive controller can go a long way toward helping your company realize its plan. However, it's your job to make sure that the finance group's goals are coordinated with those of the other departments as well as with the firm as a whole.

We want to get the most bang for our buck from the finance department. That means a significant portion of your accountant's energy should be devoted to helping the firm meet its goals.

Here are some examples of the goals an astute controller would formulate in response to the overall company and departmental goals we've come up with so far:

Increase disposable cash by an average of 15 percent over the entire year.

The finance group will likely formulate specific targets and milestones to hit in order to make this goal a reality. Such tactics might include:

■ Reduction in average accounts receivable outstanding through coordination with the marketing group whose goals include stricter credit authorization guidelines.

- Hire a trained professional collector to go after delinquent accounts.
- Accelerate cash inflow by one day through installation of a lock box or electronic funds transfer system.
- Increase the average account payable outstanding by three days. If it's done right, this often can be accomplished without impugning the creditworthiness of the firm.

Another goal of the finance department might be to:

Take advantage of trade credit discounts for early payment.

The finance action plan might include installation of an accounts payable tracking mechanism. This could identify the terms of payment for each invoice and flag it for payment on the day needed to take advantage of trade discounts. By initiating this goal, the firm's overall objectives of a net income increase by 12 percent and profit levels of $500K to $525K are made that much easier.

A third finance department goal might be:

Establish monthly financial reporting of actuals to compare against plan for each department.

This, by itself, helps every other department watch their progress toward their own goals. Where changes must be made, the responsible departments are warned early enough so they can still do something about it before they miss their goals completely.

Human Resources

If your company is large enough it might have a separate department that deals with human resources. Otherwise, administration of employee-related tasks often falls on someone who already wears two (or more) hats. Regardless, employees are a big part of every department's and company's goals.

Most human resource (HR) departments are supportive in nature. Like the accounting and finance functions, they don't really contribute directly to the bottom line. However, an astute personnel manager can greatly help the other departments meet their goals.

A case in point is the operation division's need to know the labor efficiency for each of its production workers. Wouldn't it be helpful for the human resources department to provide the labor cost per finished unit for each production worker? If the personnel manager has control over the payroll records, this type of information should be available.

Human Resources is responsible for getting the right people to help the company fulfill its goals. The human resources goals should include helping department heads evaluate the key people responsible for reaching the company's goals. The HR manager can make educated guesses of how long it will take and how much it will cost to grow, convert, or buy qualified people to meet the firm's goals.

Finally, part of the HR manager's job should be to establish the plan incentive system that rewards the firm's managers for meeting the company's goals.

Some of the goals you might see in the area of human resources include:

Formulate a manpower plan for each department based on its goals and underlying action plans by January 1.

Certainly this plan helps in identifying the number and type of workers that each department needs in order to fulfill its goals. Larger companies have personnel specialists to do this. For smaller firms, the department heads themselves often prepare a form of manpower plan and incorporate it into their action plans.

Another goal might be to increase the knowledge and skill level of specific categories of workers. A goal that accomplishes this might include:

Establish an educational reimbursement plan for employees.

Part of the action plan would identify the employees and courses the company is willing to pay for in order to upgrade their skills.

One more goal might be to formalize the employee review process:

Establish a regular timetable and format for employee performance and salary reviews.

The action plan supporting this goal might include milestones for each department and review of the actual written performance reviews by your company's head of human resources. Potential spin-offs of such a goal might be a decreased exposure to wrongful termination suits as well as employees who have the peace of mind in knowing where they stand with the company and what they can expect from it.

CAPABILITY GAP

Usually there exists a gap between business goals and the company's present capability to meet them. Identification of this gap and the specific action steps to close it comprise the next step in goal setting. This injects reality into the planning function.

Potential gaps between the firm's goals and the resources it has available to meet those goals might be found in areas such as:

- Human resources
- Finance
- Credit
- Systems
- Capital equipment

Once the company's goals are established along with the obvious shortcomings that must be filled in order to execute the plan, steps toward closing the *capability gap* begin to emerge. For example, say the overall profit improvement goals require manufacturing efficiency to cut production costs by 5 percent within a six-month period. Further, the company is small and the head of manufacturing hasn't the faintest idea how to do that. Even more likely is the possibility that the planning team lacks confidence that this goal can be achieved by the head of manufacturing. The capability gap has now been identified.

One solution is to engage a manufacturing consulting firm to identify and implement the improvements required to enhance production efficiency. The current head of manufacturing can then continue to act as the production line's caretaker (which he or she may be good at). The company's goals are met and the capability gap that once existed has been closed.

Another equally likely prospect is a gap between the financial resources available and those needed to fund working capital and capital equipment requirements. The chief financial officer should have identified this gap in the company's financial plan. Potential solutions contained in the financial action plan might include:

- Reduce working capital requirements by shaving accounts receivable and inventory levels.
- Sell the corporate office building, then lease it back. The funds generated can be used in the operation.
- Increase the working capital line of credit facility.
- Lease the necessary capital equipment rather than buy it.

Most of these potential solutions must be coordinated with other departments and included in their action plans. If the planning team discovers that a particular capability gap cannot be closed, then it must adjust the goals.

Here are the standard rules of thumb I use when assessing the existence of a capability gap for a small or medium-sized business:

■ Identify the deficiencies present that might prohibit meeting the critical objectives.

■ Specify the deficiencies in terms of people, capital, technology, systems, equipment or anything else that contributes to the capability gap.

■ Identify *potential* problems that could create a capability gap within the planning horizon that may not currently exist. This rule reflects our bottom-line orientation. We're not interested in excuses. We want results. To the extent that we're able, if an outside threat to our current capability of meeting our objectives exists, we should identify it at this point and plan for its possibility.

■ Some managers may scoff at this as trying to gaze into a crystal ball. That's not what we're doing. We're only interested in potential threats that might be classified as having a *high probability* of occurring, say, more than a 75 percent likelihood. The rest we won't bother with.

■ Identify the potential *opportunities* that could help close the capability gap. We do this in order to increase the probability of them actually occurring. For example, if the city council is considering changing the zoning of your property and this would help you, there are things you can do to move this potential along.

Closing the Capability Gap

Some companies correctly identify a hole in the capacity of their company to meet a particular goal, then fail to close it. Take, for example, the art dealer who realizes her revenue needs to increase beyond her present market. The firm doesn't appear to have the ability to market to a wider customer base. As a result, a marketing department is established. However, the salespeople, gallery, and methods remain the same—so do the still-disappointing results.

In this example, the capability gap was correctly identified—an inability to reach a wider customer base. However, the marketing department ultimately failed because closing the gap didn't include changes in the one thing that ultimately would expand the customer base—personnel and methods.

A better solution would have been to establish, say, a corporate art division, one that would not only specialize in the artwork needed by businesses for their offices, but could either lease or sell it to them. Staff the new division with personnel knowledgable about corporate image, leasing terms, and the artists whose work fits the corporate mold. *That* solution would increase sales revenue by bridging the

Table 2—4   Capability Gap Identification Worksheet

	Present capability	Planned requirements	Gap
Products and services			
Production			
Equipment			
Facilities			
Office			
Warehouse			
Production			
Distribution			
Shipping			
Paperwork control			
Marketing			
Sales			
Customers			
Promotion			
Advertising			
Human Resources			
Performance appraisal			
Salary structure			
Upward mobility			
Legal compliance			
Inventory			
Physical count			
Warehouse size			
Security			
Finance			
Available credit			
Cash management			
Working capital			
Systems			
Engineering			
Financial			
General ledger			
Accounts receivable			
Accounts payable			
Cost accounting			
Payroll			
Financial reporting			
Order entry			
Inventory control			
Purchasing			
EOQ			
Safety stock			

capability gap. Indeed, my beloved sister-in-law, Lynne Cohen, did exactly that with her wildly successful *Art Dimensions Inc.* in Los Angeles. Today, Lynne's corporate art division has taken over the company as its largest revenue producer.

Table 2-4 provides a format that may help you to identify the gap between present capabilities and planned requirements in particular areas of your company.

Now that we've identified our goals and determined where the firm's present capabilities fall short in reaching these goals, our next step is implementation. Chapter 3 demonstrates how to construct a blueprint for implementation of your planning goals.

3

Blueprint for Implementation

OVERVIEW

Now that we've figured out *what* we want to do and which departments are to do it, let's get it done. Have you ever noticed that so many so-called planners stop short of taking responsibility for the success of their plans? I've known several international consulting firms that charge well into six figures to tell their client companies what they should be doing. Some even come out of their ivory towers and assist the client in formulating a plan.

Few, however, stay on to assist in the implementation. This is the most difficult part of planning—the execution of all these ideas put on paper. Indeed, keeping all departments on track and moving in the same direction is really the purpose of the plan. With a roadmap, you wouldn't look at it once at the beginning of a long trip, then fold it up (or try to) and put it away. The same holds true for your business plan. During implementation the plan is consulted and adjusted constantly. Changes in departments are made to better assist in execution of the tasks that need to get done so the plan stays on track.

THE TASK OF THE CHIEF IMPLEMENTER

The chief implementer (usually the chief operating officer or president at a small or medium-sized business) must identify departments' action plans that either don't make sense or won't help further the overall company goals. Ideally, this identification occurs *before* the plan is executed. The chief implementer must be familiar with every phase of the operation as well as how the plan relates to each phase. There are cause and effect factors that join one department to another.

For example, if the treasurer simply cannot come up with the required working capital to support the sales and manufacturing plans, there will be fallout to most every department within the company. The chief plan implementer must be aware of each area affected and be able to take corrective action in order to keep the plan on track.

Blueprint for Implementation

The blueprint for plan implementation includes three main ingredients:

- *Who* has accepted responsibility for each action step of the plan
- *What* specific action steps are taken to accomplish the overall goals and the departmental goals
- *When* each step is scheduled for completion and the next one is to begin

With these three components, what was once a disorderly conglomeration of divergent ambitions can be transformed into a coordinated strategy with the precision of an engineering blueprint. We know *who, what, and when* for each phase of the plan. All we have to do next is work the plan and adjust for goals that aren't met or somehow become delayed.

CONVERTING GOALS INTO ACTION PLANS

The goals discussed in the previous chapter establish a linkage between the department's goals and those of the company as a whole. At the implementation stage a transformation of those goals takes place. Continuing with our map analogy, we now draw the actual detailed route from our present location to our ultimate destination.

The goals established earlier include time frames by which each is to be completed. The action plans that implement each goal break apart each time frame into mini-assemblies. Such exact specification and tracking of the steps required to meet a goal are necessary to ensure its success. The chief plan implementer is constantly asking: *what are you going to do, how are you going to do it, and when will it be done?* However, if she's smart, she'll leave the person alone to do the work without interference once she's satisfied that the approach as outlined will get them where they want to go.

Sound like a lot of busy work? You're right, it is a lot of work and it does keep everyone busy. However, without a detailed idea of how the plan is going to be implemented you leave its success to pure luck. Most successful managers take their companies and their jobs more seriously than that. Further, the fact that the implementation team actually thought about how all their goals related to one another engenders a higher degree of teamwork.

To illustrate, let's take a look at how the marketing plan at a small computer software company folds into the rest of the firm's objectives. The business has developed a regional reputation for specialized software used in computer-aided design and manufacturing work (CAD/CAM). Its sales amount to about $8 million a year with profits around $1.1 million. All of the company's stock is owned by two principals. There are about 30 employees at any one time. All the normal departments are represented by their respective managers on the planning team.

Each manager formulated the series of action steps necessary to get his or her own department where it needed to be to help fulfill the overall company goals. In this sense they were each responsible for meeting their own objectives and were held accountable for the work of their subordinates.

The head of marketing developed a time-phased plan with particular targets placed along the way for the sales force to meet. This was distributed to the other department heads as well so they both knew what was coming and when and could react accordingly as the plan unfolded. As each milestone was reached, the results of the sales effort were communicated throughout the firm.

Imagine the confidence the owners had, as well as the other department heads who relied on the marketing department doing what it promised, when they saw one milestone after another reached. There was a high degree of confidence that the overall sales revenue required in the business plan would be achieved. Further, this confidence began very early in the process since the marketing manager intentionally put his first milestones at the front of the planning horizon.

That's the kind of precision and confidence we want to impart to your business plan.

Identification of Action Steps

Everyone working on the plan must understand the actions required for each department to meet its goals. These action steps must be in sufficient detail to ensure implementation. We're not telling the department heads to show us something akin to the work movement used in a time and motion study. Instead, we want to see how they intend to go about meeting the goals they've set for themselves and that are necessary to assist other departments in meeting their own goals.

Identification of action steps is important from three standpoints:

1. The people who work the action steps are required to logically walk through the process and identify any flaws before it's too late to correct them.
2. The chief plan implementer can better coordinate actions and timing of each department as well as identify conflicts.
3. Specific action steps must be known in order to track the timing of the plan implementation.

Responsibility Within the Department

Just as the planning goals emphasized *ownership* by those responsible for meeting them, the individual departments must assign responsibility for the success of each action step. Without that commitment, the likelihood of success cannot be ensured.

Often at small businesses the responsibility for executing a department's action steps falls on just one person—usually the department head. In some cases, for very small departments, that's fine. However, meeting the goals to which these actions lead is more often a team effort. The more cohesive and committed the team, the higher the probability of success.

How many times have you seen a major problem arise that could cause a goal to be missed? It happens every business day. The person who actually set that goal and "owned" the plan to achieve the goal (was held accountable) would find some way to get around the problem. The person who was simply told what to do would be more likely to toss up his hands in exasperation and say, "I told you it wouldn't work."

The more responsibility for success of the action steps is delegated to the people who actually do the work, the higher the probability of success.

Milestones and Action Steps

Designating a completion date for each action step of the department plan provides a definite milestone against which to track progress. Having the action steps written out in front of the implementation team helps in these ways:

■ Design of the procedure to achieve the goal can be more easily evaluated and changed if necessary.

- Supervision and coordination of the effort is easier if everyone can see *what* is being done, the *expected outcome*, and *when* the results are due.
- Technical assistance and advice can be obtained if the experts can see the big picture beforehand.
- Tracking of the implementation effort is made possible through milestones.

Milestones provide a target deadline. Without a deadline it's almost guaranteed that the plan and its action steps won't be implemented. People's time—especially at small businesses where more than one hat is usually worn by the same person—gets sucked up by projects where urgency goes to according to who screams the loudest. The use of milestones and enforcement of deadlines is the only way to implement the plan.

Tie Implementation to Performance Review

Management theorists have argued for years about the best way to motivate people. Certainly implementing a plan and achieving its goals requires a high degree of motivation. Chapter 9 deals with that very topic. However, at the implementation stage everyone needs to understand how serious the company is about achieving each action step and goal.

This "management by objectives" philosophy goes a long way toward telling people how much the firm counts on them doing their part in the implementation. However, it's not the primary motivator. Nor is it the only factor by which performance should be assessed. But it does clearly tie job performance to successful implementation of each person's part of the plan.

As both managers and as employees, most of us prefer a clear understanding of the criteria used for performance appraisal. It's even better if these criteria are defined and agreed on *before* the assessment period begins! That way there's no confusion about what's required and no disputing what superior performance means.

Many times I've seen otherwise astute managers shoot themselves in the foot by not understanding the motivational linkage between performance and the review process. This more often occurs with new employees. How many times have *you* taken a new recruit aside and explained from day one the criteria you'll use to evaluate their performance and contribution to the company when they're reviewed in twelve months? I've even seen companies that deliberately keep this criteria a secret.

Don't make this mistake when implementing the business plan—it's too important to the company's profitable survival. Spell it out to each employee *before* implementation begins. Meeting each milestone for which a person is responsible should be used in determining their performance. You might even remind them what performance reviews are used for—promotions, raises, bonuses, and job stability (e.g., continued employment).

This written implementation timetable has two uses:

Performance Tracking Mechanism

If each milestone and the expected result from each is written down and understood by everyone, then monitoring and coordinating implementation is that much easier.

Documentation

In our litigious society, documentation of personnel issues is an absolute necessity. Small businesses can't afford to carry people who don't perform. One indicator of performance is meeting the plan implementation milestones already established. Counseling sessions often review these milestones and evaluate why a critical action step was missed and what the consequences of failure are to the firm. At that time a plan of action is formulated to correct substandard performance.

Such sessions provide a written chronology of the employee's situation and actions taken by both parties to raise work performance to the level required.

Table 3-1 illustrates a quantitative approach to figuring plan implementation into individual performance assessment.

Information Necessary for Implementation of the Action Plan

Business plans often fail because they are perceived by those responsible for its implementation as being *an addition to* their regular jobs. People often think of the goals they established during the planning process as being separate from what they do on a daily basis.

The implementation of a business plan must bridge the gap between every day job duties and plan objectives. Only a detailed implementation strategy can accomplish that. When done right, the action steps required to execute the plan become enmeshed in the daily rigors of everybody's job. Soon there's no difference between the implementation goals and the daily job requirements. *That's* the position in which you want to be. The *orientation* of the company's thinking changes to one of working to execute the plan rather than executing the plan only after doing the normal work. From that point people automatically implement the steps required to achieve the plan.

Table 3–1   Assessment of Implementation Performance

Assessment of Implementation Performance

Employee: _____

Supervisor: _____

Evaluation date: _____

Period being evaluated: _____

Overall company goal: _____

Departmental goal: _____

Action step: _____

Action Step #	Weight	Description	Cumulative % Completed							
			1st Qtr		2nd Qtr		3rd Qtr		4th Qtr	
			E	A	E	A	E	A	E	A

Total   100%

Weight attached to implementation effort (%): ____

Instructions:

1. The quarterly columns marked "E" are for the expected % of completion. Columns marked "A" are for the actual % of completion.

2. Column 2, Weight, is used to identify the importance each action step has with respect to the implementation effort. By multiplying the cumulative actual achieved to date by the weight attached to the implementation effort, gauge the progress of the implementation effort. Be sure, however, to account for the progress that was supposed to be made for interim periods so you don't penalize someone for work that isn't even due yet.

ACTION STEPS TOWARD IMPLEMENTATION

We've spent some time on the theory behind formulation of the action steps required for plan implementation. Now let's generate a practical example.

MTH Enterprises is a fictional company that makes those little yellow pressure-sensitive temporary notes that stick to paper. The firm also prints cute little sayings on some of its line and sells these to novelty and stationery stores. Here are the particulars that get us to plan implementation:

Overall Company Goals

Senior management decided to raise the dividend to its shareholders from $1.50 to $2.50 per share by the normal dividend declaration date for shareholders of record on October 31. Dividend payment date is December 1. The increased dividend represents a huge percentage increase and an incremental cash outflow of about $500,000. Management's reasoning for this move revolves around its past profitability and the need to boost its shareholder base to raise expansion capital in the next two years.

This is a good broad goal that is precise and has a real time limit. It's also divisible in terms of what must happen to actually meet this goal. Be sure to note how the finance department narrows the overall goal into a series of departmental targets that drives the company toward meeting its goal.

Finance Department Goals

MTH is not a huge company. It employs less than 100 people and has annual net income of about $1 million on sales of $11 million. In other words, it's a good solid company—not a superstar, but not a dog, either.

The CFO is also the controller, treasurer, and cash manager. The goals for the finance group include:

Working Capital
A majority of the cash required for the dividend payout must come from a decrease in the working capital required for running the company. Therefore, the goal is stated as:

Decrease working capital by $380,000 by September 30.

The September 30 date was set because the board needed to know the amount of cash available for the dividend when they announced it during October.

Credit Lines
The CFO wants the cushion generated by an increase to the firm's credit facilities. The goal is stated as:

*Increase unsecured working capital line of credit by $100,000
by November 15.*

The date was allowed to go to within two weeks of the scheduled dividend payment date to reduce expenses on the commitment fee for the added line of credit available.

Inventory Control

Our fictional CFO knows the background of the production and warehouse managers. They have always had free rein to order whatever volume of inventory they wished. As the company squeezes its available cash, that won't make it anymore. Therefore, the goal is stated as:

Reduce inventories by $150,000 no later than August 30.

Naturally, there are many other approaches to generating the cash needed to pay this dividend. However, these goals should suffice to illustrate our point—identification of actions that implement these goals and meet the plan objectives. Now let's watch how MTH further refines these specific targets into a series of action steps that can be quantified and placed on a timeline for execution.

Implementation Steps

The first goal our CFO addresses is the working capital reduction of $380,000 by September 30. The action steps that actually implement this part of the plan include:

Permanent Reduction in Accounts Receivable

Since A/R is a major component of MTH's working capital, it stands to reason that downsizing the receivable portfolio should be an action step toward implementation of the working capital reduction goal. Great. But how do you go about doing that?

Install a Receivable Monitoring Mechanism   Monitoring accounts receivable is something most businesses do regardless of size. The mechanism to be installed by MTH's CFO provides more information and a higher degree of control than most. The critical numbers used to manage the receivables balance include:

- A/R portfolio turnover rate—we want the turnover to *accelerate*
- Average collection period
- Aging of receivables analysis
- Computation of receivables roll rates

In order to track the current position and compare it with her targeted numbers, the CFO developed a series of tables to monitor A/R performance. Results for each of the actions steps having to do with receivables can be reported on Table 3-2. (It was reprinted with permission and appears in *CASH MANAGER'S GUIDE* by Chris Malburg, Prentice Hall, Englewood Cliffs, NJ, 1992.)

Hire Professional Collectors MTH did not have a collections staff. The CFO decided to hire two properly trained professionals to begin systematically collecting delinquent receivables.

Implement Strict Credit Review Policies MTH had routinely granted credit to just about any customer who asked for it. No more. That's part of the reason for excess aging of the receivables as well as the bad debt expenses. The CFO implemented a credit review procedure that required particular standards for customers buying on credit. This was stratified in terms of the amount of credit verification required for particular levels of credit. Further, the authorization for credit purchases went up the chain of command of the company. Here's how it worked:

- Credit purchases up to $50,000 were authorized by the credit manager.
- Credit purchases up to $200,000 were authorized by the CFO.
- Credit purchases over $200,000 were authorized by the president.

Implement a Computer Link Between the Accounts Receivable System and the Order Entry Department The CFO discovered that the sales and credit policies were too easily circumvented by the order entry clerks because they didn't have up-to-date information on the payment status of customers when they called to place an order.

This was corrected by linking the automated order entry system with the automated accounts receivable subledger. The result was that the order entry clerks suddenly had the customer's balance owed and credit history right there on the computer screen before they took the order. Customers who hadn't paid their bills were cut off from further purchases until they paid up. Specific problems were referred first to the credit manager, then to the CFO if necessary.

The four changes implemented by the CFO—a receivables tracking mechanism, professional collectors, structured credit review policies and procedures, and a computer link between receivables and order entry—reduced the receivables balance by $125,000 by the goal's deadline of September 30. But the CFO wasn't finished yet.

Table 3–2   Computation of Accounts Receivables Information

Report date: _____

Accounts receivable ratios

1. Accounts receivable turnover rate
   Equation: annual sales / average A/R balances
   Annual sales   _____

   Average A/R balances   _____

   A/R turnover rate   _____

2. Average collection period
   Equation: accounts receivable / (annual sales / 360)
   Accounts receivable   _____

   Annual sales   _____

   Avg. collection period (days)   _____

3. Aging of accounts receivable
   Equation: sum of (weighted average % of ea. aging bucket × # of days in each bucket)

A/R balances by aging bucket:	$ Amount	Weighting % in bucket	Aging bucket weighting	
Current	$			Days
30 days				Days
60 days				Days
90 days				Days
120 days	_____	_____	_____	Days
Total A/R	_____	_____	_____	Days

4. Computation of roll rate analysis

	#1 Current	#2 Current to 30–60	#3 30–60 to 60–90	#4 60–90 90–120	#5 90–120 to W/O
Month 1	$				
Month 2					
Month 3					
Month 4					
Month 5					
Total	$	$	$	$	$
Collections	$	$	$	$	$

Table 3–2 (*Continued*)

Monthly roll rate:

Current to 30–60: #1, Mo. 1 / #2, Mo. 2 =   ____ / ____ = ____
30–60 to 60–90: #2, Mo. 2 / #3, Mo. 3 =   ____ / ____ = ____
60–90 to 90–120: #3, Mo. 3 / #4, Mo. 4 =   ____ / ____ = ____
90–120 to write-off: #4, Mo. 4 / #5, Mo. 5 =   ____ / ____ = ____

Velocity with which the monthly roll rate moves from one aging bucket to the next should decline.

Eliminate Trade Discounts   The president of MTH had long been an advocate of offering trade discounts to customers who paid early. The company had standing payment terms of 1/10, Net 30 (1% discount if invoice is paid within ten days, otherwise the net is due in thirty days) printed on its invoice stock.

The CFO saw two problems with this policy that affected her ability to generate cash:

■ Too many of the customers were abusing the credit terms by taking the discount even though they paid late—many went beyond the 30 day limit.
■ This was the most expensive loan the company could obtain.

The CFO calculated that the 1/10, Net 30 terms promoted by the company president cost about 18% per year in interest expense. Here's how she computed it:

(Discount % / (Due date − Discount date)) × 360 days =
Annualized interest expense from offering trade discounts

In the example above, the annualized interest expense from offering the discount was computed as follows:

$$(.01/(30 - 10)) \times 360 = 18\%$$

MTH's aggregate borrowing rate was much less than the 18%, therefore this discount policy was actually *costing* the company more than it was helping.

The CFO's action step with regard to trade discounts was easy—eliminate them. They were too costly and many customers abused them anyway. The estimated savings per year amounted to about $30,000.

Implement a Controlled Disbursements Mechanism   The CFO wanted to *increase* accounts payable without damaging the firm's credit relationship with its vendors. She did this by implementing a payables tracking system. It began with a paper tickler file that showed when each invoice was due for payment but was later put on a microcomputer. Using this mechanism bills were paid *when due*, not before and not after. As a result the old policy of cutting checks on the fifteenth and last day of the month was discarded in favor of daily payments of those checks that were due that day.

Additionally, the company's buyer was instructed to extend the terms of payment to a minimum of 45 days for all purchases. The CFO tracked the company's average payables and watched them steadily rise from less than 30 days to the targeted 45 days. The process was scheduled to take three months. The results were expected to release $50,000 from required working capital.

Implement Revised Investment Policies for Excess Cash MTH's CFO also handled the company's short-term investment of excess cash. Until now, all investments had been in overly conservative U.S. Government paper. The CFO guided a board of directors' resolution allowing her to place these excess funds in slightly more risky investments—such as the commercial paper of AAA-rated companies and repurchase agreements collateralized by securities of the U.S. Government. This added about 150 basis points (1.5%) to MTH's overall return on its excess cash investments.

The benefits were further compounded by the fact that the measures already being taken freed up still more cash with which to either invest or to pay down the line of credit. From her cash flow plan, the CFO estimated that interest income on the short-term investment of excess cash would be increased by $20,000.

Inventory Control The CFO had long been advocating better control over the firm's warehousing of its excessively large inventories. Now was a good time to reduce the working capital tied up on the warehouse floor. Her action steps included implementing these control measures:

- Just-in-time inventory purchases and deliveries
- Ordering raw material based on an economic order quantity model
- Reducing safety stock in accordance with a stock out and cost model that minimized both the amount of safety stock required and the cost of potential inventory shortfalls

The results were estimated that working capital investment in inventory would fall to a level $175,000 below what it had been before.

Table 3–3   Financial Implementation Plan

Goal/action	Person responsible	$ impact	Imp'n date	Results date
Financial implementation plan				
Overall: Increase dividend to $2.50 per share.	CEO	$500,000	N/A	10-31-9X
Financial:				
Decrease working capital:	CFO	200,000	9-30-9X	9-30-9X
1. A/R monitoring mechanism	Acctg. Supervisor	0	1-30-9X	1-30-9X
2. Hire professional collectors	Credit Manager	130,000	1-30-9X	1-30-9X
3. Link order entry to receivables subledger	Computer Supervisor	25,000	1-30-9X	1-30-9X
4. Controlled disbursements system	A/P Supervisor, Buyer	50,000	1-30-9X	8-30-9X
Inventory:				
1. EOQ model	Production Manager, Buyer, Warehouse Supervisor	100,000	1-30-9X	3-30-9X
2. Inventory safety stock	Production Supervisor	75,000	1-30-9X	3-30-9X
Investment policies	CFO	20,000	1-30-9X	12-31-9X
Borrowing lines	CFO	100,000	6-30-9X	11-15-9X
		$500,000		

Summary of the Financial Implementation Plan

Much of the $500,000 cash requirement was met from the CFO's efforts. Table 3-3 summarizes the financial goals and the implementation plan to achieve them:

Notice that the implementation dates were not always the same as the dates when the results were due. That's because many of these measures—such as a reduction in accounts receivable—take some time to work. Also notice that in many cases the CFO allowed additional time between the results date and the actual date our scenario said the money was needed.

MTH Enterprises had a specific goal that required more funds than would have been available without a plan. Rather than trying to take the shotgun approach to solving the problem, MTH's CFO targeted her objectives precisely. Specific goals, time frames, required results, and people responsible were identified. She established the steps necessary to generate additional funds from various sources within the company. Then she set about implementing the actions that would generate those funds. The deadlines provided milestones by which to measure progress so corrections could be made while the plan was working.

That's the way to approach most complex problems—break them down into their component parts. Each part can then be dealt with by itself. Suddenly a task that may have seemed insurmountable becomes possible.

POTENTIAL PLAN IMPLEMENTATION STEPS

Every discipline within the company will likely be involved in the plan implementation. The next several sections identify areas within each department that might be useful to this effort.

Sales and Marketing

Goals impacting the sales and marketing department most likely revolve around such issues as:

■ Sales volume
■ Growth of new accounts and retention of existing ones
■ The company's position in the market
■ New product introductions
■ Competition
■ Anticipating and meeting customer demand
■ Product mix
■ Advertising and promotion

Often the implementation of a sales strategy can result from marketing goals of specific products. Conversely, implementation of the marketing plan can result directly from sales targets. This is often the case when a company must advertise in order to reach targeted sales levels.

Here are some of the areas of plan implementation that are used in the sales and marketing department.

Discretionary Expenses

Sales and marketing expenses are often looked on (by nonmarketing people) as elective. Nevertheless, sales don't appear by magic. Something has to be done to stimulate them. Different mixes of marketing expenses produce different sales results. Implementation plans often focus on the emphasis of particular products. This requires a specific mix of marketing and sales resources.

Most sales and marketing implementation plans identify the resources that will be used, their costs, and the estimated results. The amount of money that may be available to achieve a particular goal is usually finite. However, the *way* it is spent is at the discretion of the marketing department.

Another variable sometimes included in marketing implementation is the sales commission structure. This can be adjusted to reward the sales force for particular performance that is part of the implementation plan. For example, a change in the commission structure can benefit the financial group. Sales commissions can be changed to a percentage of net *collected* receivables rather than simply gross sales. This reduces bad debt and delinquent accounts.

Promotion

Promotion involves the basic task of the sales and marketing group. Particular goals that require implementation might involve adjusting the sales force focus on such variables as:

- Specific customers
- Revised sales terms such as Net 30 days
- Trade shows
- Adjustments in the company's discount policy
- Changes in the approach to returns of merchandise purchased by customers

Advertising

Most implementation plans require attention to the mix of advertising media and the markets to which they provide access. Sometimes the implementation establishes an advertising review mechanism that gauges the effectiveness of each method used. We saw how that theory worked in the scenario of MTH Enterprises. The first thing the CFO did was establish a method by which to measure performance of the changes made. Though it contributed nothing to the hard dollar targets, the plan probably could not have been implemented without it.

Product Development

Part of marketing implementation often has to do with working alongside the engineering staff when a new product is on the drawing boards. Questions regarding product features, demand, color, packaging, and price (to mention just five) are often researched by the marketing department. Hard quantitative data using sophisticated statistical sampling techniques are sometimes used to answer these questions. Further, the implementation plan may call for the engagement of an independent consultant to provide expertise (or manpower) that the present staff lacks.

Distribution

Sometimes distribution of the product is directed by a part of the marketing department. The timeliness or method of distribution can often be a marketing tool. Part of the implementation plan specifies product distribution. A good example is the success of Domino's Pizza Corp. Their marketing niche is more a function of timely distribution than superlative pizza.

Customer Service

Marketing related customer service extends to the handling of complaints as well as warranty programs. Warranty work can be extremely costly both in terms of not matching policies offered by the competition as well as maintaining a cost-effective program that meets both customer requirements as well as those of the company.

These are some of the elements that a sales and marketing organization controls during plan implementation. They are often set apart from the overall goals of the marketing department and their costs and results are reported separately.

Operations

Many smaller businesses lump a variety of functions into a catchall called *operations*. This is often the largest and most critical area of plan implementation. Functions most often found in the operational plan include:

- Manufacturing
- Purchasing
- Capital expenditures
- Facilities

Goals established in the plan for each of these areas must be separated into a series of action steps that fulfill the overall operational objectives.

Manufacturing

Most goals of manufacturing or assembling departments revolve around cost control and production targets. Among these are such things as:

- Overtime wage expense
- Management of the number of shifts on the production line
- Quality control rejects
- Costs of reworking substandard finished goods
- Accounting for production costs

An example of one goal in a manufacturing department that assembles automotive aftermarket car antennas might be something like this:

Reduce the overall cost for assembling the entire antenna product line by 10% before the end of the second quarter.

That's a laudable goal. However, without some sort of blueprint for implementation, it probably won't be accomplished within the time frame required. Therefore, let's determine the steps to accomplish this goal.

First, many small businesses have little idea of the actual costs associated with manufacturing (or assembling, in this case) particular products. Therefore, our initial step might be to establish a reliable cost accounting system. Here are the implementation steps to achieve this goal:

Standards   Establish a series of standards for each product whose cost is being measured. This should include standards for direct and indirect labor, cost of materials purchased, fixed and variable costs associated with overhead, selling and G&A expenses, number of QC rejects.

For many small businesses, installation of a standard cost system can be a lot of paperwork. It requires research and study of the operation. Nevertheless, even though the standards initially may not be as exact as they eventually will be, having something is better than nothing. Further, the standards should approach the objective established by the goal of the operations group.

Comparison of Actuals Against Standards   Next, a mechanism to track how each cost of product assembly performs against the standards is implemented. Many desktop automated accounting systems contain a cost accounting module that tracks standards against actuals and reports variances. MAS-90 (by State of the Art, Inc.) and ACCPAC (by Computer Associates, Inc.) are two of the most popular.

Action Now that we have information on material cost variance, labor costs, rework expenses, and allocation of overhead, we're in a position to begin changing things to meet our objectives.

Additional implementation steps to reduce product assembly costs might include such things as:

- Reorganize the assembly line to make it more efficient. This increases production without increasing labor costs, driving down the cost of labor per item produced. Managers might call this a *positive labor efficiency variance.*
- Negotiate fixed-price contracts for the purchase of materials used or assembled on the line. In a period of rising prices, this injects a badly needed constant into the assembly cost equation.
- Replace some of the old worn-out assembly line equipment with new more efficient machines. This reduces the cost of idle labor due to equipment downtime. Further, QC rejects drop as a result of the new and better equipment.

Purchasing

The purchasing function often lies within operations. Depending on how material-intensive the company is, this task may be more or less vital. Further, if the company buys goods whose terms are not negotiable (a rare occurrence, but sometimes the case) the emphasis on buying will also fall. However, the overall operational goals usually tie in some significant way to the purchasing department.

Plan implementation guidelines for the purchasing department might include such issues as:

Prices Our goal was to reduce the overall cost of assembling the antennas. One of the logical places to start is in the raw materials bought for the assembly line. The purchasing department has several potential implementation steps to assist in achieving this goal:

- Change to cheaper vendors.
- Purchase in larger quantities that allow for bulk discounts.
- Alter purchase terms (such as payment date) to reduce costs.
- Adjust the time of year certain purchases are made to obtain a discount.

Availability One operational goal (or concern) may be that an uninterrupted supply of raw material be available to the company. This can be particularly important in companies that require materials from manufacturers subject to strikes or other events (such as weather conditions) that could disrupt shipments. The purchasing department can implement safeguards to ensure a steady supply by the following methods:

- Arrange for standby vendors to fill the gap a disruption in supplies could cause.
- Develop a resource sharing plan with other companies to allow the trading of goods and facilities back and forth in the event of a supply disruption or other interruption. The newspaper industry, for example, does this as do many large computer installations.

Capital Expenditures and Facilities

Both capital expenditures and facilities may fall under the operations umbrella. Often a company's facilities are inadequate for the production or volume of business the plan requires. In this case a major part of the implementation plan is to provide the additional space by the time it is needed. If this is a major construction project, chances are the project manager will have a schedule of all the steps needed to get the job done. This schedule is incorporated into the implementation plan.

Capital expenditures refers to (capital) assets the firm buys in order to conduct its business. In the operations area of MTH Enterprises where the goal is to reduce assembly cost of its antenna line, capital expenditures might refer to buying new production equipment. If the equipment needs to be designed first, then manufactured, the firm's operational personnel will be involved from the engineering standpoint as well.

Finance

Implementation steps for the plan in the finance area generally include a combination of support functions and hard financial goals. Here is a list of some implementation steps often found in finance:

- Develop a financial performance reporting system that compares actual to planned performance in each key area of the plan.
- Reduce float in the cash management system.
- Decrease the compensating balance requirements for existing loans.
- Increase the line of credit available.
- Install a viable system of internal accounting controls.
- Increase the annualized average return on excess cash invested. The actual implementation step to achieve this would be to increase the risk taken with investment of excess cash by

transferring a predetermined percentage of the portfolio from conservative instruments to more risky instruments.

Human Resources

Many small businesses don't have a dedicated human resources (HR) department. Often this function is delegated to an administrative person. Still, the tasks associated with human resources are important to implementation of the plan and achieving its objectives. Here are some of the critical steps often employed to integrate the HR function into implementation of the overall business plan:

■ *Personnel:* Most growth-oriented companies hire people who have the capacity to grow with their jobs. Often the job requires a more experienced person to handle tasks whose function has outgrown the incumbent. In these cases, a senior position is created and staffed from the outside with the incumbent retained as support.

The HR department works with each discipline within the company to target positions (and sometimes create them) that fulfill the implementation goals of that department. The positions, job functions, salaries, and type of person required all form action steps for the HR department (or whoever is responsible) to help the company implement its plan.

■ *Recruiting:* Getting the right people and developing a skilled labor pool from which to draw is often a primary HR implementation step. In order to know how many people are needed, when, and what skills they require, the HR department often produces a manpower plan for each department. For example, they incorporate the production department's direct labor plan for the entire year into the HR recruiting plans.

■ *Compensation levels:* Most personnel managers have a good idea of the compensation level for each job function in the company. Part of the implementation plan is to make sure these levels are competitive. If they are too high, the firm unnecessarily pays for something it doesn't need. If it is too low, there will be a turnover of valuable personnel.

A component of the implementation plan often includes regular salary survey in the open market to verify that the company's compensation levels are correct.

A big part of HR implementation has to do with the incentive plan to motivate achievement of the firm's goals. The HR manager usually has more experience in developing motivation in people than the other managers in the company. Therefore, the HR manager should be responsible for designing, implementing, and managing the performance incentive plan.

▪ *Labor union contracts:* If your company is a union shop, chances are the union contract will be up for negotiation sometime in the next few years. The personnel manager often spearheads these negotiations. To be effective, a plan outlining terms the company can live with and that fulfills the business plan's requirements becomes part of the HR plan implementation process.

▪ *Compliance with federal and state labor laws:* It's up to the HR manager to ensure the company complies with labor laws. In our litigious society, failure to do so can be very expensive in lawsuits, settlements, and attorneys' fees.

Part of the mechanism should provide for notification and implementation of changes in the laws. A second part should provide for periodic audit of the firm to make sure its managers and staff continue to comply with the law.

MILESTONES

We establish milestones to chart progress toward our goals. They're important so we can track the plan implementation step by step. Usually milestones come in the form of target numbers such as sales levels and production costs that are due by a particular date.

Most significant steps toward implementing the plan should have points at which performance is assessed. Milestones should be:

▪ Meaningful to the implementation step being tracked
▪ Important to the overall plan
▪ Representative of a goal that other departments need to know was reached so they can continue with their own implementation steps

Scheduling Milestones

A milestone represents a deadline by which a specified performance is to be achieved. The best time to have such a deadline is at the completion of an important step in the implementation of a goal.

Additionally, the deadline should recognize other departments needs as well. For example, let's say the manufacturing department needs to purchase additional raw materials. These materials must be purchased 30 days before setup of the production run that makes the additional goods the sales department says it will sell. However, before the purchase order can be issued, the company must have the ability to pay for it. Therefore, the controller's negotiation of an increased working capital line of credit becomes critical to placement of that order. In this case, the milestones would be:

- Closing the deal for the line of credit
- Issuing the purchase order
- Completion of the special production run
- Selling the additional goods produced

Responsibility

There must be a single individual responsible for successfully completing each milestone by its scheduled deadline. Without that, the likelihood of a task being accomplished diminishes. Many companies spell out the milestones particular individuals are committed to meet in their annual review. Further, they link the person's bonus or other incentive compensation with achieving these milestones. Table 3-4 illustrates a simple milestone chart.

Milestone charts aren't complicated. They simply need to state *who, what, and when* about the particular phase of the goals being implemented.

COORDINATION OF ACTION PLANS

Artful use of milestones places the critical path toward completion of each action step into perspective. Many departments need to coordinate their activities with other departments in order to continue from one step to the next. We saw that in Table 3-4.

Some companies carry their milestone charts into the overall plan by drafting a *master implementation chart* that shows all action milestones for each department. Using such a chart, one look reveals the sequence of the action steps. A careful review shows the order in which each step must take place before the next can begin. This is called the *critical path*. At the initial stages of the implementation process, it's easy to see if some steps are out of sequence and must be rearranged.

PLANNING POINTER

Be sure to carefully review each department's implementation plan with particular attention paid to due dates and the critical path. We don't want one department having to wait for another to finish a task when the problem could have been prevented by coordinating the effort from the start.

Table 3–4 Milestones

TDO Partners, Ltd.
Table of Milestones
New Product Introduction: Computer Keyboard

Due date	Milestone	Person responsible
2–1	Completion of prototype	Smith
3–1	Completion of engineering specifications	Jones
3–10	Line of credit increased to $500,000	Adams
3–11	Raw materials for production ordered	Allen
3–15	Preliminary sales of 1,000 units are received	Waters
4–11	Production line is set up and first run is done	Berens
4–15	First customer shipment is completed	Conly

INTERDEPARTMENTAL CAUSE AND EFFECT FACTORS

Coordinating all the implementation steps of a business plan is a little like putting together a puzzle. Each piece has a particular place it fits to make the whole project work. Further, the actions of most departments have some sort of impact on at least one other department (and usually more than one). These are what we'll call *interdepartmental cause and effect factors.*

As you review your implementation plan for the entire company, be conscious of the risks and opportunities in the rest of the firm. There is fallout risk if a given department is late, or fails in meeting their milestone. Conversely, there's an opportunity if a department is early or exceeds its target. One thing is certain—there will be some effect.

Table 3-5 illustrates two interdepartmental cause and effect factors you should watch out for. You'll probably come up with many more that are germane to your business.

From this table we can see the domino effect of just two changes somewhere in the implementation plan that react throughout the company. In the first case, sales increases beyond what was originally planned, that's normally a good thing. However, suddenly the company's available cash is sucked up by the additional inventory needed to produce the products already sold. An emergency loan may be required at a higher rate than the profit margin can support. Since the credit authorization department is suddenly inundated with additional work, the approval process breaks down and delinquent customers or just plain deadbeats enter the receivables system. The company could soon become a victim of its own success.

Table 3–5   Interdepartmental Cause and Effect Factors

Interdepartmental cause and effect factors			
Cause	*Department*	*Effect*	*Department*
Sales increase	Sales	Production increases	Manufacturing
		Inventory shrinks	Operations
		Working capital rises	Finance
		Shipping schedules	Operations
		Credit approval workload increases	Finance
		Delinquency and bad debt rises	Finance
Increase in bank borrowing denied	Finance	Working capital investment must shrink	Finance
		Purchasing must be adjusted downward	Operations
		Manufacturing schedule slows	Manufacturing
		New product development delayed	Operations

Be aware of the cause and effect factors in your company. Identify them and make sure to figure them into the implementation plan.

IDENTIFICATION OF ACTION STEPS THAT DON'T MAKE SENSE

How do you identify goals or action plans that don't have a prayer of being realized? It's not easy. Especially when you really want to believe the company can perform like that. As we have seen, overoptimistic implementation plans have negative fallout for the rest of the company. They must be spotted from the start and corrected.

One quick way is to look at the assumptions behind particular goals. Ask:

■ Are the results coming from these assumptions similar to what other companies could expect?

■ Has the company ever performed as predicted before?

- What is the risk of not meeting (or exceeding) the projection— how is the rest of the company affected?
- What corrective actions can we take to minimize damage if the goal is not met?
- What does the person responsible stand to loose if he or she is wrong?
- Do these assumptions make sense?

Review Cause and Effect Factors

Once you've become familiar with the interdepartmental cause and effect factors at your company, use them to assess the logic behind the implementation plan. Go through each step of the implementation plan, asking, "How does the target specified by this department affect the targets of every other department?" The answer should be readily apparent if these causal factors were considered in the first place. If the cause and effect factors were ignored, then it's back to the drawing board.

Plan For Uncertainty

OVERVIEW

Business plans are literally crawling with uncertainty. With that uncertainty comes risk to successful implementation of the plan. As business managers we must know how to identify these key areas of concern. This chapter illustrates:

- Ways to identify risk due to uncertainty
- Techniques to assess potential return for risk deliberately undertaken
- Some of the techniques planning professionals use to deal with uncertainty
- How to build in safeguards against uncertainty
- Contingency planning for your worst nightmares

THE KEY IS FLEXIBILITY

The most effective business plans are those with enough flexibility so that when something goes wrong the damage is contained. In a sense this *compartmentalization* is similar in theory to the watertight doors used aboard ships. If there's a leak, entire portions of the vessel can be shut off from the rest, thus localizing damage. In this way a small portion is sacrificed for the good of the whole.

Our business plan needs to include enough flexibility so that departures can be absorbed without affecting the overall outcome. Within reason, well-organized business plans can take a hit if some departmental goals are not met. Indeed, that's the point:

We want to win the whole war, not just a few minor battles.

Plans formulated with an understanding of risk insulate their overall goals from uncertainty. When something doesn't go just right, other variables within the plan—designed to minimize that very risk—kick in to bring us back into line.

We expect uncertainty to affect our plans. However, this uncertainty and the hazards it brings does not make the plan or its creation less valuable. In fact, one of the most important parts of the business plan recognizes risks and formulates contingency actions to deal with them. Indeed, during my career, I've met many executives who shy away from committing to specific planning goals simply because of the uncertainty. "How can I tell you how many widgets we'll make when the sales projections might be so far off," they ask.

Nonsense. That's just an excuse to avoid being held accountable for the responsibility that's part of the job description. By definition, planning involves uncertainty. The trick is to create enough flexibility so the plan *reacts* to areas that don't go the way you thought they would.

ELEMENTS OF UNCERTAINTY

When you begin talking to your staff or your boss about how the business plan should address uncertainty, you're likely to get some skeptical reactions. Many hard-driving executives claim to have little time for gazing into a crystal ball. Neither do we.

Instead, we want to recognize uncertainty and the risk it brings to our plan in a scientific manner. We do this using a technique that isolates and quantifies risk due to uncertainty throughout the plan. From there, we'll take steps to deal with it before it happens. When we're done, the planned targets for our company can be achieved throughout a range of specific performances by uncertain variables.

Decision Making Under Uncertainty

The uncertainty contained in any business plan comes from many areas including:

- Demand for the product
- Competition
- Technological development
- Legislative and regulatory actions
- Price and availability of raw materials
- Manufacturing machinery downtime

Get the idea? Techniques for decision making when the assumptions are likely to move around can be separated into five components:

■ *Options:* There are usually several alternative actions you can take given a particular decision.

■ *Possible events:* For every decision there is a given set of possible events that can occur. An example of one such event would be a tightening of bank credit requirements when you are deciding on the size of a loan to ask for.

■ *Probabilities of events:* The probability of specific events occurring affects the risk of each option. Most planners at small and medium-sized companies think of probability in terms of three gradients:

- ☐ Highly probable
- ☐ Possible
- ☐ Unlikely

An alternative when we want to quantify a particular possibility is to assign it a numerical *probability percentage* of a given event occurring. This technique is called *expected value analysis* and is discussed later.

■ *Consequences:* When we make decisions under uncertainty we usually ask, "What's the worst that could happen?" That's human nature. Emotion rather than logic tells us that if a particular event occurs and it puts us out of business, that's a risk we can't tolerate—regardless of its probability. Indeed, insurance companies make their living by preying on people's irrational fear of disaster regardless of the probability.

■ *Profit from the decision:* If we're going to make a decision with an uncertain outcome, we'd better get rewarded for taking that risk. A big part of any decision made under uncertainty involves identifying the potential profit. That's how the state lotteries and other gambling establishments entice their players into making what is almost assuredly a sucker bet. They peg the loss low enough to be of no consequence when compared with the potential reward.

Capacity to Absorb Risk

Everyone's capacity to absorb the risk associated with uncertainty is different. Further, this capacity changes with every decision. Some people are naturally conservative. They are said to be risk-averse—the reward has to outweigh the risk before they'll put their money on the table. The capacity for risk by someone who is risk-averse is illustrated in Figure 4-1.

Note the concave shape of the curve. This means that the outcome (or reward) of a given decision must always be greater than the risk to obtain it. However, there comes a point of diminishing return near where the curve begins to flatten. At this point more risk will not be undertaken *regardless* of the potential return.

As managers, we need to be aware of our risk and make an informed judgment as to whether we're being adequately compensated for it.

METHODS TO DETERMINE UNCERTAINTY AND RISK

Some people think of risk and uncertainty as dirty words. This applies only if the consequences catch you by surprise. Without risk, there is usually no worthwhile reward. As managers, we're paid to take risk. However, we *manage* that risk by:

- ■ Identifying it
- ■ Taking it down to a point that meets our risk/reward tolerance
- ■ Controlling the uncertainty that can move what was a previously acceptable risk to one that is suddenly unacceptable

A major part of our business planning effort includes assessment of uncertainty and the risk it creates. Once we establish this, we're in

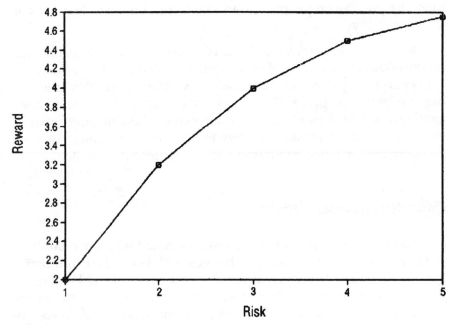

Figure 4—1 Risk-averse decision

a position to refine our plan goals and implementation action steps to control the risk. We accomplish this using three methods:

■ Multiple planning scenarios
■ Sensitivity analysis
■ Simulation

These techniques only sound complicated. Large corporations with the trained staff who are paid to do this work make it complicated. But it doesn't have to be. Let's investigate.

Multiple Scenarios

Each phase of the business plan should include several scenarios that play out possible outcomes of uncertain assumptions. Sales level is usually a good uncertainty to investigate. There are things behind the sales level assumptions that contribute to its uncertainty. Competition or consumer demand are two such possibilities.

We want to put a bracket around the impact of uncertainty so we know the potential damage it can cause to the overall plan. An easy way to do this is to create various scenarios—best case, worst case, and most likely case are good for starters. By running the consequences of specific uncertainties through the entire plan we can readily see three things:

■ Areas of the plan this uncertainty is most likely to affect
■ Damage the event can inflict
■ What must happen within the company to counteract the effects of events whose outcomes are uncertain

Running through various scenarios should be part of the planning team's job. Most companies use these studies on the impact of uncertainty to:

■ Adjust their planning targets and implementation strategies
■ Formulate contingency plans
■ Monitor each uncertain assumption during the planning period to make sure it isn't moving out of acceptable limits

SENSITIVITY ANALYSES

Assessment of your plan's sensitivity to uncertainty is nothing more than measuring the degree to which costs or benefits may change due

---

PLANNING POINTER

Often the performance assumptions for one department are used by another to formulate its implementation plan. Using various scenarios for uncertain conditions, the dependent department may use a worst-case scenario from another department as the most likely outcome when formulating its own implementation plan.

For example, say that sales levels are planned around a worst case of $1 million. The financial department uses sales projections to create its cash plan. By using the worst-case sales levels as a base from which to start, finance will know the *maximum* cash shortfall it is likely to encounter. With this worst-case uncertainty identified, it's easier to create action steps that deal with it. In this case, a greater reduction in working capital required to run the firm and maybe a larger line of credit might be appropriate.

---

to outside influences. For example, the size of a farm's crop will vary with rainfall. A drought drives the total volume available for sale down and the price up (due to scarcity).

Assessment of Sensitivity

We measure sensitivity of the plan to identify the impact of the occurrence of key assumptions. Let's say, for instance, that our business plan has these implementation goals to hit our $1 million net income target:

- Sales must reach $12 million.
- Cost of goods sold cannot be greater than $5 million.
- Direct labor expense cannot exceed $2.1 million.
- Interest expense is targeted at $1.2 million.

Wouldn't it be nice to know how changes to each of these uncertain variables impact our target net income? To find out, we'll use a simple form of sensitivity analysis. Let's start with an imaginary firm we'll call T-D-O Corporation. Page 1 of Table 4-1 shows T-D-O's simple income statement.

This company has a simple goal—hit $1 million in net income before tax by year-end. The question is how serious a threat is presented by uncertainties such as cost of goods sold, direct labor expense, and interest expense. To answer that question we need to determine the impact to the target net income before tax figure *over a range of possible values* for each variable in question. From there we identify those goals in the plan that are absolutely critical and those that are less important. Usually, the variables that present a problem are those that move only slightly but can produce huge profit swings. Direct labor is one such variable. As you can see from page 2 of Table 4-1, a 2% movement in direct labor cost produces an 8% swing in net income before tax.

Note that we know the table is accurate when we can see the direct labor cost of $2.1 million and see that it produces the correct net income figure of $1 million.

Sometimes variables work synergistically. That is, if two variables move together, the impact of their total movement on our goals

Table 4–1   Sensitivity Example, pg. 1

T-D-O Corporation profit plan ($ in thousands)	
Sales	$12,000
Cost of goods sold:	
Raw materials	2,150
Direct labor	2,100
Indirect labor	750
Subtotal cost of goods sold	$ 5,000
Gross margin	$ 7,000
Overhead:	
Administration	4,800
Interest expense	1,200
Subtotal overhead expense	$ 6,000
Net income before tax	$ 1,000

Table 4–1   Sensitivity Example, pg. 2

T-D-O Corporation sensitivity analysis direct labor to net income ($ in thousands)	
Direct labor	Net income
$2,500	$ 600,000
2,450	650,000
2,200	900,000
2,100	1,000,000
1,850	1,250,000
1,600	1,500,000
1,350	1,750,000
1,100	2,000,000
850	2,250,000

Table 4–1 Sensitivity Example, pg. 3

T-D-O Corporation sensitivity analysis
direct labor and administrative cost to net income
($ in thousands)

Direct labor	Administrative cost					
	$5,500	$5,200	$4,800	$4,500	$4,200	$3,900
$3,500	$−1,050	$−,750	$−,350	$ −50	$ 250	$ 550
3,300	−,850	−,550	−,150	150	450	750
3,100	−,650	−,350	50	350	650	950
2,900	−,450	−,150	250	550	850	1,150
2,700	−,250	50	450	750	1,050	1,350
2,500	−50	250	650	950	1,250	1,550
2,300	150	450	850	1,150	1,450	1,750
2,150	300	600	1,000	1,300	1,600	1,900
1,950	500	800	1,200	1,500	1,800	2,100
1,750	700	1,000	1,400	1,700	2,000	2,300
1,550	900	1,200	1,600	1,900	2,200	2,500
1,350	1,100	1,400	1,800	2,100	2,400	2,700

is greater than if they moved independently. Page 3 of Table 4-1 illustrates the change in net income if two variables, direct labor and administrative costs, move together.

Note that, when combined, relatively minor changes in either of these variables can produce huge swings in net income. For example, a favorable drop in direct labor from $3.5 million to $3.3 million is a 5.7% change. A helpful drop in administrative costs from $4.8 million to $4.5 million is just a 6.3% change. However, when combined, they cause net income to *rise* from a loss of $350,000 to a profit of $150,000, a swing of 143%!

Sensitivity Analysis Using a Computer

Sensitivity studies of uncertain variables don't require a computer, but using one does help. Table 4-1 was prepared using a simple spreadsheet program (LOTUS 1-2-3). In fact, most of the popular spreadsheet packages contain some sort of data table management capability from which to draw conclusions regarding sensitivity of uncertain variables.

Further, using a computer, the movement of variables can easily be plotted on a graph. This readily illustrates how a change in the velocity of movement in one variable can affect targeted results. Look at Figure 4-2 to see the movement in net income before tax resulting from changes in direct labor costs (see page 2 of Table 4-1):

SIMULATION ANALYSIS

Simulation is a more sophisticated version of sensitivity analysis. Where sensitivity tested only one or two variables at a time, simulation can test how the entire plan reacts to various uncertainties all occurring at the *same* time. We use simulation techniques for a variety of purposes:

■ They aid in identifying possible weak links in our plan.
■ They assist in preparing multiple case scenarios.
■ They are used to prepare contingency plans to implement when the uncertainties you were afraid of actually occur.

For many years the value of simulation was known only to the largest corporations with the most sophisticated computers and an army of MBAs to interpret the data. No more. With the arrival of personal computers and the user-friendly software that goes with

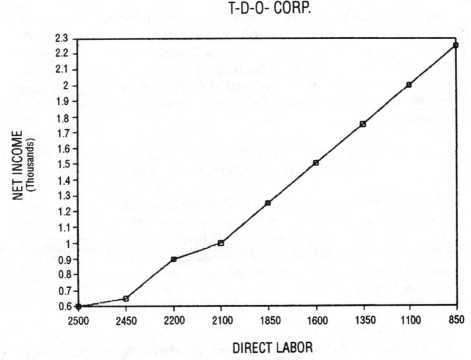

Figure 4—2   Direct labor versus net income

them, even the smallest companies can profit from modern simulation techniques. Furthermore, you don't have to be a programming genius or even a stellar mathematician to benefit.

By the way, in developing this section of the book I talked with my fellow consultants and some college professors about the subject of simulation. Several told me not to bother. They said that small business people and entrepreneurs lacked the sophistication to use this tool. Then I asked the maligned small business people and entrepreneurs. Guess what—they not only used simulation (although they often called it something else) but many included it as part of their ongoing efforts to reduce business risk.

Here are some of the steps we'll take in using simulation analysis to reduce the risk of uncertainty to our plan:

- Identify the risk factors inherent in our plan (called *embedded risk*).
- Formulate alternative strategies to reduce that risk.
- Implement these risk-reduction strategies.
- Monitor the effectiveness of our decisions and modify them as required.

Embedded Risk

Our first step is to identify the risk due to the uncertainty of the key variables of our plan. For example, let's say the price of raw materials is a key factor in maintaining the profit margins necessary to meet specific financial goals. If we did nothing else to our plan to ease the risk caused by this one uncertainty, then *the profit margin projections over the range of possible raw material prices defines embedded risk.* Stated differently:

> *Embedded risk is that risk that already lies in the company without doing anything to control it.*

We identify embedded risk first to determine our starting point. From there we work to reduce that risk. Some people at this point say, "Fine, now all we have to do is predict what the uncertain variable will be, then target our plan to take full advantage of it." These are the gamblers talking. That's exactly *not* what we want to do. For two reasons:

Inconsistency
The probability of consistently predicting where the uncertain variables will be is practically nil. Besides, that's not our business.

Certainly, the gamblers may get lucky and correctly guess once or twice. When they're right, profits will be greater than those of us who are more conservative. However, over time, they'll be wrong more often than they will be right. And when they're wrong, profits will be lower than those of the rest of us. Remember, we're here for the duration. We want to win the whole war, year after year—not just a few minor battles.

Purpose of Risk Control

Controlling business risk through simulation means *insulating* the company's plan from uncertainty. We don't go out and "play the market." Instead, there are specific things we can do to take advantage of these uncertainties when they go our way, and to limit our exposure when they don't. Of course, there's a price we pay for being risk-averse. When the variables go our way, our profits usually aren't as large as those of the gamblers. However, when uncertainties go against us, our losses aren't nearly so large.

Determination of Embedded Risk

The computations required to assess embedded risk aren't complicated. However, they are numerous. That's why a computer is handy. Let's assume that you have put the section of your plan you wish to simulate into a simple automated spreadsheet. Continuing with our example of insulating the company from potential price swings in raw materials, we'll simulate the gross profit margin results. We run the spreadsheet many times over the likely raw material costs (both up and down). We note both the prices and the results of each simulation run.

If we were to graph our results, they might look like those shown in Figure 4-3.

The figure shows how gross margin changes over time given possible movement (both favorable and unfavorable) in the prices of raw materials. Note how the downside risk is much greater than the upside potential. This is entirely realistic, although not the position in which we want to be. If we're going to take risk, we must be compensated for it on the upside.

Therefore, we now have our starting point from which to simulate various strategies to *insulate* our company from movement in raw material prices.

Formulation of Strategies

We use the same spreadsheet (or whatever software was used to determine embedded risk) to create risk-reduction strategies. We retain the same possible values to the uncertain variable(s) we are trying to control. However, this time, instead of not doing anything,

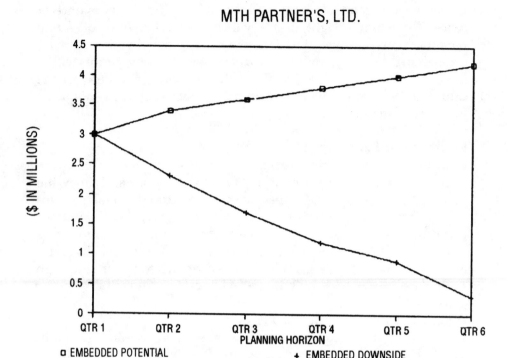

Figure 4–3   Embedded risk: Gross margin

we implement our action plans. Continuing with our example, there are many things that can be done to control something like raw materials prices. Among the possible strategies are:

■ Reengineering the product to use smaller amounts of raw materials or to use other materials less subject to price fluctuation
■ Negotiating a bulk purchase of the raw materials
■ Working with the supplier on a fixed-price contract
■ Hedging exposure to raw materials price increases using commodity futures contracts

You've probably thought of others as well. The point is, we're now doing something to insulate our risk. Observe also, that the strategies listed above all carry a price. In other words, we're buying an insurance policy against price increase. That policy is expensive, but it lessens our exposure. Further, the cost of that insurance is not nearly what the expected value of the loss would be if the market goes against us.

Usually, the formulation of these risk-control strategies slices the bottom part out of the downside risk *and* at the same time trims a small part from the upside potential. Since we're not in the business of gambling with our company, the narrowed risk suits us just fine. Figure 4-4 illustrates how a risk-reduction strategy might alter exposure to uncertainty.

As you can see, we've accomplished our goal. The upside potential is slightly reduced (by about $200,000) if the price swings go our way. Generally, upside potential is decreased only by the cost of implementing the risk-reduction strategy. Fixed-price contracts, for example, are often slightly more expensive and don't allow us to reap the benefits if the market price declines. However, we have succeeded in reducing our downside risk by a little over $1 million if prices move against us. That's what simulation is all about—investigating alternatives that allow us to maintain our profit margin in spite of uncertainty.

Risk Versus Reward

Every uncertainty implies risk. There's nothing wrong with risk; we just want to be aware of it and measure the probable costs if we lose against potential profits if we win. With this information we can make an informed judgment as to how much risk we wish to undertake, if any.

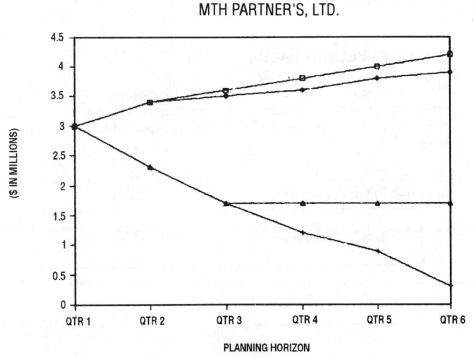

Figure 4-4   Risk-reduction strategies

Many businesses shoot themselves in the foot by undertaking too much risk for the potential reward. Still others fail to consider the reward probability associated with risk they accept. Table 4-2 puts this in perspective. (This exhibit was reprinted with permission from *CASH MANAGER'S GUIDE* by Chris Malburg, Prentice Hall, Englewood Cliffs, NJ, 1992.)

Too many companies find themselves in the lower-right quadrant (high risk/low reward). An example would be a company that planned on making up lost profit from the high prices they had to pay for materials by raising their prices. Except they failed to consider how easy it was for competitors to enter their market with lower prices. In this case, their profits were at high risk by the inflated prices they paid. Their reward potential turned out to be too low due to an almost nonexistent entry barrier. It was a sucker bet.

Instead, we want to be in the upper-left quadrant (low risk/high reward). An example of this position was seen in Figure 4-4 where we cut off a substantial part of the downside risk without severely curtailing the upside potential. Companies afraid of uncertain raw material prices that lock in their costs using commodity futures contracts are a case in point. They reduce their exposure to rising prices and at the same time improve their potential for reward. How can they do this? By keeping intact the upside benefits if prices move in their favor and limiting the downside costs.

When evaluating uncertainty, make sure you keep the risk/reward ratio in your favor.

USE OF EXPECTED VALUE

When dealing with uncertainty and risk management, there are a variety of statistical techniques commonly used. The easiest, however, is the concept of *expected value*. Here is expected value analysis in a nutshell.

Table 4–2   Risk/Reward Matrix

R E W A R D		
	Low risk/high reward	High risk/high reward
	Low risk/low reward	High risk/low reward

RISK

Table 4–3 Computation of Expected Value

	Probability	×	Outcome	=	Expected value
	10%		$100,000		$ 10,000
	20%		200,000		40,000
	30%		150,000		45,000
	25%		175,000		43,750
	10%		300,000		30,000
	5%		500,000		25,000
Expected value	100%				$193,750

- The probabilities of several possible outcomes to an uncertain event are identified.
- These are multiplied by the profit or loss of the outcomes being tested.
- The products are added together to arrive at the overall expected value of the uncertainty.

Table 4-3 illustrates the concept of expected value computations.
As you can see, there's a considerable range between the possible outcomes—from $100,000 to $500,000. However, 75 percent of the probabilities are concentrated between $150,000 and $200,000. Indeed, the expected value of the outcome ($193,750) is within that range. The most difficult part of expected value analysis is accurately gauging the probabilities of each possible outcome. Certainly the probabilities you come up with aren't going to be perfect. However, they should represent your best guess as to the likelihood of each outcome. Beyond that, it seldom makes sense to bear the cost of getting it more precise.

We can employ expected value to identify the most likely outcome of a series of uncertain events. In Table 4-3, if we were trying to determine a production schedule based on projected sales, our most likely sales would be around the $194,000 level. This provides us with a base from which to start. From there, we can work with the uncertainties in terms of action plans if sales levels hit above or below $194,000.

Now we've got a quantifiable reason to support our assumptions and the uncertainty surrounding them. Keep in mind, however, determination of the expected value of an uncertain outcome doesn't mean it will happen. This only provides a logical assessment of the most likely level we may be dealing with. If the possible outcomes are scattered across the board, reliability of the analysis is less certain.

TOLERABLE ERROR

In cases where there's risk that a key target may not be met, we can isolate the damage it might cause. One logical approach to uncertainty is the concept of *tolerable error*. This simply means that as long as a particular uncertain variable stays within a specified range, its impact to the overall plan is acceptable. The company, then, plans accordingly.

The first step to determining the range of tolerable error is to identify those assumptions in the plan that cause the uncertainty. For example, let's say the cash plan assumes that 75 percent of accounts receivable are collected within 45 days after sale. The range of error acceptable before levels of available cash drop so far that our vendors begin delaying shipment because we're stretching our payables may be 65 percent and 50 days. That is, 65 percent of our receivables will be collected within 50 days of sale. Therefore, our *range of error* that we can tolerate and still implement the rest of our plan is:

Between 65 and 75 percent of all receivables are collected between 45 and 50 days.

We can live with actual performance falling anywhere between the limits of these two assumptions. If the firm's history and your own good common sense indicate that the performance will likely fall somewhere within that range, then the assumption makes sense. Otherwise, it's back to the drawing board.

Banking institutions use the concept of tolerable error when determining their exposure to interest rate fluctuations. They can forecast what their net interest income (interest income from outstanding loans less interest expense paid to depositors and other sources of lendable funds) will be if interest rates move. By playing out rising and falling interest rate scenarios over their planning horizon, a bank can identify its exposure to interest rate movement. If found to be unacceptable, the smart bankers take steps to decrease this vulnerability. Contrary to popular belief, banks don't usually play the interest rate markets. They are supposed to be partly insulated from rate movement. The way they go about doing this uses the same theory the rest of us employ in our own small businesses.

BRACKETING THE ACTION PLAN

Bracketing assesses each critical element in the action plan. It then measures the impact of movement of the uncertain variable on the target and identifies the range of tolerable error. In this way each critical element is "bracketed" for a required range during plan implementation.

The real value to bracket planning is that it breaks down the individual elements into action plan components. These are categorized by importance. It then identifies the feasibility of the action plan. Where there is unacceptably low likelihood that the action plan can be achieved, the implementation is adjusted until the plan becomes more feasible.

Not all departments need be bracketed. Generally, only areas in the company containing uncertain variables that include these characteristics are involved:

- The uncertainties of the variable affects the overall plan for the entire firm.
- The impact of an uncertain variable is not obvious just by looking at it.
- Management must be able to exert some degree of control over the outcome of the uncertain variable—otherwise, there's no point in doing the work.

Here's the way bracketing uncertain variables works:

- A sensitivity analysis is run on the action plan to identify the variables most critical to achieving the target.
- Management determines the range over which each of these critical variables could fall.

The exercise identifies risk to the action plan caused by a few critical variables. We can then determine how far away we are from the range of tolerable error, and take steps to bring it in line.

For example, let's assume that production capacity must be 100,000 units. This capacity can vary no more than 10% or 10,000 units and still keep the entire company on track. However, there are five critical uncertainties that affect our production capacity. One of these, *variable A*, impacts capacity by 2,000 units if changed just 1%. Therefore, the maximum tolerable error of *variable A* (assuming everything else stays the same) is 20% (2,000/10,000 = 20%). This becomes its bracket. The other variables are similarly tested.

Offsetting and Synergistic Variables

Many times the impact of movement by one critical variable will be offset by that of another. These two circumstances may neutralize the positive or negative effects of either change on the target plan. Likewise, two variables that move simultaneously might cause an impact greater than if they had moved separately.

These possibilities are usually determined in the bracketing exercise as well.

BUFFERS AGAINST UNCERTAINTY

Now that we've identified the ways by which to recognize and measure uncertainty, how should we deal with it? Even now, different departments within your company probably employ a variety of methods to insulate the company from risks over which they have control.

Manufacturing

Risks most manufacturing departments must deal with include:

- Production capacity sufficient to meet sales demands without creating oversupply
- Inventory management of raw materials, work in process, and finished goods
- Adequacy of the labor pool at targeted costs
- Warehousing and storage facilities
- Shipping facilities

Every manager uses the approach that works best for his or her company in its particular circumstances. However, here are some of the techniques that have worked before to reduce the risk of uncertainty in these areas:

Production Capacity

Too much capacity can be just as bad as having too little. Both extremes can be expensive and present a risk to meeting planned targets. Some companies establish their production capacity at the most likely sales level. If more capacity is required, they might rent it or subcontract out the added production necessary.

Depending on the likelihood of the need for extra capacity, some companies maintain additional production facilities and close relationships with subcontractors. Often there is a contract already in place that identifies the specifics and prices for what might be required. In this way, the price of obtaining additional capacity can be boiled into the implementation plan and included in the range of tolerable error. Further, startup lead-time is minimized.

Inventory

Inventory management seems to be the bane of many small business managers. Like production capacity, inventory levels must be established to satisfy demand without burning up working capital by having so much inventory on hand that turns too slowly. Understanding the principals behind inventory management can reduce the risk (and costs) of uncertainty. Let's spend a few minutes reviewing two of the major inventory management tools: economic order quantity and safety stock.

Economic Order Quantity (EOQ)   There is a point of diminishing returns beyond which it doesn't pay to buy in larger orders. Managers afraid they will run short of raw materials often ignore the correct order quantity. EOQ provides a method to determine the optimum order quantity of a particular item. It's more of a theory than a rule cast in stone. However, using the EOQ principles provides a mathematical benchmark against which to assess inventory risk.

Here is the EOQ formula:

$$EOQ = \sqrt{[(2QP)/AC]}, \text{ where}$$
Q is the annual quantity of the item used in units.
P is the purchase order cost.
A is the annual cost of carrying a unit in
stock for one year. The carrying cost of
inventory includes such items as allocated
warehouse expenses and interest costs on working
capital requirements. This is expressed as a
percentage.
C is the purchase price of the inventory item.

Let's run the equation assuming:

- We will need 100,000 units this year.
- The cost of one completed purchase order including receipt of the goods and shelving is $100.
- The annual carrying cost of inventory is computed to be 12%.
- The cost of each item is $2.00 for order quantities between 5,000 and 10,000.

The economic order quantity size for this product is 9,129 units, determined as follows:

$$\text{EOQ} = \sqrt{[2 \times (100,000 \times \$100)]/(12\% \times \$2.00)} = 9,129$$

Assuming an even production run, there will be about eleven of these orders during the year (100,000/9,129 = 10.95). Beyond that volume per order or order frequency, the benefits derived from bulk purchases are not optimized.

PLANNING POINTER

Some suppliers offer discounts for bulk orders. Make sure your EOQ analysis includes these costs reductions.

Safety Stock   To counter the risk perceived by carrying too little inventory, some managers carry a safety stock. This is a good idea as long as the safety stock is appropriate for the costs of running short. Too often, the inventory manager is not accountable for the *costs* of carrying excess inventory—only for running short. Therefore, safety stock is higher than it need be. This sloppiness eats up working capital that could (and should) be used more profitably in other parts of the company.

The trick is to peg the safety stock at a level where it's cost effective. We do this by considering variables such as the probability and cost of running short, the number of orders placed per year (taken from EOQ calculations), and the cost of inventory carry.

Here's the equation to find the optimum safety stock level:

Probability of stock out at a given level of safety stock
× Stock out cost
× Number of orders per year (Demand/EOQ)
Equals expected stock out cost
+ Carrying cost of safety stock
Equals total inventory carrying cost

The easiest way to find the appropriate safety stock is to set up the computation in tabular form. Compute the cost of the various units of safety stock under consideration. Then choose the one with the lowest total cost. See Table 4-4.

The optimum level of safety stock has the lowest inventory carrying cost. In this example, the optimum safety stock level is 60 units. An unnecessary safety stock of inventory exceeding 60 units wastes valuable working capital without contributing to overall profitability.

Table 4–4 Computation of Safety Stock

Units of safety stock	Probability of stock out	Cost of stock out	# of orders per year	Stock out cost (A)	Carrying cost (B)	Total cost (C)
60	40%	100	15	$600	$300	$900
70	60%	100	15	900	350	950
80	35%	100	15	525	400	925
90	22%	100	15	330	450	780

(A) Stock out cost is computed as the probability of stock out × cost of stock out × # of orders per year (EOQ).

(B) Carrying cost is computed as the carrying cost of one unit per year (assumed to be $5.00) × safety stock.

(C) Total cost is computed as stock out cost + carrying cost.

Labor Pool

The right mix of workers with the necessary skills at the right cost can be a source of uncertainty for any business. Companies in the service sector or retail tend to be more greatly influenced by labor than do capital-intensive companies.

A major uncertainty in planning labor cost can be upcoming union contract negotiations. Smart managers keep a close watch on the contracts that other companies have negotiated with the same union. Additionally, they maintain a close working relationship and ongoing dialog with union executives and the shop stewards in their own company. When it comes time to negotiate the contract, the union's demands don't come as a surprise and they are able to work with them within the constraints of their own business plan.

In cases where managers see the costs of their normal labor pool rising, they begin seeking alternative sources of skilled workers. Sometimes companies are able to import the needed people from outside the city or even outside the state and still come out ahead. If the problem is seen as being long term, many companies begin making provisions to move some of their labor-intensive operations offshore. Parts of Asia and the Far East are notorious among American workers for undercutting domestic wages.

Having too many workers on the payroll can be just as disastrous to the business plan as not having enough. In cases where cutbacks are required, smart managers have already planned for them. Such contingencies as severance pay, outplacement, and a fund for legal fees and settlement of lawsuits for the multitude of labor-related issues attendant to cutbacks are usually included in the business plan. Further, a policy on settlement versus pursuit of litigation is usually in place before the fact.

Warehouse and Storage Facilities

Companies are often uncertain as to the requirements for their warehouse and storage facilities. There is usually a direct link between the manufacturing action plan and the amount of space required to house inventories of raw materials and finished goods.

If additional space is needed, an option on a lease for another facility is often the solution. This provides an insurance policy that reduces a potential uncertainty. Further, it fixes the potential excess costs so they can be entered into the business plan. Another solution to reduce storage requirements is to implement an early shipment schedule of finished goods to customers. This gets the goods off the warehouse floor, making room for other items that must be stored.

If excess warehouse and storage capacity is anticipated, the company can rent out the part of its facility that won't be needed. This recovers at least a part of the cost that would have otherwise been lost.

Shipping Facilities

Shipping is probably one of the easiest uncertainties to control. If additional shipping capacity is required, more trucks can always be leased to move the merchandise. If the problem is purely short term, trucking companies can be hired to take up the required capacity.

If your company anticipates having excess shipping capacity, you can always do contract work for other companies that have the opposite problem. Indeed, if you are already leasing out some of your excess warehouse space, the most likely customers for your excess shipping capacity are your present lessees.

Marketing

The marketing plan usually contains the most uncertainty. There's not a great deal managers can do about sales shortfalls caused by customers who simply refuse to buy. However, the problem may be related to a variety of other things such as:

- Incentive of the sales force
- Advertising
- Failure to target the correct market

Nevertheless, if the company needs a particular sales level and it's not forthcoming, immediate corrective action must be taken. If not, the entire business plan is in jeopardy.

Believe it or not, some firms have the opposite problem—they are blessed with excess demand for their products. It takes a savvy manager who knows when to turn away business. Here are three instances where this might be a good idea:

■ Acceptance of a huge order would place overreliance on a single customer—professionals such as CPAs are prohibited from taking on a single client that is so large it could compromise their independence.
■ The firm doesn't have the working capital to finance inventory purchases and receivables carrying costs of additional orders without reducing its profit margin below acceptance levels.
■ The company does not possess the manufacturing capacity to make additional goods without incurring unfavorable labor variances due to overtime and excess machine downtime resulting from overutilization.

Finance

The financial plan is probably the easiest to formulate. It depends on input from the rest of the company. The results are mathematically computed. The greatest uncertainty lies in whether the assumptions that went into the financial plan will occur.

For small and medium-sized businesses, probably the most critical factor in the financial plan is the cash balance. Uncertainty associated with the rest of the plan affects cash all along the planning horizon. To control this risk, most financial managers do at least two things:

■ They formulate the cash flow plan on a most-likely to worst-case basis—if the firm can survive that, then they have adequate cash reserves.
■ They plan for the availability of additional cash resources.

Some of the other factors used to further control uncertainty in the financial plan include the following:

■ Accounts receivable and payable balances are managed to a predetermined level.
■ Sales terms are controlled—specifically the payment due date.
■ Payment terms for purchases are controlled—again, specifically the payment due date.
■ Tax liabilities are recognized and their payment timing is planned.
■ Interest rates on borrowing are locked in by a hedging mechanism.

Table 4–5 Commonly Encountered Variables Subject to Uncertainty

- Sales
- Sales-related expenses including:

  □ Sales commissions

  □ Travel and entertainment

  □ Telephone

  □ Postage and express mail delivery

  □ Auto

  □ Advertising

- Sales price of products sold (driven in part by competition)
- Actions by competition
- Interest rates
- Labor rates
- Terms of vendor payments—accelerates cash outflow
- Customer payment habits—drives receivables aging, which affects cash flow
- Prices of raw materials
- Bank lending requirements
- Foreign exchange rates
- Energy prices
- Legislative changes, such as changes in the tax law
- Governmental spending, such as defense spending

CONTINGENCY PLANS

The planning process with which we've been working has a built-in contingency strategy. By definition, arriving at the changes required in various departments' action implementation plans given the best case, worst case, and most likely cases, produces a contingency plan.

Changes in the business environment seem to happen quickly—especially when they go against you. There's a lot to be said for having a predetermined response in the event of a disaster. Usually there's no time to try and figure out what to do. Analysis paralysis sets in and by then it's too late.

We saw the beginnings of contingency planning above when we discussed ways to reduce uncertainty. A good example is having alternative manufacturing facilities firmly committed in the event demand outstrips capacity.

Just like the main business plan, contingency plans must be continuously evaluated to measure the risk/reward ratio in the event they must be implemented. As long as contingency plans are routinely updated to make sure they are still current and provide an appropriate response, they can help reduce uncertainty.

Commonly Encountered Uncertainties

Every business has its own set of variables that can make or break the business plan. Some variables can move way out of their planned range without severely affecting the plan. Others need only move a bit before there's a significant risk to the plan. Earlier in this chapter we determined the importance of these variables using sensitivity analysis.

If you are formulating your business plan for the first time, Table 4-5 will help you identify some of those uncertain variables that are sure to be encountered in business.

Cause and Effect

Business planners pay close attention to the impact of seemingly unrelated events. What may appear to affect only one department often can have major repercussions in other areas of the company.

Say that your bank tightens its credit criteria. Interest rates move 10 percent over the top of the planned range as demand for funds exceeds supply. Consequently, customers stretch their payment habits. The result is that your cash flow begins to slow and the potential money available from your bank becomes more expensive. This domino effect impacts other parts of the company that were depending on using borrowed money to fund particular actions.

Identify the cause and effect factors that can make your business plan go astray. Watch them closely and formulate a contingency plan for those you think are critical to the company meeting its objectives.

Operations

OVERVIEW

Chapter 5 features the techniques used to synthesize departmental plans into the overall goals. We do this using the same top-down approach established for the overall planning process. In this way, requirements of the corporatewide plan are filtered through the entire organization.

Think of business planning as you would a symphony orchestra. The composer sets the overall goals by writing the music. The conductor performs the plan by coordinating various groups who execute the composer's ideas. The individual musicians—*at the operating level*—perform their particular parts in concert with each other and in harmony with the conductor's instructions. Only through such organized effort from the composer, the conductor, and the individual musicians can the desired results be achieved.

The operational plan tells each manager the results that are required from their particular department to achieve the necessary objectives. This can be tricky since it involves two phases:

1. The various departmental plans must be integrated into a single coordinated unit that fulfills overall requirements of the companywide plan.
2. The personal agendas of individual department managers must be adjusted to move toward the larger goal, rather than one *they* may have in mind.

INTEGRATION OF DEPARTMENTAL PLANS

One way to determine how the various parts of the plan relate to one another is to trace the generation of profit through the company. This process identifies the critical path of what must happen in order for the business to make money. With this exercise comes an understanding of how each department's individual goals fold into the plans and action steps of every other department.

Identification of the Business Cycle

Most companies have a business cycle through which their purchases of raw materials are converted into saleable goods. From that point, vendors are paid, receivables are collected, and the process begins again. Some firms run many complete business cycles every year. Some don't. An example would be a construction company whose projects take years to complete.

Let's identify the business cycle of a small manufacturing company and see how each step relates to the plans of other departments.

Inventory Purchase

The first step in most business cycles is either manufacturing or buying the goods that your customers will eventually buy from you. However, to do that we need to know what the firm's *cash capability* is before purchases are made.

The concept of cash capability is similar to a football quarterback throwing a pass to a receiver not yet in the target area. By the time the ball gets there, however, he should be. We can compute the amount of cash available to purchase inventory by using this formula:

■ Disposable cash currently available
■ *Plus* short-term investments maturing within the business cycle
■ *Plus* scheduled collection of already existing accounts and notes receivable
■ *Plus* available lines of credit and other borrowing facilities scheduled to be drawn during the business cycle
■ *Less* payment obligations due within the cycle
■ Equals cash capability

With the available cash determined throughout the business cycle, we are now in a position to determine the amount of inventory we can purchase (without throwing the company into receivership).

Key link: Cash capability is compared with the amount of inventory the sales department says is required to fulfill its scheduled sales levels. This is subtracted from current cash balances as a cash outflow.

> *Key link:* Inventory purchases drive the terms required by the company's buyer in order to mesh with the cash available for disbursement to vendors.

Manufacturing

The manufacturing production schedule is one of the most important pieces of the business cycle and operational plan. From this comes such critical information as:

- The number and skill level of workers needed
- The manufacturing cost estimates for things such as utility expenses incurred in the manufacturing process
- Sufficiency of the manufacturing and inventory storage facilities

> *Key link:* This manufacturing production schedule feeds the personnel requirements plan.

> *Key link:* The manufacturing production schedule dictates amount and timing of capital expenditures required to purchase equipment for the manufacturing operation.

> *Key link:* The manufacturing production schedule is required by the finance department to determine the timing of cash payments to employees, vendors, and suppliers.

The Sales Cycle

The sales cycle dictates the time frames for particular sales targets to be met. It begins when the company's sales people first call on prospective customers. The next step is to evaluate the customer's creditworthiness and make a decision on credit limits. Once credit is approved and the goods are shipped, the company cuts an invoice, which is then entered into the accounts receivable system.

> *Key link:* Bonds between the sales cycle and other parts of the business plan include:

- Credit criteria—often handled in the finance area
- Terms of sale including pricing, trade discounts (if any), and payment due dates
- Timing and method of invoice release

Disburse Payment Obligations

Sometime after the inventory is purchased, it must be paid for. Along with input from the manufacturing department's inventory purchasing schedule comes such information as:

- Payment obligations scheduled by due dates
- Determination of payment aging policy as dictated by the finance department (also used by the purchasing department to plan terms of its purchase contracts and negotiations)

Collection of Customer Payments

The finance department uses the business cycle and the plans that comprise it to determine its own receivables collection action plan. Accelerating the collection of accounts receivable can be expensive. It often requires the presence of trained collectors, dunning notices, and sometimes legal remedies.

Key links between the business cycle and the financial department include the following:

- Timing of the sales plan is done for purposes of computing *when* collections should be forthcoming.
- Terms of sale offered by the sales and marketing department should be determined.
- Expenditures are scheduled for such things as advertising.
- Geographic dispersion of the customer base should be determined as the cash flow plan unfolds. The farther customers are away from corporate headquarters, the longer it takes for payment to arrive. This information is contained in the sales plan. The finance department may use it to establish an accelerated cash inflow mechanism, such as a lock box.

MANAGING COMPETING AGENDAS

Business planning is a human endeavor. As such, you'll find the priorities of some managers aren't in sync with those of the company's goals. The operational plan brings together the diverse goals of most of the line managers in the company. It organizes and controls this effort so the end products of one department dovetail into the requirements of another.

Recognize that every part of the operational plan won't be met with open arms by all managers. The expected results from some departments may adversely impact the ability of others to meet their targets. Further, the timing of results from one department may not be what's required by others. Such problems need to be addressed and corrected in the operational plan.

Sometimes management makes the mistake of creating an environment where competing agendas are actually *promoted*. This results largely from three areas:

1. Incentive motivation
2. Promotion policies
3. Resistance to change

Incentives

We'll be talking in detail about the right way to initiate an incentive policy in Chapter 9. But for now you should know that incentives must be established at the operating level to drive performance in the direction needed to achieve the plan objectives. When it's done incorrectly, incentives can undermine the operational plan. Such problems occur when obtaining the incentive becomes more important than coordinating the plan results of the company as a whole.

Typically, such problem incentives are too large and overshadow competing manager's sense of teamwork. It becomes a *win at all cost* motivation. Other times the criteria for successfully meeting goals necessary to get the incentive reward are not thought through by management. Incentives that reward a specific performance in one department can actually *diminish* overall performance of the company as a whole. An example is the inventory level managed by the manufacturing department. An incentive is given to keep the inventory down to a specific level. The target is hit. However, the cost of backorders shoots up and the climb in sales revenue is hindered due to lack of availability of goods to ship. As a result, the revenue targets are missed and overall profitability falls. That's called *getting no bang for your buck.*

To prevent this from happening, incentive components of the HR operating plan can be tiered:

- The first part—usually the largest part—is based on the person meeting his or her individual goals.
- The second part—proportionately smaller—is based on the person's *department or division* meeting its goals.
- The third part—smaller still—is based on the company meeting its overall goals.

Promotion Policies

The same problem can exist when the incentive for meeting operational planning objectives is a job promotion. Unless the promotion criteria are clearly defined and emphasize success of the company as a whole, the sense of teamwork required by the operational plan is lost. I know of one New York money center bank that promotes its people on a two-year cycle. As a result, short-term programs and fixes are established with results that appear to be working but at a cost to other areas.

Resistance to Change

By necessity, plans cause change. However, there is a force in nature that's resistant to change—*inertia of rest*. The operational plan breaks down this resistance to change. Department heads are responsible for creating both the environment and mechanism that gets results that are different from those that were obtained before.

A case in point is the manufacturing department's idea of the appropriate level of raw material inventory. The manufacturing manager naturally wants to schedule long production runs. That's the most cost-efficient use of his production line setup costs. Further, he can buy the raw materials in bulk at a discount, thereby creating a favorable material price variance.

The controller, however, sees things differently. Large buildups in raw materials suck up working capital. Eventually, these purchases must be paid for. Further, a production run that exceeds sales levels just sits on the warehouse floor in the form of finished goods inventory—another waste of working capital that takes too long to be turned into sales, then accounts receivable, and finally disposable cash.

Both managers have valid points. The manufacturing head may have always done long production runs because they were so cost efficient. His planning targets may even require him to cut cost of goods sold to a new and lower level. The production run may be the method he chooses to accomplish this task.

The controller, on the other hand, is responsible for the company's cash position and how best to employ limited working capital. She sees the production manager as not employing his allocation of working capital in the most efficient way.

See the quandry? The operational plan must identify such conflicts and resolve them so that:

■ The plan moves ahead toward its goals.
■ The managers are still appropriately motivated to succeed in their areas of the plan that promote the overall good of the firm.
■ Everyone's best interests are served—the company's as well as the managers who execute the plan.

INTERCOMPANY SALES AND TRANSFER PRICING

If your company has more than one division, issues of intercompany sales and transfer pricing will probably surface during the planning process. This tends to be a sore point between operating managers because their plan targets are often influenced by the costs of goods they are required to purchase from another division of the same company. Therefore, the success of one division *could* come at the expense of another all because of the transfer pricing rules employed.

This is troubling for the planning team since intercompany sales are all "funny money" anyway. You are just taking funds from one pocket and putting them in another. Any success or failure due to intercompany sales and transfer pricing means little.

When judging the performance of an operating unit where intercompany sales are an issue, it's best to either factor them out completely or make them competitive with the market place. After all, both divisions work for the same parent company and are executing operating plans that promote the overall parent's goals.

For example, many companies centralize their treasury function on the parent level. When operating divisions need to borrow money, it's from the parent. In this way, all the company's borrowing requirements are consolidated at the parent level. The leverage of a larger single credit facility can be used on the lender by the corporate treasurer.

The parent then charges each division the going market rate on funds borrowed for that day, as if it were a bank. This is called a *capital charge*. Each division is aware of this price and makes its decisions on the profitable use of these funds based on real market information. This works just like any other independent company—except the divisions don't have to worry about a credit rating.

Consequently, artificial costs or savings resulting from transfer pricing are eliminated from divisional borrowing decisions.

SALES AND MARKETING

Most of the operational plan depends on answers derived from the sales and marketing plan. Specifically, we need answers regarding:

- Sales volume and method, such as direct selling media, the sales force, sales representatives, and brokers
- Promotions such as price changes, premium programs, special store fixtures, and trade show participation
- Advertising both in terms of products and the firm's market image in the various advertising media used

- Products offered and new products under development
- Customer service areas such as repair, warranty service, customer training, and complaints
- Distribution of the products, such as method of shipment, distributors, and use of warehouse facilities

Each of these areas is important in generating a solid sales and marketing plan as well as to those departments responsible for support of these programs.

Controls Provided by the Sales and Marketing Plan

A benefit spun off by the sales and marketing plan includes control over some of the costs associated with selling the product. These include:

Selling Expenses
The sales plan provides information regarding the sales levels of each particular product or area of the business. If a department or item is not performing as required, changes can be made before it's too late.

Promotion and Advertising
Sales promotions can quickly get out of control—especially where expensive in-store displays are concerned. Be sure to watch the costs and benefits of each promotion and advertising program. As soon as they become marginal, cut them off.

Trade shows can be a large expenditure for little sales increase if the sponsoring organization doesn't live up to its promises. Additionally, giveaway promotions should be carefully watched so that the right goods are getting to the right people.

Product Development
Expenditures of product development commonly include packaging, features, styling, and the potential market. The best way to control the expenses for this research is on a *project basis*. That way, the costs and benefits for particular programs can be judged independently of one another. Each project becomes integrated into the sales and marketing plan.

Customer Service
Warranty repairs, complaints, and product recalls all fall under customer service. By incorporating this significant cost center into the sales and marketing plan, managers can be held responsible for controlling its costs.

Key statistics used in formulating the customer service plan include:

- Failure rate percentages and history of each product
- Comparative trends for warranty service costs
- Customer complaints and requests for new features

Distribution

Product distribution is important for both the warehouse and shipping departments. Additionally, if part of the marketing plan includes an increased level of customer service and responsiveness to orders, the distribution network plays an important part.

The inventory manager also needs to know how the plans for product distribution are going to change. This enables her to plan for swings in the inventory demand both for raw materials and finished goods.

HUMAN RESOURCES PLAN

Employees are one of the most expensive and critical areas of the operational plan. The human resources (HR) plan objectives include:

- Fulfilling the short- and long-term staffing needs of the firm
- Implementation of action steps to attract qualified people having the required skills
- Development and maintenance of a compensation plan to retain valued employees
- Establishing a competitive system of benefits, such as group health insurance
- Managing employee risk through an appropriate workers compensation program
- Establishing a mechanism that motivates employees and develops skills necessary for the company to achieve its plan objectives

If any of these four targets fall short, the company's operating plan could be at risk.

Components of the Human Resources Plan

Most HR plans address these issues critical to the company's operations:

- Developing and maintaining an appropriate incentive compensation system
- Staffing requirements in terms of changes necessary in existing positions and new positions required by the plan
- Systematic employee performance evaluation
- Maintenance of competitive salaries, perks, and overall compensation levels

Staffing Requirements

The most basic issue addressed by the HR plan is that of *who and how many*. Having enough people with the right combination of skills and motivation goes a long way toward meeting the overall company's plan objectives.

To this end, the human resources plan focuses on determining the personnel requirements for each department. This isn't always as easy as it may seem. Included in this part of the plan are variables such as:

- Needs for temporary personnel
- Overtime expenses for existing employees where neither an additional full-timer nor an interim person can be justified

Special Situations

Temporary personnel and overtime are special situations. This is the most expensive form of labor the company can buy. There comes a point of diminishing return for both overtime and temporary personnel expenses. Generally these are so expensive that they're used as stopgap measures only.

The HR manager's operational plan deals specifically with both temporary employees and overtime expenses. Often each project that requires temporaries and OT are identified. The exact tasks of the temps and OT personnel are pinpointed. Sometimes, the number of hours they'll be working are recognized. With this level of detail, control over this most expensive form of labor can be managed.

PLANNING POINTER

Failure to properly consider the increased efficiency of experienced personnel when establishing headcount targets is a prime source of what we call *sandbagging*. Department managers have been known to argue for the inclusion of added personnel resources in order to pad their expense targets. This provides a nice cushion against which to make up other planning shortfalls.

Another way to judge the reasonableness of headcount targets is to measure them against an index. For example, when evaluating the number of sales people, you might link these with projected sales revenues. If sales revenues per person suddenly changes from what it has been in the past, then something has shifted.

Another index often used is net income per person. When the operational plan is compared against actual results, you can quickly see how much each employee brings to the bottom line.

Employee Performance Evaluation

Part of the HR plan should include maintenance of an employee evaluation mechanism (or its initial implementation if one doesn't currently exist). It's only good business to periodically evaluate every employee's performance. Benefits of this practice include the following:

- Employees rest easier knowing exactly what their boss and the company thinks of their performance.
- Specific goals are put into writing and act as a standard against which to gauge future performance.
- The company has a verifiable tracking mechanism of each person's performance on which to base its employment decisions.

Goals are useful in implementing the popular *management by objective* program. Under this system, incentive compensation is paid based on the goals attained.

Compensation

The HR manager's operating plan should include a series of action steps to evaluate and adjust employee compensation for each level in the company. This includes salaries, perks, bonuses, and other forms of compensation such as insurance and retirement plans.

The HR operations plan incorporates compensation schedules for every employee. Included here are:

- Each employee's compensation history
- Competitive compensation levels in other companies
- Copies of job descriptions that tell what the person does for the company
- Performance reviews by supervisors
- Scheduled raises

Based on these data, the HR manager is able to determine appropriate compensation levels and schedule out salary expense for the company over the planning horizon.

The HR plan usually includes a review of compensation levels to ensure that the firm is competitive with what the market thinks specific skills are worth. Part of the HR manager's job is to ensure the firm pays at a level that attracts and retains qualified employees without being overly generous. Such surveys are often conducted by trade associations. For example, the Printing Institute of America regularly publishes a wage and salary survey for HR managers in that industry to use as a guide.

Tracking the Manpower Plan

The HR plan can be quantified to better gauge efficiency. We won't get deeply involved in the cost accounting aspects of labor standards and variances here. That level of sophistication is greater than our purposes require. However, many small companies identify key manpower performance targets and track their operating plans against them.

Here's how it's done:

Step 1: Identify Benchmarks
The first step determines the meaningful benchmarks that tie into the manpower plan. Look for something that identifies the performance of the people you wish to track. In a manufacturing environment, this could be the labor costs directly and indirectly associated with making the product. In a service company, this could be the salary expenses involved in performing the service being sold.

Step 2: Determine What the Costs Should Be
Step 2 links the labor costs with the actual operating plan that makes the product or delivers the service. Experience tells us what these costs should be. Most manufacturing companies have some sort of labor cost breakdown for their operations.

For our purposes, the excruciating detail provided by a cost accountant is not necessary. All we want to know is how close our labor costs are to what we had originally planned them to be. Using this information as the planning year unfolds, we can take corrective action in the event labor costs are getting out of hand.

Step 3: Include Indirect Costs
There are two different types of costs associated with employees: direct and indirect. The direct costs are the most obvious. These include salaries and wages paid to the employees. Indirect costs are somewhat more elusive. They include insurance, 401(k) plans, sick time, absenteeism, state employment department and OSHA re-

quirements, and preparation of employee manuals. The list goes on but you get the idea.

Often the indirect costs are the toughest to control. They are usually administered by the HR manager and should be included in his or her plan. A good way to measure the indirect labor costs is to compare it against the sales revenue for one unit sold. For example, say we sell boxes for $10 each. The indirect labor costs associated with selling one box are $1. That means 10 percent of the revenue for every box we sell is eaten up with overhead expenses associated with our employees.

These overhead costs don't contribute directly to making the box; however, they are no less necessary. Without competitive indirect costs (some people call them perks), the company would not attract the type of people able to meet the firm's goals.

ALLOCATION OF CORPORATE OVERHEAD

If your company has more than one division, chances are it incurs some costs associated with running the whole show. This is what we call corporate overhead. Since the parent company of the divisions (sometimes called the holding company) has no way of recouping its costs, they are frequently allocated to the operating divisions.

This allocation is a constant source of irritation to division managers. Not only are they responsible for meeting their own planning targets, now they must make a profit *above* that to pay for their share of the corporate overhead. Even when they do, they've just broken even. To add insult to injury, the division managers often view involvement by the corporate executives as an unwelcome intrusion on their territory that adds little to their bottom line.

The good news (as if any exists in this sensitive area) is that the parent company has an operational overhead plan too. If it doesn't, you should make sure it gets one. The holding company plan does several things:

- It identifies just what these administrative people intend to do for the operating divisions.
- It specifies levels of cost for the services it provides.
- It allocates percentages of its total cost to each operating division.

With a credible operating plan created at the corporate level, everyone understands what services they get and what their costs will be.

MATERIALS REQUIREMENTS PLANNING

Materials requirements planning (MRP) coordinates the production of products having several components or substages that must be assembled. Most companies begin their MRPs from the bottom up—that is, they start with the number of end products required. From there the parts and assemblies necessary are "backed into" throughout the production (or assembly) process.

Since the parts and assemblies are based on the requirement for finished goods, their input stages are interdependent. That often means one part of assembly must be finished so that it can be used in another, which goes into another . . . until the final product is put together.

Coordination of the MRP

Depending on your company, raw materials can be almost as expensive to purchase as the labor used to turn them into finished goods. This part of the operational plan feeds directly into the:

- Cash disbursement schedule located in the financial plan
- Schedule of disposable cash
- Facilities plan for warehouse storage
- Capital expenditures plan for additional material handling equipment

Some of the inventory decisions that come out of the materials requirements plan include:

- Size of material orders
- Safety stock of material to be kept on hand
- Timing of material orders
- Which vendors to use (those that fulfill the delivery schedules)

These items are usually the responsibility of the purchasing manager. Table 5-1 illustrates the computation of planned material purchases.

Naturally, from a financial point of view, the controller wants to have the materials arrive on the shop floor just before they are needed. This cuts down on the buildup of excess raw materials inventory. Further, it accelerates manufacturing inventory turnover. Both serve to decrease working capital requirements.

However, the production manager doesn't want to risk interrupting the steady flow of his manufacturing line. That's expensive in terms of employee downtime as well as that of the production line equipment. Therefore, the MRP portion of the operating plan becomes a coordinated effort between production, finance, and the sales force.

PLANNING POINTER

When changing vendors for some of your subassemblies or raw materials, be sure to track the rejected parts that come from the new vendor. Often it doesn't pay to switch to a cheaper vendor whose parts require more rework costs than if the more expensive but better goods were originally purchased.

To do this, you should have some idea of the normal reject rate of each part or subassembly. Compare this "standard" number against actuals all along the planning horizon.

Anatomy of the MRP

Large corporations can explode the MPR into an extremely complicated document, manageable only by computer. For our purposes, however, it can be much simpler. Don't forget, the MRP's primary function is to coordinate the efforts of sales, manufacturing, purchasing, and finance.

The purists will notice that we're not really designing what most people know as a material requirements plan. Instead, we're constructing a combination of several schedules based on an MRP—but it gets the job done. Components of our blended schedule should include the following:

Table 5–1 Materials Requirements

Computation of materials purchases requirements	
Units required for production	200,000
Plus safety stock	25,000
Total units required	225,000
Less beginning inventory on hand	(10,000)
Units to be purchased	215,000
Purchase price per unit	× $5.00
Cost of material purchases	$1,075,000.00

Basic Format

Begin with the basic format shown in Table 5-1. We want to see how the material requirements are derived for every part that we'll be purchasing. This also tells us the amount of money we'll spend and when.

Timing

For the purchasing and finance departments, timing of the MRP is everything. They have to know when the goods are needed and when they'll be paid for. To accomplish this, the MRP takes on the appearance of a schedule with the months (or even weeks or days, if necessary) across the top.

The first quarter of the schedule shows the timing necessary for the sales department's forecast. This tells production *when* they must have the goods ready for shipment.

The next quarter shows the production department's timing requirements to have the goods ready for feeding into the production or assembly line. Therefore, each component is entered on its own line with the number of units and their costs required in the appropriate time. This should anticipate the sales schedule. It must also reconcile to the sales forecast.

The next quarter shows the purchasing department's purchase order schedule for each raw material and subassembly. Be sure to take into consideration vendor lead-times and a timing cushion for delivery problems.

The final quarter of the report illustrates the finance department's vendor payment schedule—again listed by component. Whatever your policies with respect to vendor payment terms and aging of accounts payable, they should be included here.

With these four items, we've identified:

1. When the finished goods need to be shipped
2. When the raw materials and subassemblies must be ready for the production line
3. The cost of subassemblies used on the production line
4. The number of subassemblies required on the production line
5. When these items need to be purchased
6. When these items must be paid for and how much that will be

CAPITAL REQUIREMENTS PLANNING

Capital requirements usually represent the largest expenses of the company during the planning year. Capital assets are simply those things the company needs in order to earn revenue or reduce future costs. An example of a capital asset is the new forklift used in the warehouse. It may also include renovations or additions to property, plant, equipment, patents—anything durable that the firm needs to earn revenue.

The most successful business plans identify capital requirements by *project*. This provides two things:

- Control over how the capital plan ties into the overall operating plan
- A better monitoring mechanism that tracks the separate components of the capital plan

Items to Include in the Capital Plan

There are three elements crucial to the capital expenditure plan:

1. Cash outflows to pay for the capital assets
2. Cash inflows resulting from the capital assets
3. Timing of both

Cash Outflows
Not only do we need to include the amount of money expended for the asset we're buying, but there are other considerations. There may be a residual value of the old equipment (if any) that is being replaced. This cash inflow offsets the outflow to determine a *net cash outflow*.

Additionally, there may be certain tax implications such as a capital gain or loss on disposition of the old equipment. Finally, many capital assets are so expensive they can't be funded internally and require borrowing. Don't forget to include the interest expense on any loans in the capital plan.

Cash Inflows
Cash inflow is the reason for making the capital expenditure in the first place. The operating plan must contain the cash inflow as a result of the capital expenditures. It's best to include this by each capital project so we can better track its performance.

Timing
Both cash inflows and outflows must be *time-phased* into the operating plan. The cash flow of each capital project figures in determining whether they are deals the company should make or not. Further, the finance department needs this information to plan its funding activities for borrowing and investment.

Additionally, most capital expenditure plans run beyond the one-year planning horizon we're dealing with here. That's due to the durable nature of the assets being purchased. Don't ignore the multiyear impacts of these acquisitions. They'll be used later to compute the overall return on investment.

Assessment of Capital Expenditure Merits

This is not a finance book. However, there are three simple measures commonly used to determine the merit of a potential capital investment. When evaluating a possible capital acquisition, use these computations as an indicator to help in your decision.

Present Value of the Cash Inflows

When judging between two capital expenditures, we often discount future cash flows back to their present value. This number can be used to judge the gross present value of cash returned or it can be used to compute the return on investment. Here's how it's done.

Step 1: Discount Cash Flow Back to Present Value   Let's assume we're deciding between two projects, A and B. The cost of borrowing the money for both projects is 12 percent. Here are the assumptions for both projects:

- Project A: Cost is $500,000 and the net cash inflow is expected to be $75,000 for 10 years.
- Project B: Cost is $400,000 and the net cash inflow is expected to be $65,000 for 15 years.

The present value of both projects can be found using the Net Present Value (NPV) tables in any finance book or by using a sophisticated calculator (such as the HP 12-C).
The NPV of both projects is:

- Project A: $423,767
- Project B: $442,706

Step 2: Compute Return on Investment   The return on investment (ROI) is computed by dividing the NPV of the cash inflows by the initial investment, then dividing the result by the number of years over which the cash flow takes place.

- Project A: ($423,767/$500,000)/10 years = 8%
- Project B: ($442,706/$400,000)/15 years = 7%

If we consider nothing else, Project A is the better decision.

Internal Rate of Return
Unlike the NPV calculation above, the internal rate of return (IRR) discounts all future cash flows back so that they exactly equal the initial net capital outlay. Here's how it is done:

Step 1: Determine the Annuity Table Factor We'll be using a table of the present value of an ordinary annuity of $1 (found in most finance books). That tells us the IRR percentage. To find the table factor use this formula:

$$\text{Net cash outlay/Average annual net cash inflow} = \text{Annuity table factor}$$

For our projects, these are:

- Project A: $500,000/$75,000 = 6.67
- Project B: $400,000/$65,000 = 6.15

Step 2: Use the Annuity Table to Determine IRR Look up the two factors using the table of the present value of an ordinary annuity of $1. Be sure to use the row corresponding with the number of years over which the investment returns cash.

- Project A: For 10 years, the table factor of 6.67 gives us an approximate IRR of 8%.
- Project B: For 15 years, the table factor of 6.15 gives us an approximate IRR of 14%.

Using the IRR, Project B is the best.

Rules of Thumb
Here are three shortcut rules that may help when comparing results of your net present value analysis against the IRR:

- If the NPV (in $) and the IRR (in %) equals the cash outlay or the cost of capital (respectively), the project is a break-even and probably won't be done except under special circumstances.
- If the NPV (in $) is negative or the IRR % is less than the cost of capital, the project is a dog and should not be done.
- If the NPV (in $) is positive and the IRR is greater than the cost of capital, the project is profitable and bears further investigation.

Payback Period

Most small and medium-sized businesses are concerned with the time an investment takes to pay for itself. We compute this *payback period* as follows:

Net cash investment/Annual net cash inflow = Payback period

Here is the computation for our two projects:

■ Project A: $500,000/$75,000 = 6.7 years
■ Project B: $400,000/$65,000 = 6.2 years

Project B is the best because we're at risk a shorter period of time to recoup our cash outlay.

Postcompletion Review

We want to maintain accountability for the success of our capital expenditures. A good way to do this is to conduct periodic postcompletion reviews of most capital expenditure programs. This accomplishes several goals:

■ Data on previous decisions is maintained.
■ It provides a forum in which to take corrective action if necessary.
■ Those who pushed for the expenditure are forced to take responsibility for the results.
■ It demonstrates management's commitment to the plan and its success.

MANUFACTURING

Of the operating groups within a company, manufacturing seems to be the least inclined to participate willingly in the planning process. Manufacturing managers tend to be hands-on oriented and often see planning as a staff job. Nevertheless, the product that comes out of the manufacturing plan drives other significant parts of the operations plan.

To be effective, the manufacturing plan should address:

■ What will be made or assembled, and when
■ What will be shipped, and when

- What materials, labor (both direct and indirect), and supplies are required, and when
- How much time will be used, by whom, and when
- Who is responsible for each of these things

When viewed as a worthwhile exercise on those results the rest of the firm can count, the manufacturing plan becomes a source of profit enhancement or cost reduction. Specifically, the manufacturing plan can identify nonproductive assets that are no longer in use. These can be retired and disposed of, freeing up needed storage space and working capital.

Additionally, the physical layout of the production operation can sometimes be more efficiently arranged. This leads to savings such as less direct labor required and more efficient feeding of raw materials into the production line.

A well-organized manufacturing plan can identify underutilized personnel and reassign them to more productive tasks. The planning process in the manufacturing area considers the uptime of its machinery and personnel. When either are out of range, changes are made to reduce downtime costs. In one of the purest senses, the manufacturing plan provides the engineering blueprint for actual execution of the operations plan.

Specific Issues in the Manufacturing Plan

There are at least nine things we want the manufacturing plan to address:

1. Units produced and timing
2. Engineering of the plant, production line, and products
3. Quality control
4. Distribution
5. Capital investment of manufacturing equipment
6. Machinery downtime due to unscheduled repairs and preventive maintenance
7. Work force required to make the product
8. Inventory required
9. Employee training

Depending on how sophisticated your plan needs to be, these next five items provide a level of detail that supports the manufacturing plan:

1. Cost of goods manufactured—often the most significant of any costs

2. Production rates used to support the sales plan—unless production timing and volume ties to the sales plan, the goods won't be available for shipment when needed
3. Plant capacity and capital expenditures (or divestitures) required for the planned level of production
4. Ancillary manufacturing costs such as overhead
5. Required inflow of raw materials and subassemblies—used in the purchasing plan and becomes a key component of the working capital plan

Each of these items communicate the intent as to how the manufacturing department intends going about its task.

Manufacturing plans deal both in units produced as well as dollars spent. Some of the costs we're interested in seeing include:

- Supervisory salaries
- Direct labor costs
- Indirect labor costs
- Raw materials or components
- Maintenance labor
- Maintenance parts
- Supplies
- Depreciation allocation
- Insurance
- Tax allocation
- Telephone
- Power utilities
- Fuel

All of these contribute to the bottom line number. In the manufacturing area, that is the cost of goods sold.

INVENTORY AND WAREHOUSE

There's a difference between inventory levels and replenishment. *Inventory* is a level of raw materials, work in process, and finished goods that we want to maintain. *Replenishment* is the plan to keep the inventory at that level.

The first thing to identify is the person responsible for inventory and its warehousing. In a manufacturing organization the head of production is the one most often responsible for maintaining required inventory levels.

The inventory plan ties both the production and sales plans together. The aim is to avoid the jerky starts and stops in both these areas that cause inefficiency. Additionally, the inventory plan is a compromise between competing forces within the firm.

On one side are manufacturing people who want long production runs to minimize retooling costs and take advantage of economies of scale. They want to buy inventory in bulk. In the other camp is the sales force. They want product on the warehouse shelves ready for shipment when a customer says "Go." They care little for economic order quantities or safety stock levels. Yet a third area that must bring these competing factions together is the finance department.

Reasonable Inventory Levels

The inventory plan reconciles these competing areas of the company. Here are some areas to look at when evaluating planned inventory levels:

Basis for Planned Levels

We talked earlier about using the economic order quantity to know how much inventory to purchase and in what size lots. Certainly, there are many times when this theory simply does not work in a given situation. However, it does provide a good basis from which to begin. When evaluating the inventory purchase plan, find out *how* the purchase amounts and frequencies were derived—you just may be surprised at the lack of support and the questionable assumptions!

We've said before that safety stock levels are ripe for getting out of hand. Often, excessive inventory levels are blamed on the need for safety stock. This only masks poor inventory control. When confronted with an inventory plan that identifies a specific level of safety stock, be sure you understand the supporting logic.

Another index of inventory is the computation of *days of sales in inventory* (DSI). This tells us in easy-to-understand terms how long at current sales levels our present inventory will last. Here's how to compute it:

$$DSI = (\text{Inventory balance/Cost of goods sold}) \times \text{Number of days in the period}$$

Note that the cost of goods sold (CGS) is for the period being analyzed. Let's run the computation assuming we have a CGS for last year of $500,000 and a beginning inventory of $175,000.

$$(\$175,000/\$500,000) \times 365 = 128 \text{ days of sales in inventory}$$

At this rate, our inventory turns over less than three times during the year (365/128 = 2.9). For many companies, such a large inventory (therefore, low turnover) is unacceptable. A meat packer, for instance, manages inventory by the credo, "Sell it or smell it."

Composition of Inventory

The amount of inventory contained in your plan depends to some degree on what it's made up of. Raw materials, for example, may have become scarce so the purchasing manager loaded up when he could. Finished goods may be inordinately low due to a fear that they may become obsolete in the near future.

Here are some considerations when looking at the size and composition of your inventory plan:

- Lead-time to get the items
- Expected demand
- Terms of purchase for the items—sometimes getting a great deal on certain purchases means that inventory *should* be allowed to temporarily balloon
- Potential price fluctuations (either up or down)
- Possible labor disputes that could disrupt the manufacturing line
- Potential interruption of inventory supply lines
- Durability of inventory items—how long they can be kept before they are no longer usable (or saleable)

Cautions Regarding Inventory

Small and medium-sized businesses get their lunch eaten more by poor inventory management than almost any other problem. Here are a few simple things you can do to control your inventory.

Obsolete Inventory

Track the movement of each inventory item. Be sure that particular items are moving at an acceptable rate so that you make an appropriate return on that investment of working capital. When items begin to slow down, find out why. Either fix the problem or discontinue the item.

Items that don't move after an acceptable time can be considered obsolete. This determination depends on your company and industry. When obsolete inventory is identified, get rid of it. Sell it at a discount if necessary, but free up the warehouse space and the working capital this unproductive asset consumes.

Physically Inspect the Warehouse

Don't be afraid to spend some time in the warehouse. Look at the inventory stock. Where there's an inch of dust on certain items, find out why. Often that's a sure sign that the item isn't moving.

Look at the security of the facility. If the items are extremely valuable, there should be appropriate security to prevent theft and pilferage. Often something as simple as an unlocked back door can spell an *attractive opportunity* for inventory to walk out.

Lastly, be sure to conduct periodic physical inventory counts. These should be done by people not directly involved in the safe-keeping of the inventory. Reconcile any differences between the physical count and the balances appearing on the books.

6

Finance—How Much Do We Need and When Do We Need It?

OVERVIEW

Chapter 6 shows how to formulate a logical financial plan to measure results of the operation and achievement of overall goals. This chapter describes the components of a financial plan—what they mean, how to pull them together, and how to use them as a management tool.

How much money do we need and when do we need it? To many small and medium-sized business managers that's the only question the financial plan needs to answer.

Cash flow planning is certainly important. And it *does* answer the question of how much and when. However, smart business planners *derive* their cash flow plans from an overall financial plan, not vice versa. Doing otherwise allows your borrowing requirements to dictate how you run your business. In fact, it should be the other way around—we manage our business and require funds to help us meet our goals.

The business plan flows through the firm by department and onto the prospective financial statements. The resulting financial plan quantifies objectives, tactics, and policies for the company over a specific operating period. It puts them all into a standardized format that everyone can understand.

For our purposes, the financial plan has three major segments:

1. The *operating plan* which is presented as the company's projected income statement. It includes assumptions from such subplans as sales, production, administrative expenses, distribution and advertising.
2. The *financial position* plan is presented as the company's projected balance sheet. It includes the assets, liabilities, and owner's equity of the firm.

3. The *cash flow plan*. This is the part that tells us how much to borrow and when.

Financial plans sometimes scare people because of their apparent complexity. However, you don't have to be a CPA to prepare *or understand* a financial plan. The dependency of one department's performance on another only makes a financial plan *seem* complicated. Indeed, because of their linkage, components of financial plans are like dominos—as one falls, the others topple on down the line. We get around that complexity in two ways:

1. We'll isolate the impact of key variables on the financial plan—such as the sales revenue estimates. Once we know all the areas each variable can change, the mystery goes away.
2. We'll use a simple spreadsheet computer model to create the financial plan. This relieves us from having to do the arithmetic when cranking through changes to the financial plan. The computations are easy, but again, their volume makes the financial plan *seem* complicated. A simple spreadsheet program was used to create the samples shown at the end of this chapter. We'll discuss how to use the computer in financial planning later on.

Computers are not a requirement for financial planning. However, they speed the process along and allow for more creativity as ideas can be quickly tested without much effort. Even if you don't use a computer for your financial planning, you'll find the discussion helpful.

Each department's operating goals can be plugged into the financial plan and examined to see how they further the company's overall objectives. The fact that results are presented in a consistent format (using *generally accepted accounting principals,* according to the CPAs) gives everyone a common point of reference.

Financial planning requires two key steps to ensure success:

1. The operational plan must be distilled into a set of projected financial statements and supporting schedules.
2. A convenient mechanism must be designed to compare actual performance against the plan each month. Only by such review can mid-course corrections be made quickly and efficiently.

COMPONENTS OF THE FINANCIAL PLAN

The purpose of a financial plan differs only slightly between companies. It is created to put the business plan into a financial orientation. Our mission when preparing a financial plan is to:

- Project the financial results of the business over the planning horizon.
- Identify the financial position of the company at key milestones.
- Determine what financial resources are required to meet the plan and when they are needed.

There's nothing difficult about answering these questions. To do so, we'll work in three areas:

1. *Assumptions:* These are not only our own financial assumptions, but the product of other subplans within the company.
2. *Workpapers:* We want a permanent record of how the financial plan was developed.
3. *Financial Schedules:* These are the work product of our financial plan.

ASSUMPTIONS

Assumptions are the keys to creating a credible financial plan. We derive most of our assumptions from the subplans of other departments. These are used to create the revenue and expense numbers that eventually feed into our financial plan.

Additional assumptions specific to the financial plan, such as interest rates or borrowing capacity, are usually obtained from outside sources.

Customarily we have a separate section of the financial plan devoted to explaining the assumptions used and their derivation. Often this is extensive, especially in the workpapers. The objective is to logically explain how each assumption was derived.

Of course, such thoroughness should be tempered with the need and benefit. Smaller businesses have less need for extensive documentation because everyone is closer to the numbers. However, as time goes on, people forget what they were thinking when they created these assumptions. The assumption section becomes more valuable as time goes on.

Time Horizon

The first assumption decision made in the financial plan is the time horizon. Most likely this matches that used in the business plan. For our purposes, this will be just one year. However, many companies produce multiyear financial plans.

If you are in the position of going out more than one year in your financial plan, look carefully at the level of detail produced. Accuracy of financial projections falls off dramatically beyond one year. This is true especially if, for example, interest is a material expense item. How much credibility do you think a five-year financial plan has when one of its major assumptions turns out to be a forecast of interest rates? Not much!

In cases where you have less confidence in the accuracy of your assumptions because of an extended time horizon, reduce the detail contained in the financial plan. For example, the income statement may be abbreviated to show only major revenue and expense items. These don't produce a number that could be called net income. However, they often suffice for purposes of the business plan. *And* they are credible management tools because the underlying assumptions are based on solid analysis. That's the important thing.

Additionally, we want the interim milestones presented by the business plan to exactly coincide with the financial plan. If we plan out one year by month, maybe with quarterly subtotals, that's usually sufficient.

In terms of assumptions, we have two categories:

1. Driver assumptions
2. Secondary assumptions

Driver assumptions are usually stated in terms of dollars while the secondary assumptions are a *percentage* of the drivers. Therefore, as the driver assumption changes, so does the secondary assumption automatically.

Driver Assumptions

Drivers are key assumptions on which the rest of the plan depends. For example, sales is a driver assumption. Such things as cash inflow from collections depend on sales.

The fewer the driver assumptions, the better. That way, if our financial plan is done on a computer, change in a key variable automatically flows through the entire financial plan without much additional work.

Secondary Assumptions

Most of the financial plan assumptions should be dependent on the few driver assumptions. For example, advertising expenses are often stated as a percentage of the sales they are known to generate. So are accounts receivable.

Input from Other Departments

Each department's operating goals can be "plugged" into the financial plan and examined to see how they further the company's overall objective. When the impacts of changes can be computed quickly and accurately the financial planning mechanism becomes a useful and creative planning tool.

Departmental subplans, stated in dollars, are fed into the financial plan. Such input items include, for example, projected sales revenue resulting from the marketing subplan and cost of goods sold coming from the manufacturing subplan.

Financial plans have a habit of being used as the performance benchmark of the business plan. That's because it's so easy to compare actual results against those planned on a monthly basis. Financial plans are also changed many times before they become finalized and are accepted by everyone responsible for the plan's execution. Finally, third parties often base their decisions regarding the firm (such as lending) at least in part on the financial plan.

For these reasons we want all the assumptions documented. This is true particularly of the assumptions derived from other departments. Often the person who prepares the financial plan isn't as familiar with the details of each departmental assumption as the group that produced them. For this reason, assumptions must be *traceable* back to their source.

Here are the items contained in the financial plan that generally come from other departments:

Sales and Marketing
The financial plan doesn't recreate the sales plan. However, there are some key pieces of information the financial plan requires. Generally, these assumptions are specific in terms of dollar level (or percentage of another variable) and timing.

Here are the assumptions used by the financial plan that come from the sales and marketing plan:

Sales   This is usually one of the primary driver assumptions. Many parts of the overall plan are based on particular levels of sales. If your company carries several products or product lines, the financial plan often identifies specific sales levels for each. This makes it easier to identify where sales revenue comes from. However, the financial plan keys on one number—total revenue.

If you choose not to provide the detail of how sales revenue was generated in the financial plan, be sure to have it readily available in your workpapers. Questions regarding sales revenue are almost guaranteed from anyone reviewing the financial plan.

Customer Mix   Customer mix is a key ingredient in the accounts receivable and collections segment of the financial plan. After all, if the sales and marketing plan targets a new type of customer with different (or unknown) payment habits, an allowance is going to be made in the collections area for cash flow purposes.

Further, the sales plan may identify a new geographic location of customers. This also affects the speed of collections and the effort expended (such as possible use of a lockbox system).

Credit Criteria   Often the marketing plan adjusts credit-granting rules for specific campaigns. This is important to the financial plan in forecasting future receivables balances and bad debt expenses.

Sales Commissions   This is a secondary assumption based on sales, net of returns, and allowances. It changes automatically as sales change. Commissions are usually a large expense and should appear as a separate line item in the financial plan.

Warranty Service Expense   Warranty programs are often part of a marketing campaign. Their expenses are real nevertheless. If the item is material in its relation to gross sales, it probably should be included as a separate line item in the financial plan. Regardless, it should be boiled into the sales and marketing assumptions that are included in the financial plan.

Product Development   Programs from which new products (or enhancements to existing products) spring should be included in the assumptions used in the financial plan. More often than not, we detail all the various projects in the workpapers. From this, total product development cost is obtained. *That's* what goes into the financial plan.

Along with the costs are also the benefits of product development. These should already be included in the sales forecast provided by the sales and marketing department. Be sure that these aren't buried in the workpapers. We want to easily identify the returns obtained from these costs.

Manufacturing: Cost of Goods Sold

Cost of goods sold is the bottom line number we are interested in from the manufacturing department. If they have done their job in preparing the action plan, all of the costs associated with manufacturing the firm's products are included.

In many cases, this means allocating certain overhead, and indirect and fixed expenses shared by all of the items produced. Two examples would be rent for the space occupied by the production line and salary of the production manager. All products benefit from these expenses and should bear their fair share.

Even though the cost of goods sold is often the single largest expense, it's best presented in the financial plan as a secondary assumption—usually as a percentage of the gross sales revenue before returns and allowances. That way, as the sales level fluctuates, we maintain an accurate cost of goods sold expense without having to recompute this complex number. The difference between the 100 percent sales price and the cost of goods sold (stated as a percentage of the sales price) is called the *gross margin*.

Some companies take a more top-level view of their financial plan. Others like very detailed financial plans and want to tie back each product's cost against its gross revenue. This causes a lot of work and makes the financial plan more complicated. However, it allows us to track the critical gross margin all along the planning horizon for each product. To be of any real use, however, the projected income statement must show each product separately on its face. Using this technique, tracking performance of the manufacturing department and detailed gross margin becomes much easier.

Other Manufacturing Costs

Cost accounting is a complex subject and beyond the scope (or necessity) of our job here. We do, however, want to be sure all the expenses of the manufacturing department are included somewhere in the financial plan. Most of these will be in cost of goods sold. Those that are not should be included somewhere else within the financial plan.

Depending on the company, these other costs may include such things as:

■ Shipping and packing
■ Warehousing
■ Repair and maintenance of material handling equipment
■ Quality control
■ Production engineering

A point to be made here is one regarding financial planning sophistication. When companies—especially smaller ones—first begin financial planning they often try to make it overly complex. Don't make this mistake. Even if the plan is less than 100 percent accurate, it's still better than having no plan at all. As time goes on the firm's ability to create and execute its financial plan grows. With that growth may come added sophistication and complexity of the financial plan—but only if it adds to the final product.

Transfer Pricing

We introduced the concept of transfer pricing in Chapter 5. Now, at the financial planning level, it's time to assign actual price policies to these "sales."

There are three methods from which most firms choose:

- *Market value of the goods sold from one division to another.* This is the most favored way because it places the purchase decision in terms of the real world.
- *Cost plus a markup.* If the financial plan uses this technique, it's liable to pass along operating inefficiencies of the selling division without penalty. The higher the manufacturing cost, the greater the profit dollars to the "seller."
- *Actual cost.* Using this method, no profit is shown. This isn't fair to the selling division, which could have sold the same goods to a third party at a profit.

When selecting a transfer pricing policy consider these factors:

- Organizational goals
- Performance evaluation and fairness to the buyer and seller
- Autonomy of divisions
- Legal and regulatory requirements

The last item, legal conformity, is important. The IRS takes a dim view of firms managing their profit (and therefore their tax liability) using transfer pricing schemes.

Human Resources

If cost of goods sold is the single largest expense item, salaries, wages, and benefits often run a close second. The detail associated with these cost projections is already contained in the HR subplan. We don't need to include them again in the financial plan except by reference.

Some of the HR components we *do* want in the financial plan include:

- *Scheduled salary expense* for every month over the planning horizon. This must include raises *as they are scheduled to occur* in the HR plan.
- *Overtime expense.* Some companies want specific control of overtime expense. The only way to gain that control through the financial plan is to include OT as a separate line item.
- *Bonuses.* Show them separately in the periods where they are granted. The bonus policy (percentage of net income, for example) and those who are eligible are usually included as part of the assumptions in the financial plan workpapers.
- *Recruiting expenses.* These are another component of the HR plan that flows to the financial plan.
- *Legal fees.* Unfortunately, litigation has become a more significant part of many HR plans. Although a separate line item in the financial plan is probably not required, the portion of legal fees allocated to HR-related activities should be traceable back to the assumptions.
- *Outside services.* Include here such things as temporary workers and consultants. Depending on the degree of accountability and control you want over these costs, they may or may not be shown as a separate line item in the financial plan.

Financial Assumptions

Along with the assumptions flowing into the financial plan from all the departments throughout the company, there are some significant assumptions required just for the financial plan. These include:

Interest Rates Depending on the nature of the business and its investments or need for borrowed funds, interest income and expense may be a material item to the financial plan. Interest rates dictate the level of interest income and expense.

But where do we get a reliable interest rate forecast? Economists are poor at projecting the value of future interest rates. However, they're good at projecting a *range* in which the rates will likely fall. That's what most companies use in their financial plan when they need an interest rate as a critical driver assumption. There are many economic forecasting firms that supply interest rate forecasts (such as Chase Econometrics and Data Resources, Inc.).

We want two things from the interest rate assumptions we use:

1. The appropriate interest rate for our purposes—maybe it's Treasury Bills, maybe it's prime or the Fed's 11th District cost of funds. Some plans use several rates in various parts of the plan.
2. Three interest rate scenarios: best case, worst case, and most likely—we'll use all three in creating a *range of tolerable error.*

This is especially important if the interest income or expense item has a significant influence on the financial plan results.

Collections Forecast   Not only is the collection of accounts receivable needed to produce the cash flow forecast, the financial plan uses it to help produce the ending cash number appearing on the balance sheet each month throughout the planning period.

Some of the assumptions that are included in the collections forecast are:

- The percentage of sales that are expected to be cash and the portion that are on credit—these items are secondary assumptions, driven by sales
- The percentage of receivables that historically pay within 30, 60, 90, and 120 days
- The percentage of receivables that roll through the system to write-off as a bad debt
- If the financial plan calls for factoring or selling accounts receivable, the timing and amounts received
- The rate at which receivables will be collected

Payables Forecast   Accounts payable also play an important part in the cash forecast that evolves from the balance sheet projections. We want to know several things about our accounts payable in the financial forecast:

- How much trade credit our vendors will allow us—this helps us project the balance in payables all along the planning horizon
- The timing of major payables due dates such as inventory purchases and taxes
- The trade discounts and due dates for taking advantage of them

Minimum Level of Required Cash   This is almost like a safety net. We don't want cash to fall below our minimum established floor in the event that something unforeseen happens. Further, some of our bank loans may require that we maintain compensating balances in non-interest-bearing accounts. If so, these are included in the minimum level of cash required.

Borrowing Capacity   This is one of the major assumptions we'll use in creating the financial plan. We want to know the funds available and the timing necessary to obtain them. If our line of credit is adequate, timing is no problem since all it takes is a phone call to execute the draw.

However, if our company's funding requirements are more sophisticated and require secured loans, capital infusion, debt or equity offerings, then part of the financial plan should be to get started on securing these funds *well before* they are needed.

Capital Expenditure Plan   The cash outflows and inflows (if financing is used) of capital expenditures are often included in the financial plan. We want this part of the plan to be detailed in terms of:

- Specific project
- Amount
- Timing
- Sources of funding if coming from outside the firm

Specifying each project is especially important. The workpapers for the financial plan, if not the face of the financial statements themselves, should show cash inflows and outflows associated with each capital project. These have a habit of undergoing changes both in timing and in amount. We want to use this part of the plan as a control mechanism. For that reason, we need to know which projects are tracking according to plan and which aren't.

General, Administrative, and Overhead Costs

If most of the company's revenue and expenses are included in the various other parts of the plan, general and administrative (G&A) and overhead costs shouldn't be very large. However, be sure not to overlook them. We don't want any surprises as the plan unfolds.

Here are some of the G&A items you might look for:

- Income from investments
- Executive and supervisory salaries including bonuses that don't belong to any single department
- Office staff salaries and wages
- Repairs and maintenance
- Utilities expenses
- Telephone
- Postage and messenger service
- Office supplies
- Travel and entertainment
- Depreciation and amortization of office equipment
- Insurance
- Taxes—federal, state, local, and property taxes
- Auto expenses not already allocated to the consuming department
- Professional fees, such as legal and accounting

Management Fees Companies with several divisions allocate their corporate office expenses to each division in the form of a management fee. Like the transfer price of intercompany sales, this is "funny money." Your accountants will find this and factor it out through what they call *intercompany eliminations*.

The financial plan must eliminate this misleading effect as well. Here's how:

Corporate office financial plan:

Revenue from management fees charged	$ 50,000
Overhead expenses	(50,000)
Net income	$ -0-

Division A's financial plan:

Management fee expense charged by corporate office	$ 35,000

Division B's financial plan:

Management fee expense charged by corporate office	15,000
Total management fees paid by divisions	$ 50,000

The management fee expenses are *added back* at the division level, thus eliminating them as expense items on the financial division plans. At the corporate level, the management fee revenue is *removed* as an income item. All this adding and subtracting leaves the overhead expenses originally charged at the corporate level intact so they don't fall through the cracks.

For purposes of producing the projected income statement, these costs are absorbed by the divisions that benefit from them. However, for cash flow purposes, this funny money is eliminated and the firm is left with just one corporate office expense that must be paid.

Opening Balance Sheet

Once we have all the assumptions that feed into the financial plan, it's time to crank through the math. Though this isn't an accounting textbook and we won't dwell on the mechanics, there *is* a starting point. We begin the financial plan with an opening balance sheet, considering the accounts from the end of the prior period. They comprise the beginning numbers used in the financial plan.

Ratios and Statistics

Many experienced financial planners take some of their opening financial benchmarks from the beginning balance sheet. That way they have benchmarks against which to track changes as the financial plan spins out over the planning horizon. Some of these financial statistics include:

- *Current ratio:*

Current assets/Current liabilities

This identifies the company's ability to meet its current obligations using just current assets—those assets that are scheduled to be converted to cash during the operating period. A current ratio of about 2:1 is considered appropriate for many industries.

- *Quick ratio:*

(Cash + Marketable securities + A/R)/Current liabilities

The quick ratio, or acid test as some call it, tells us something about the firm's ability to repay its current obligations using just receivables and cash or cash equivalents. A quick ratio of about 1:1 is considered generally acceptable.

- *Liabilities covered by working capital:*

Working capital provided from operations/Total liabilities

This ratio illustrates how much of the current liabilities can be repaid using internally generated working capital.

- *Financial structure:* There are two things we want to measure concerning the ways we're financing our assets:

- Term financing:

Fixed assets/Short-term debt

If too much of our fixed (long-term assets) are financed using short-term debt, two things can occur:

  □ The debt matures prior to the assets earning enough money to repay the obligation.
  □ If interest rates spike upward, the cost of funds is likely to rise along with it, changing the assumptions used to acquire the asset in the first place.

- Proportionate term of debt:

Short-term debt/Long-term debt

Ideally, we would like to have long-term debt (sometimes referred to as the core borrowings) exceed short-term debt. If not, the company is subject to a liquidity squeeze if it attempts to roll over maturing short-term debt when cash is scarce. This happened to some real estate developers during the early 1990s when banks all but stopped lending on real estate.

These are a few of the benchmarks you may wish to monitor from the beginning balance sheet, throughout the time horizon of the financial plan. If you see the numbers deteriorate at the financial planning stage, you are in a position to do something about it.

Your company may already have debt on its books. Buried somewhere in the covenants and restrictions of the loan indenture are likely to be specific financial benchmarks the firm has promised not to fall below. If it does, the loan may be subject to immediate call and repayment. *These* are benchmarks to which you definitely pay attention. It's a good idea to have your financial plan compute them for each month.

In the event you see that the firm is going to breach one of the loan covenants you can bring the lender into the picture. Generally, he needs to know how serious the problem is and what you are doing to correct it. Be sure to secure a written waiver of the breached covenant (if it actually does occur). Otherwise, the loan is still subject to call.

WORKPAPERS

As time goes on the sources of information that went into the financial plan become more valuable. That's why we want to be sure we've documented them. This is contained in the workpapers that support the plan. Very few of the people who receive a copy of the plan ever see the workpapers. They generally remain in the financial director's possession. However, they'll be consulted frequently.

Contents of the Workpapers

Our workpaper files contain these items:

- A marked copy of the financial plan, showing workpaper references for each assumption and number appearing in the financial plan
- Derivation of assumptions and explanation or reference back to the originating department's subplan

■ Subschedules that compute specific figures that flow up to the financial statements

Examples of the subschedules would be items such as the collection plan for accounts receivable. Sales create receivables. But from there the collections plan cranks through using such assumptions as:

■ Customer payment habits
■ Percent of accounts receivables that rolls through the various aging buckets in the receivables system
■ Bad debt

The result is a comprehensive illustration of how we plan the collections system to work in order to produce the cash inflow and receivables balances seen on the face of the financial plan statements.

Cash outflow from payment of accounts payable as well as funds inflow from borrowing are two more examples of detailed workpaper subschedules that support the financial plan.

The rule to follow when creating the workpapers that support the lead schedules of the financial plan is:

Every number should be explained.

If it isn't obvious from looking at the face of the financial plan, then a workpaper schedule or narrative explanation should be made to clarify it.

Two-Way References

The easiest reference convention is to number the workpapers at the bottom using a colored pencil. This facilitates quickly flipping through them to find the right one.

We want to be able to go from the lead financial schedules in the plan to the workpaper that explains each number. However, we also want to go the other way: from the workpapers back up to the right number on the lead schedule. To do that we mark references to the financial plan on the workpapers. In some cases we'll reference these back up to the appropriate line on the financial statement.

FINANCIAL SCHEDULES

This is the product of the financial plan that everyone sees. The level of detail you should include varies according to the familiarity of your audience with the operation being planned. Larger firms with people who may be unfamiliar with the financial operations of the company often want to see more detail.

In any case, the financial plan should be detailed enough so that the audience gets a clear picture as to exactly *how* the firm's financial goals are met. Anything beyond that is fluff that we don't need. Besides, including unnecessary data, schedules, and charts tends to confuse people more than it helps. It's better to quit while you're ahead.

Statements, Schedules, and Illustrative Aids

The financial plan must tie to accounts in the general ledger for purposes of conveniently tracking performance. Additionally, the plan needs to be in a format generally understood by most people. For these two reasons, most financial plans begin with three financial statements:

1. Balance sheet
2. Income statement
3. Statement of changes in financial condition

Part of a sample financial plan is included at the end of this chapter. (Figures 6-1 to 6-4, Tables 6-2 to 6-5)

Balance Sheet

The company's projected balance sheet starts with the beginning balances we described above. From there, it evolves according to the rest of the company's business plan.

Many of the figures contained in the planned balance sheet are the result of computations from subschedules. On these subschedules we have the space and the level of detail to demonstrate how a particular number on the balance sheet evolves.

Accounts receivable is a case in point. A/R begins with the prior period ending balance. Sales are added to it. However, the receivables balance is reduced as payments are received and as bad debts are written off. It rises again as more sales are made.

See how the receivables balance flows as a result of the assumptions? That's why we put many of the balance sheet numbers on subschedules and let them flow up to the actual balance sheet—similar to information contained on our workpapers that flows up to a lead schedule.

Table 6-1 shows some of the sources of balance sheet information that flow from the assumptions as well as from the other financial statements and subschedules.

Table 6–1   Balance Sheet Information Sources

Balance sheet item	Source of information
Cash	Statement of changes and/or statement of cash flows
Accounts receivable	Schedule of accounts receivable
Inventory	Production schedule/raw material purchase schedule
Prepaid expenses	Financial assumptions
Investments	Investment maturity schedule
Property, plant, and equipment	Schedule of fixed assets, capital expenditure schedule, and depreciation schedule
Furniture and fixtures	Schedule of fixed assets, capital expenditure schedule, and depreciation schedule
Other assets	Financial assumptions
Trade accounts payable	Schedule of trade accounts payable
Inventory accounts payable	Schedule of inventory accounts payable
Short-term debt	Debt repayment schedule
Deposits and advance payments	Schedule from sales department
Accrued income taxes payable	Computed from rate assumption and income statement
Accrued property taxes payable	Financial assumptions
Long-term debt	Debt schedule
Other liabilities	Financial assumption
Partner's capital	Financial assumption
Capital stock	Financial assumption
Retained earnings (if a corporation)	Prior period balance sheet plus net income for this period

Income Statement

Information from the income statement drives the balance sheet and the statement of changes in financial position. This is probably the most interesting report produced by the financial plan. It tells us the profitability of the company all along the planning horizon. Usually at least some of the planning goals for the firm are linked with profitability. The income statement provides a convenient gauge to track actual performance against the plan.

The bulk of the assumptions used in the business plan usually go into the income statement. Major sections of the income statement include:

Revenue   Revenue comes from a variety of sources. The largest is the main line of the company's business. However, be sure not to forget income from the lesser product lines, sale of assets such as equipment, and interest income. Additionally, many firms carry some sales over from one year to another due to accounting cutoff requirements. If your company falls into this category be sure that you are consistent when applying these carryover and cutoff rules. We don't want to compare apples with oranges when tracking the actuals versus the plan or from one year to the next.

Cost of Goods Sold Many financial plans compute the cost of goods sold (CGS) on a separate detailed subschedule and allow the result to flow up to the income statement. CGS is often the most important cost number since it's the largest.

Here's how to compute cost of goods sold:

> Beginning inventory
> + purchases
> + all direct and indirect manufacturing costs
> − ending inventory
> = Cost of goods sold

The manufacturing plan should contain all the inventory purchases and costs necessary to compute CGS. The ending inventory figure usually combines the safety stock with the amount left over after the planning period in preparation for the next time frame.

Other Costs and Expenses All other costs associated with running the firm go in this section. These include such things as legal and accounting, interest expense, rent, and utilities. Make sure that *all* costs not previously accounted for in the manufacturing operation are included in other costs.

Statement of Changes in Financial Position

The statement of changes combines results from both the balance sheet and the income statement. It doesn't use assumptions from the rest of the business plan. Instead, it is purely a mathematical product of the interaction between these two financial statements.

The most valuable presentation of a statement of changes for a small business seems to emphasize cash. The format to follow includes:

Sources of Working Capital This converts net income (which is not a cash number) from the income statement into a source of working capital. The working capital items added to net income include such things as:

- Depreciation and amortization
- Cash inflows from sale of capital stock, partnership contributions, and financing
- Paydowns of accounts receivable
- Reduction of inventory

Anything from the income statement or balance sheet that can be considered a source of working capital or cash goes into this section of the statement of changes.

Uses of Working Capital　Working capital is used by the company when, for example, capital equipment is purchased, a loan is paid down, or accounts payable are repaid without replacing the balance with more credit purchases. Additional uses of working capital might include payment of:

- Taxes
- Deposits
- Prepaid expenses

One of the easiest ways of making sure that you've counted all of the sources and uses of working capital is to go down the balance sheet line by line, making sure each change is accounted for on the statement of changes.

For financial planning purposes, many analysts prefer to have the statement of changes compute the ending cash balance. This is done at the bottom as follows:

$$\begin{aligned}
&\text{beginning cash} \\
&+ \text{ cash sources} \\
&- \text{ cash uses} \\
&= \text{ ending cash}
\end{aligned}$$

The ending cash number then flows up to the cash balance on the balance sheet. If the balance sheet balances, then it's a pretty good assumption that all three financial statements tie in with each other.

CASH FLOW PLAN

The cash flow plan is often the most important section of the financial plan for medium and small businesses that are strapped for cash. It answers the all-important questions of *how much* money we need and *when* we need it.

Companies that find themselves with surprise cash flow problems have usually failed at producing their cash flow plan. This part of the planning process won't pull your firm out of a cash crunch. However, it will identify the problem before it becomes a crisis and give you time to fix it.

Here are the steps we use to produce a cash flow plan.

Identify Cash Generated From Operations and All Other Sources of Cash

These are the funds generated from cash sales as well as the collection of accounts receivable. Here's a list of some likely sources of cash inflow:

- Cash sales, net of credit card service charges
- Collection of accounts receivable, net of bad debt expense and collection fees—don't forget that this schedule should be time-phased as it was in the collection subplan (indeed, A/R collection can often be taken right from the collection subplan)
- Collection of loans receivable (if any, such as from officers)
- Investments maturing
- Receipt of interest income from loans and from investments
- Receipts from sale of assets not normally associated with the regular operations of the firm

Identify Cash Outflows

All operating expenses are cash outflows. However, these are usually in the form of payment on accounts payable. Many companies successfully avoid major purchases of items whose terms are *cash on delivery*.

Along with the payments for operating expenses come such things as:

- State and federal income taxes
- Property tax
- Sales tax
- Payroll tax
- Debt service (both principal and interest)
- Capital expenditures
- Insurance premiums
- Dividends to shareholders

By scheduling out the inflows and outflows for each month of the planning horizon a fairly accurate picture of the cash balance at any point in time emerges. Using this technique we can see where disposable cash drops below our minimum required balance.

One of the most effective ways to illustrate how much cash is required by the firm and when, is to graph the difference between inflows and outflows. If the balance dips below the established minimum, the amount needed to bring it back up is the borrowing requirement.

USE OF COMPUTERS IN FINANCIAL PLANNING

Using computers to help prepare the financial plan is not a requirement. But it certainly can be a tremendous help. The greatest contribution a computer makes to the financial planning effort comes in terms of:

- Mechanical number crunching
- Organization of the data
- Presentation of the results
- Preparation of alternative scenarios and analyses

For small and medium-sized companies the most effective use of computers in financial planning comes from a desktop computer using simple spreadsheet software. Among the most common spreadsheet products available are:

- Lotus 1-2-3
- Excel
- Framework
- Javelin
- VP-Planner
- Multiplan

More sophisticated readers may scoff at this simplicity. However, consider the four purposes of using a computer in financial planning listed above. We *want* simplicity. We want the ability to quickly change anything in the plan at a moment's notice. Finally, those who use the plan should be the ones working with the planning model, not some computer professional separated from the issues at hand. For all of these reasons, a bigger, more sophisticated computer with more complex software usually just gets in the way and doesn't further the ultimate objective.

Care must be taken in constructing your automated financial planning model so that it has a high degree of credibility and accuracy. Here are some of the ways to do it.

Use of Submodels

We've emphasized how the details from other department plans should feed directly into the financial planning model. One example we've used was the sales revenue plan. If there's a way for you to get changes made to the subplans to flow directly into the financial planning model, do it. This saves time and greatly reduces the chance of error in transferring the data from one plan to the next. Additionally, it provides an excellent trail as to the derivation of the most important pieces of data.

Normally we take the time to electronically link the financial plan with only the most important departmental subplans. These might include:

- Sales
- Manufacturing and production costs
- Accounts receivable and payable inflow and outflow schedules

Most of the other data, while important, probably won't change that much during the planning process. Nor does it usually impact the overall financial performance of the firm to as great an extent. Therefore, we include it in the assumptions.

Assumption Section

Structurally, the financial plan should have an assumption section built into it. Planners using a spreadsheet often put the assumption section at the top of the model. The actual "body" of the plan then reaches up into the assumption section to take the data required for its computations. Finally, the assumption section should be printed separately from the rest of the plan.

Programming Techniques

Everybody has his or her own pet programming techniques. Here are a few you may find useful:

Soft Programming

This is a technique of programming the financial planning model. It simply means that no quantitative variables are programmed into the logic of the computations (the equations). Rather, any variables required to perform a logical operation are retrieved from the assumption section.

Here's an example:

$$\text{Loan balance} \times \text{Interest Rate} = \text{Interest Expense}$$

Using a soft programming approach, the loan balance is computed by the model using assumptions and computations having to do with cash requirements. The interest rate is obtained from the assumption section. See how *nothing* is left in the equation that cannot be changed as the result of changes in the model? An inexperienced financial planner might have put the interest rate on the loan right into the equation.

Soft programming takes a little longer than "hard" programming your assumptions right into the logic. However, financial plans that use soft programming techniques can be updated and changed with a minimum of time and effort.

Financial Statements That Flow

Information generated from the financial statements should flow between one another. This ensures that they are all consistent. For example:

■ Net income, depreciation, and amortization all should flow from the income statement to the balance sheet and statement of changes.

■ All changes to balance sheet accounts should flow to the statement of changes.

■ The ending cash balance should be computed on the statement of changes and flow back up to the balance sheet.

■ Subschedules of line items that were derived elsewhere should flow into the financial plan—accounts receivable and payable are two examples.

Use of Abbreviations

Don't use slang or acronyms to describe line items in the financial plan. Imagine how irritating that is to a banker, unfamiliar with your business and its jargon. The rule in financial planning is:

When in doubt, spell it out.

Clearly Label Columns and Number Pages
This may sound basic. However, most of us in the business have seen financial plans where it was difficult to tell just what time frame a column of numbers fell into. Usually this happens after the first page of a schedule. The person programming did not understand how to get the column headings to repeat at the top of each successive page.

Page numbers are another thing to include in the header at the top of each page. Remember, our objective is to make the financial presentation as clear as possible—not to confuse the reader.

Sensitivity Analyses

Computers are great workhorses for quickly computing the sensitivity of the financial plan to specific assumption changes or a combination of changes. Most simple spreadsheet products have a module that computes sensitivity quickly. Additionally, often we'll just change a series of assumptions, compute the model, and take a look at the results.

We want to get a couple of things out of our assessment of sensitivity:

- Determining the *relative importance of specific variables* to the overall financial plan of the company. We use this in calculating how much work to put into nailing down the precision of certain assumptions.
- Establishing a *range of tolerable error* for specific assumptions. We've talked about this earlier. The financial plan helps pinpoint where specific assumptions can fall and still meet our financial targets.

Validating the Computer Model

Once the financial plan has been created on a spreadsheet there are some tests we need to make. Chances are that whoever did the programming is not a professional—nor is there need for one. We want to make sure the programming:

- Is arithmetically correct
- Is logically consistent with the way we know the company operates
- Produces a verifiable result

Here's how:

Test Arithmetic

This is a simple but boring task. *Every* number must be tested. For assumptions that are brought down from the assumption section, verify that the program grabbed the right one. For columns of numbers that are added down (*footed* is the accounting term), make sure they do. In cases where several subtotals are taken from various places in the spreadsheet and foot to a grand total, make sure that the right subtotals were taken.

Finally, columns usually add across (*cross-foot*) by month to give a year-end total. Make sure they cross-foot.

PLANNING POINTER

One obvious error that can impugn the credibility of a financial plan is cross-footing numbers that should not be. Percentages are a good example. The gross margin percentage is not cross-footed, nor is it computed as the average of all the months. Rather, the year-end gross margin is computed by dividing the year-end gross profit by year-end sales—the equation is the same as was used in each month.

Test Logic

Go over every equation for computational accuracy and for possible faulty logic. Even though an equation may have been copied across an entire column of numbers, make sure the copy was done correctly.

Validate the Model

Validation means simply loading into the model known assumptions that have a known result and observing the outcome. This is most easily done with last year's actual performance numbers. Load them into the planning model and run it. The results should come out close to the prior year's actuals. If not, find out why. It could mean there's an error or inconsistency in the planning model.

TESTING FINANCIAL STATEMENTS

If you've done all of the above there's a high probability that your automated financial planning system will be correct. However, there are several quick tests we can do that are designed to find glaring errors. If you do these, you are less likely to distribute something that clearly has computational problems.

Balance Sheet Checks

Here are some things to look for on your financial plan's balance sheet:

Does the Balance Sheet Balance?
Imagine how much credibility a balance sheet has if total assets don't equal total liabilities and equity. That's the first thing you should check.

Cash
The cash balance (usually shown at the top of the balance sheet) should equal the ending cash balance throughout the rest of the financial plan. Depending on the format, it might be found in the cash flow plan or in the statement of changes in financial position.

Agreement of Subledgers with the General Ledger
This is more important when looking at the financial statements that track actual performance against the plan. Make sure that all subledgers tie out to the general ledger. For example, the accounts receivable subledger should show a balance that exactly ties to the accounts receivable balance appearing on the general ledger.

The same holds true for these subledgers and schedules:

- Accounts payable
- Inventory
- Capital assets
- Accumulated depreciation and amortization

Retained Earnings
Retained earnings (one of the last lines of owner's equity in the balance sheet) should tie to the income statement. Here's how: Retained earnings is the prior period's balance in retained earnings *plus* the current period's net income after tax.

Agreement of Subplans
There should be consistency between the numbers that appear in the departmental subplans and those that are used in the financial plan. For example, the accounts receivable plan should show a balance at the end of each operating period that should tie into the receivables balance on the balance sheet of the financial plan. Additionally, these sales levels that produced the collection of accounts receivable should tie back into the sales plan.

The same thing should be true of the balance in the accounts payable plan compared with the purchasing plans for equipment and inventory. This all should tie out to accounts payable appearing on the prospective balance sheet.

Income Statement Items

Income statement items appear in other places besides the income statement itself. For example, net income before taxes also appears at the top of the statement of changes for conversion to working capital sources. Depreciation and amortization, two costs that appear on the income statement, are added back to net income before taxes on the statement of changes.

Sales   The sales revenue schedule appears on the income statement. This should tie back into the production schedule. You should be able to see how the production schedule *leads* sales. Often a graph of these two schedules reveals potential timing problems.

Salary Expenses   Salaries are one of the largest expenditures. Make sure that the salary expense appearing on the prospective income statement ties back into the salary schedule prepared as part of the human resources plan.

Operating Expenses   The operating expenese for each department as well as the corporate office overhead expenses should tie out to the place they appear on the financial plan income statement. If they are not itemized, then they should tie back into the assumptions that were used to develop the consolidated number.

SAMPLE FINANCIAL STATEMENTS

The following (Figures 6-1 to 6-4, Tables 6-2 to 6-5) are sample financial statements that demonstrate some of the principles discussed above.

Table 6–2A Peaches Corporation Prospective Balance Sheet, 199X

	Beg balance	Month 1	Month 2	Month 3	Month 4	Month 5
Current assets:						
Cash	$ 100,000	130,160	211,408	305,061	470,172	657,866
Accounts receivable	350,000	347,000	354,500	386,250	425,850	442,500
Inventory	200,000	220,000	258,750	325,000	315,000	270,000
Total current assets	$ 650,000	$ 697,160	$ 824,658	$1,016,311	$1,211,022	$1,370,366
Fixed assets:						
Corporate offices	2,500,000	2,500,000	2,500,000	2,500,000	2,500,000	2,500,000
Machinery & equipment	1,500,000	1,500,000	1,500,000	1,500,000	1,500,000	1,500,000
Furniture & fixtures	1,000,000	1,000,000	1,000,000	1,000,000	1,000,000	1,000,000
Leasehold improvements	750,000	750,000	750,000	750,000	750,000	750,000
Subtotal fixed assets	$5,750,000	$5,750,000	$5,750,000	$5,750,000	$5,750,000	$5,750,000
Accumulated depreciation	800,000	807,750	815,500	823,250	831,000	838,750
Fixed assets	$4,950,000	$4,942,250	$4,934,500	$4,926,750	$4,919,000	$4,911,250
Total assets	$5,600,000	$5,639,410	$5,759,158	$5,943,061	$6,130,022	$6,281,616
Current liabilities:						
Accounts payable	325,000	229,000	206,438	227,516	238,344	221,188
Accrued income taxes payable	0	55,518	113,865	180,623	252,838	322,025
Revolving line of credit	250,000	250,000	250,000	250,000	250,000	250,000
Current liabilities	$ 575,000	$ 534,518	$ 570,303	$ 658,139	$ 741,182	$ 793,213
Bank note	500,000	500,000	500,000	500,000	500,000	500,000
Stockholder's equity:						
Common stock	3,800,000	3,800,000	3,800,000	3,800,000	3,800,000	3,800,000
Preferred stock	625,000	625,000	625,000	625,000	625,000	625,000
Retained earnings	100,000	179,892	263,855	359,922	463,840	563,403
Total stockholder's equity	$4,525,000	$4,604,892	$4,688,855	$4,784,922	$4,888,840	$4,988,403
Total liability & stockholder's equity	$5,600,000	$5,639,410	$5,759,158	$5,943,061	$6,130,022	$6,281,616

(continued)

Month 6	Month 7	Month 8	Month 9	Month 10	Month 11	Month 12
841,962	1,021,759	1,177,726	1,333,368	1,484,847	1,629,732	1,768,029
442,050	435,450	428,550	421,350	413,850	406,050	397,950
227,500	187,500	180,000	172,500	165,000	157,500	150,000
$1,511,512	$1,644,709	$1,786,276	$1,927,218	$2,063,697	$2,193,282	$2,315,979
2,500,000	2,500,000	2,500,000	2,500,000	2,500,000	2,500,000	2,500,000
1,500,000	1,500,000	1,500,000	1,500,000	1,500,000	1,500,000	1,500,000
1,000,000	1,000,000	1,000,000	1,000,000	1,000,000	1,000,000	1,000,000
750,000	750,000	750,000	750,000	750,000	750,000	750,000
$5,750,000	$5,750,000	$5,750,000	$5,750,000	$5,750,000	$5,750,000	$5,750,000
846,500	854,250	862,000	869,750	877,500	885,250	893,000
$4,903,500	$4,895,750	$4,888,000	$4,880,250	$4,872,500	$4,864,750	$4,857,000
$6,415,012	$6,540,459	$6,674,276	$6,807,468	$6,936,197	$7,058,032	$7,172,979
192,875	163,531	149,469	141,688	136,344	131,000	125,656
388,326	451,790	512,421	570,220	625,190	677,333	726,652
250,000	250,000	250,000	250,000	250,000	250,000	250,000
$ 831,201	$ 865,322	$ 911,890	$ 961,907	$1,011,533	$1,058,333	$1,102,309
500,000	500,000	500,000	500,000	500,000	500,000	500,000
3,800,000	3,800,000	3,800,000	3,800,000	3,800,000	3,800,000	3,800,000
625,000	625,000	625,000	625,000	625,000	625,000	625,000
658,811	750,138	837,386	920,560	999,663	1,074,699	1,145,671
$5,083,811	$5,175,138	$5,262,386	$5,345,560	$5,424,663	$5,499,699	$5,570,671
$6,415,012	$6,540,459	$6,674,276	$6,807,468	$6,936,197	$7,058,032	$7,172,979

Table 6–2B Peaches Corporation Prospective Income Statement, 199X

	Month 1	Month 2	Month 3	Month 4	Month 5	Month 6
Sales	$550,000	$575,000	$650,000	$700,000	$675,000	$650,000
Cost of goods sold	165,000	172,500	195,000	210,000	202,500	195,000
Gross margin ($)	$385,000	$402,500	$455,000	$490,000	$472,500	$455,000
Gross margin (%)	70%	70%	70%	70%	70%	70%
Advertising	27,500	28,750	32,500	35,000	33,750	32,500
Bad debt expense	6,940	7,090	7,725	8,517	8,850	8,841
Commission expense	55,000	57,500	65,000	70,000	67,500	65,000
Depreciation:						
Corporate offices	2,800	2,800	2,800	2,800	2,800	2,800
Machinery & equipment	1,700	1,700	1,700	1,700	1,700	1,700
Furniture & fixtures	1,250	1,250	1,250	1,250	1,250	1,250
Leasehold improvements	2,000	2,000	2,000	2,000	2,000	2,000
Insurance	5,000	5,000	5,000	5,000	5,000	5,000
Salaries & wages	82,500	86,250	97,500	105,000	101,250	97,500
Payroll taxes	9,900	10,350	11,700	12,600	12,150	11,700
Utilities	27,500	28,750	32,500	35,000	33,750	32,500
Travel & entertainment	27,500	28,750	32,500	35,000	33,750	32,500
Total costs and expenses	$249,590	$260,190	$292,175	$313,867	$303,750	$293,291
Net income before tax	$135,410	$142,310	$162,825	$176,133	$168,750	$161,709
Tax accrual	55,518	58,347	66,758	72,215	69,188	66,301
Net income	79,892	83,963	96,067	103,918	99,563	95,408

(continued)

Month 7	Month 8	Month 9	Month 10	Month 11	Month 12	Total year
$625,000	$600,000	$575,000	$550,000	$525,000	$500,000	$7,175,000
187,500	180,000	172,500	165,000	157,500	150,000	2,152,500
$437,500	$420,000	$402,500	$385,000	$367,500	$350,000	$5,022,500
70%	70%	70%	70%	70%	70%	70%
31,250	30,000	28,750	27,500	26,250	25,000	358,750
8,709	8,571	8,427	8,277	8,121	7,959	98,027
62,500	60,000	57,500	55,000	52,500	50,000	717,500
2,800	2,800	2,800	2,800	2,800	2,800	33,600
1,700	1,700	1,700	1,700	1,700	1,700	20,400
1,250	1,250	1,250	1,250	1,250	1,250	15,000
2,000	2,000	2,000	2,000	2,000	2,000	24,000
5,000	5,000	5,000	5,000	5,000	5,000	60,000
93,750	90,000	86,250	82,500	78,750	75,000	1,076,250
11,250	10,800	10,350	9,900	9,450	9,000	129,150
31,250	30,000	28,750	27,500	26,250	25,000	358,750
31,250	30,000	28,750	27,500	26,250	25,000	358,750
$282,709	$272,121	$261,527	$250,927	$240,321	$229,709	$3,250,177
$154,791	$147,879	$140,973	$134,073	$127,179	$120,291	$1,772,323
63,464	60,630	57,799	54,970	52,143	49,319	726,652
91,327	87,249	83,174	79,103	75,036	70,792	1,045,671

Table 6–2C   Peaches Corporation Prospective Statement of Changes in Financial Condition 199X

	Month 1	Month 2	Month 3	Month 4	Month 5
Financial resources provided:					
Cash from operations	$ 79,892	$ 83,963	$ 96,067	$103,918	$ 99,563
Add nonworking capital expenditures:					
Depreciation	7,750	7,750	7,750	7,750	7,750
Tax accrual	55,518	58,347	66,758	72,215	69,188
Total working capital from operations	$143,160	$150,060	$170,575	$183,883	$176,500
Effects of changes in components of working capital on cash:					
Increase in accounts receivable	3,000	(7,500)	(31,750)	(39,600)	(16,650)
Increase in inventory	(20,000)	(38,750)	(66,250)	10,000	45,000
Decrease in accounts payable	(96,000)	(22,563)	21,078	10,828	(17,156)
Cash from operations	$ 30,160	$ 81,248	$ 93,653	$165,111	$187,694
Draw down on line of credit	0	0	0	0	0
Proceeds from bank note	0	0	0	0	0
Issuance of common stock	0	0	0	0	0
Issuance of preferred stock	0	0	0	0	0
Total financial resources provided	$ 30,160	$ 81,248	$ 93,653	$165,111	$187,694
Financial resources applied:					
Purchase of capital assets	0	0	0	0	0
Dividends paid to pref'd stock	0	0	0	0	0
Dividends paid to common stock	0	0	0	0	0
Total financial resources applied	$ 0	$ 0	$ 0	$ 0	$ 0
Increase (decrease) in cash	$ 30,160	$ 81,248	$ 93,653	$165,111	$187,694
Beginning cash balance	100,000	130,160	211,408	305,061	470,172
Ending cash balance	$130,160	$211,408	$305,061	$470,172	$657,866

(continued)

Month 6	Month 7	Month 8	Month 9	Month 10	Month 11	Month 12
$ 95,408	$ 91,327	$ 87,249	$ 83,174	$ 79,103	$ 75,036	$ 70,972
7,750	7,750	7,750	7,750	7,750	7,750	7,750
66,301	63,464	60,630	57,799	54,970	52,143	49,319
$169,459	$ 162,541	$ 155,629	$ 148,723	$ 141,823	$ 134,929	$ 128,041
450	6,600	6,900	7,200	7,500	7,800	8,100
42,500	40,000	7,500	7,500	7,500	7,500	7,500
(28,313)	(29,344)	(14,063)	(7,781)	(5,344)	(5,344)	(5,344)
$184,097	$ 179,797	$ 155,967	$ 155,642	$ 151,479	$ 144,885	$ 138,297
0	0	0	0	0	0	0
0	0	0	0	0	0	0
0	0	0	0	0	0	0
0	0	0	0	0	0	0
$184,097	$ 179,797	$ 155,967	$ 155,642	$ 151,479	$ 144,885	$ 138,297
0	0	0	0	0	0	0
0	0	0	0	0	0	0
0	0	0	0	0	0	0
$ 0	$ 0	$ 0	$ 0	$ 0	$ 0	$ 0
$184,097	$ 179,797	$ 155,967	$ 155,642	$ 151,479	$ 144,885	$ 138,297
657,866	841,962	1,021,759	1,177,726	1,333,368	1,484,847	1,629,732
$841,962	$1,021,759	$1,177,726	$1,333,368	$1,484,847	$1,629,732	$1,768,029

Table 6–2D   Peaches Corporation Schedule of Accounts Receivable Planning Period, 199X

	Month 1	Month 2	Month 3	Month 4	Month 5
Beginning balance	$350,000	347,000	354,500	386,250	425,850
Plus credit sales	330,000	345,000	390,000	420,000	405,000
Less collections:					
From 90 days ago	45,500	45,500	45,500	42,900	44,850
From 60 days ago	70,000	70,000	66,000	69,000	78,000
From 30 days ago	52,500	49,500	51,750	58,500	63,000
From current sales	165,000	172,500	195,000	210,000	202,500
Ending accounts receivable	$347,000	$354,500	$386,250	$425,850	$442,500

Table 6–2E   Peaches Corporation Schedule of Accounts Payable Planning Period, 199X

	Month 1	Month 2	Month 3	Month 4	Month 5
Beginning balance	$325,000	$229,000	$206,438	$227,516	$238,344
Plus credit purchases (Inventory only)	165,000	194,063	243,750	236,250	202,500
Less payments:					
For current purchases	66,000	77,625	97,500	94,500	81,000
For purchases 30 days ago	113,750	57,750	67,922	85,313	82,688
For purchases 60 days ago	48,750	48,750	24,750	29,109	36,563
For purchases 90 days ago	32,500	32,500	32,500	16,500	19,406
Ending accounts payable	$229,000	$206,438	$227,516	$238,344	$221,188

Month 6	Month 7	Month 8	Month 9	Month 10	Month 11	Month 12
442,500	442,050	435,450	428,550	421,350	413,850	406,050
390,000	375,000	360,000	345,000	330,000	315,000	300,000
50,700	54,600	52,650	50,700	48,750	46,800	44,850
84,000	81,000	78,000	75,000	72,000	69,000	66,000
60,750	58,500	56,250	54,000	51,750	49,500	47,250
195,000	187,500	180,000	172,500	165,000	157,500	150,000
$442,050	$435,450	$428,550	$421,350	$413,850	$406,050	$397,950

Month 6	Month 7	Month 8	Month 9	Month 10	Month 11	Month 12
$221,188	$192,875	$163,531	$149,469	$141,688	$136,344	$131,000
170,625	140,625	135,000	129,375	123,750	118,125	112,500
68,250	56,250	54,000	51,750	49,500	47,250	45,000
70,875	59,719	49,219	47,250	45,281	43,313	41,344
35,438	30,375	25,594	21,094	20,250	19,406	18,563
24,375	23,625	20,250	17,063	14,062	13,500	12,937
$192,875	$163,531	$149,469	$141,688	$136,344	$131,000	$125,656

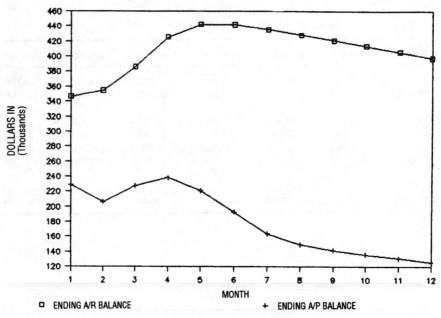

Figure 6–1   Peaches Corp. Receivables versus Payables, 199X

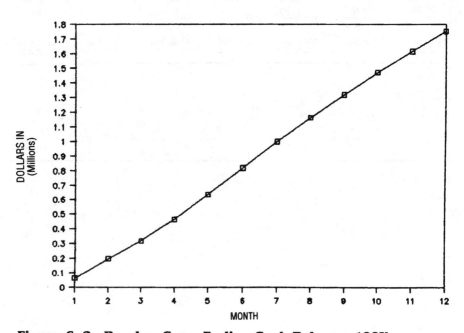

Figure 6–2   Peaches Corp. Ending Cash Balance, 199X

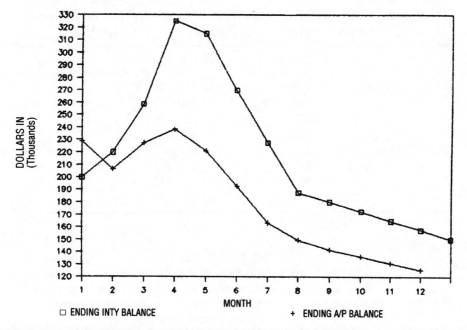

Figure 6–3   Peaches Corp. Inventory versus Payables, 199X

NET INCOME, 199X

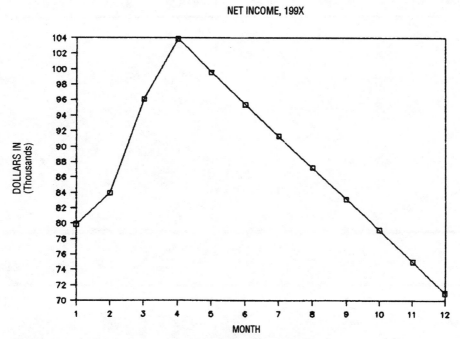

Figure 6–4   Peaches Corp. Net Income, 199X

Table 6–3 Peaches Corporation Sensitivity Analysis, Cost of Goods Sold vs. Year-End Net Income, Plan Year 199X

CGS%	Net income
50%	$ 199,021
45%	410,683
40%	622,346
35%	834,008
30%	1,045,671
25%	1,257,333
20%	1,468,996
15%	1,680,658

Table 6–4 Peaches Corporation Sensitivity Analysis Cost of Goods Sold & Salary vs. Year-End Net Income, Plan Year 199X

Salary %	Sales commission %				
	14%	12%	10%	8%	6%
19%	$ 686,691	$ 771,356	$ 856,021	$ 940,686	$1,025,351
17%	781,516	866,181	950,846	1,035,511	1,120,176
15%	876,341	961,006	1,045,671	1,130,336	1,215,001
13%	971,165	1,055,830	1,140,495	1,225,160	1,309,825
11%	1,065,990	1,150,655	1,235,320	1,319,985	1,404,650

Table 6–5 Peaches Corporation Financial Plan Assumptions 199X

	Beg balance	Month 1	Month 2	Month 3	Month 4	Month 5	Month 6	Month 7	Month 8	Month 9	Month 10	Month 11	Month 12
Balance sheet assumptions:													
Cash	100,000												
Accts receivable assumptions:													
Note: The A/R schedules assumes collections from prior periods not shown in the planning horizon.													
Additionally, A/R is assumed to be a fixed percentage of sales. This percentage can be altered in the assumptions.													
Accounts receivable (% of sales)	350,000	60%	60%	60%	60%	60%	60%	60%	60%	60%	60%	60%	60%
Beginning balance	350,000												
Percentage of sales on credit		100%	100%	100%	100%	100%	100%	100%	100%	100%	100%	100%	100%
Collection rates:													
% collected current		50%	50%	50%	50%	50%	50%	50%	50%	50%	50%	50%	50%
% collected w/in 30 days		65%	65%	65%	65%	65%	65%	65%	65%	65%	65%	65%	65%
% collected w/in 60 days		85%	85%	85%	85%	85%	85%	85%	85%	85%	85%	85%	85%
% collected w/in 90 days		98%	98%	98%	98%	98%	98%	98%	98%	98%	98%	98%	98%
Bad debt %		2%	2%	2%	2%	2%	2%	2%	2%	2%	2%	2%	2%
Inventory (% of sales)	200,000	40%	45%	50%	45%	40%	35%	30%	30%	30%	30%	30%	30%
Corporate offices	2,500,000	2,500,000	2,500,000	2,500,000	2,500,000	2,500,000	2,500,000	2,500,000	2,500,000	2,500,000	2,500,000	2,500,000	2,500,000
Machinery & equipment	1,500,000	1,500,000	1,500,000	1,500,000	1,500,000	1,500,000	1,500,000	1,500,000	1,500,000	1,500,000	1,500,000	1,500,000	1,500,000
Furniture & fixtures	1,000,000	1,000,000	1,000,000	1,000,000	1,000,000	1,000,000	1,000,000	1,000,000	1,000,000	1,000,000	1,000,000	1,000,000	1,000,000
Leasehold improvements	750,000	750,000	750,000	750,000	750,000	750,000	750,000	750,000	750,000	750,000	750,000	750,000	750,000
Accts payable assumptions:													
Note: The A/P schedule assumes that only inventory is included in the A/P balance. In practice this is not usually the case.													
Accounts payable (beg. bal. only)	325,000												
Accounts payable (% of inventory)		75%	75%	75%	75%	75%	75%	75%	75%	75%	75%	75%	75%
Beginning balance	325,000												

Table 6–5 (Continued)

	Beg balance	Month 1	Month 2	Month 3	Month 4	Month 5	Month 6	Month 7	Month 8	Month 9	Month 10	Month 11	Month 12
% of inventory purchases on credit		75%	75%	75%	75%	75%	75%	75%	75%	75%	75%	75%	75%
Payment rates:													
% paid current		40%	40%	40%	40%	40%	40%	40%	40%	40%	40%	40%	40%
% paid w/in 30 days		75%	75%	75%	75%	75%	75%	75%	75%	75%	75%	75%	75%
% paid w/in 60 days		90%	90%	90%	90%	90%	90%	90%	90%	90%	90%	90%	90%
% paid w/in 90 days		100%	100%	100%	100%	100%	100%	100%	100%	100%	100%	100%	100%
Accrued income taxes payable	0												
Bank note	500,000	500,000	500,000	500,000	500,000	500,000	500,000	500,000	500,000	500,000	500,000	500,000	500,000
Revolving line of credit	250,000	250,000	250,000	250,000	250,000	250,000	250,000	250,000	250,000	250,000	250,000	250,000	250,000
Retained earnings	100,000												
Common stock	3,800,000	3,800,000	3,800,000	3,800,000	3,800,000	3,800,000	3,800,000	3,800,000	3,800,000	3,800,000	3,800,000	3,800,000	3,800,000
Preferred stock	625,000	625,000	625,000	625,000	625,000	625,000	625,000	625,000	625,000	625,000	625,000	625,000	625,000
Dividends pd on common stock	N/A	0	0	0	0	0	0	0	0	0	0	0	0
Dividends pd on preferred stock	N/A	0	0	0	0	0	0	0	0	0	0	0	0
Income statement assumptions:													
Sales		550,000	575,000	650,000	700,000	675,000	650,000	625,000	600,000	575,000	550,000	525,000	500,000
Cost of goods sold (% of sales)		30%	30%	30%	30%	30%	30%	30%	30%	30%	30%	30%	30%

Note: CGS as a % of sales keys off of the assumption in month #1 and computes that assumption for every other month. The purpose was to use this in the sensitivity analysis.

	Beg balance	Month 1	Month 2	Month 3	Month 4	Month 5	Month 6	Month 7	Month 8	Month 9	Month 10	Month 11	Month 12
Advertising (% of sales)		5%	5%	5%	5%	5%	5%	5%	5%	5%	5%	5%	5%
Bad debt expense (% of A/R)		2%	2%	2%	2%	2%	2%	2%	2%	2%	2%	2%	2%
Commission expense (% of sales)		10%	10%	10%	10%	10%	10%	10%	10%	10%	10%	10%	10%

Note: Commissions as a % of sales keys off of the assumption in month #1 and computes that assumption for every other month. The purpose was to use this in the sensitivity analysis.

	Beg balance	Month 1	Month 2	Month 3	Month 4	Month 5	Month 6	Month 7	Month 8	Month 9	Month 10	Month 11	Month 12
Depreciation													
Corporate offices	500,000	2,800	2,800	2,800	2,800	2,800	2,800	2,800	2,800	2,800	2,800	2,800	2,800
Machinery & equipment	100,000	1,700	1,700	1,700	1,700	1,700	1,700	1,700	1,700	1,700	1,700	1,700	1,700
Furniture & fixtures	75,000	1,250	1,250	1,250	1,250	1,250	1,250	1,250	1,250	1,250	1,250	1,250	1,250
Leasehold improvements	125,000	2,000	2,000	2,000	2,000	2,000	2,000	2,000	2,000	2,000	2,000	2,000	2,000
Insurance		5,000	5,000	5,000	5,000	5,000	5,000	5,000	5,000	5,000	5,000	5,000	5,000
Salaries & wages (% of sales)		15%	15%	15%	15%	15%	15%	15%	15%	15%	15%	15%	15%
Payroll taxes (% of salaries)		12%	12%	12%	12%	12%	12%	12%	12%	12%	12%	12%	12%
Utilities (% of sales)		5%	5%	5%	5%	5%	5%	5%	5%	5%	5%	5%	5%
Travel & entertainment (% of sales)		5%	5%	5%	5%	5%	5%	5%	5%	5%	5%	5%	5%
Tax accrual %		41%	41%	41%	41%	41%	41%	41%	41%	41%	41%	41%	41%

Note: Salaries as a % of sales keys off of the assumption in month #1 and computes that assumption for every other month. The purpose was to use this in the sensitivity analysis.

PART II
IMPLEMENTATION
OF THE PLAN

7

Benchmarks

OVERVIEW

We need to establish a link between the blueprint for plan implementation and the company's everyday operations. Well-chosen benchmarks provide that link. They are the yardsticks by which we measure progress toward our goals. This chapter illustrates the methods used to establish meaningful performance measurement benchmarks and use them as your business plan's compass.

We want benchmarks that can be quickly put together at the end of each operating period (and sometimes during them). Benchmarks should be quantitative and track plan implementation. They should also tell us something about where to look in order to fix a problem that could sidetrack the plan.

Establish benchmarks *during* construction of the business plan. After all, we know from the start that we are going to monitor our progress toward implementation of the plan. So we may as well establish meaningful devices to measure that progress. Everyone on the planning team must understand the benchmarks, including:

- What they mean
- How they are computed
- The particular part of the plan tracked by each
- The people who are responsible for achieving each

Without benchmarks, implementing a business plan is like flying an airplane without a compass. It's hard to tell if you're on course just by looking out the window at the ground whizzing by. Same thing with your business plan.

SELECTING BENCHMARKS

Benchmarks indicate progress toward implementing the plan. They give everyone an idea of how well the firm is doing in attaining *specific* goals. If they are chosen correctly, a benchmark can point to a potential problem that might cause deviation from the plan.

A case in point might be the financial manager negotiating a larger line of credit for expansion of working capital requirements. This benchmark is critical to financing the receivables generated by the sales department's action plan. It also demonstrates funds available to pay for the raw material purchased by the production department. This benchmark is critical to implementation of the plan. Further, its timing is important.

In this example we've identified five attributes the most useful benchmarks possess:

1. They are easily identified and quantified.
2. Time can be specified.
3. The person responsible for attaining them can be identified.
4. They are important to implementation of the plan.
5. There is no question of when they are achieved.

Identification

Ease of Recognition
Benchmarks are like anything else in business—the easier the better. There's nothing complicated about choosing benchmarks. Just make sure they can be easily recognized. In the example above, we used a line of credit. The company received an amendment to the borrowing agreement stipulating that the amount available had been raised. Simple. There was no question about definitions.

Use Numbers as a Common Denominator
The second part of benchmark identification is the ability to communicate it in a form everyone can understand. Numbers most easily tell us if a benchmark has been reached. Therefore, select quantifiable benchmarks against which to track plan implementation. The line of credit certainly was quantifiable. The amount was the increase in the line unambiguously stated in dollars.

If you can avoid it, don't use benchmarks that are amorphous blobs of opinion. An example would be a benchmark that calls for "raising the overall quality of employees." Not only are such benchmarks hard to nail down, but they are open to dispute. Further, experience tells us that such qualitative objectives usually don't help us reach the short-term targets set forth by our business plan.

Timing

Business plans are really a series of action steps that take place in a specific sequence. Often for one part of the plan to begin working, another part must have already been completed. This is true of our line of credit example. We need reasonable assurance that the LOC can be increased before we commit to selling more products and building our receivables and payables balances. Once we actually buy the components, assemble, and sell them, we're committed. The line *must* be increased before the first payable comes due.

Once we have identified the benchmarks, we need to determine *when* each must be reached to keep implementation of our plan on track. Careful thought must be given to the needs of each plan component when arriving at the due date for each benchmark.

Here are two things to ask yourself when arriving at the order and timing for benchmarks:

1. Which departments are dependent on this task being completed before they themselves can begin (or end)?
2. What is the impact if the benchmark is achieved early (or late)?

Timing the benchmarks, then, becomes the most basic of the yardsticks by which we measure implementation of our business plan.

Responsibility

Responsibility for meeting specific benchmarks must be assignable to an individual. We've talked before about the necessity for assigning responsibility and accountability for creation of the different plan components. The same principles hold for meeting our benchmarks.

Choose your benchmarks in such a way that there is no question who is responsible for meeting them. Make sure these people know they're being held responsible. Finally, give them the tools they need to get the job done.

Often this includes providing the authority to make decisions that may have formerly been held by senior management. Without that authority to act, most people's commitment to a goal diminishes. The ultimate responsibility still rests with the person who can get things done.

Relevance to the Implementation Plan

We want benchmarks that tell us how we're progressing. Engineers find such relevant benchmarks by using critical path charts. Such technology here would be overkill. However, briefly, the critical path identifies those parts of the plan around which all the other components revolve. Unless each of the critical factors is met, the plan implementation does not move forward.

That's what we want our benchmarks to be—critical parts of the plan that could cause implementation to stop if they weren't met on time. Often such crucial factors hinge on changes to the infrastructure of the company. For example, installing a new order entry (OE) system so the increased amount of orders can be handled. This might be considered a benchmark.

However, ask yourself what it is you're measuring. Is it the order entry system? That's only a secondary goal. By itself, the OE system doesn't do the company any good without the *critical factor* of increased sales. Therefore, the relevant benchmark would be specific levels of sales—probably established at key time frames along the plan implementation timeline.

Bringing the OE system up is an important action step, but the need for it depends on the sales level. Without sales, the new system is irrelevant.

Hitting Benchmarks

The last criteria for selecting benchmarks has to do with knowing when they've been reached. If benchmarks were selected with their measurement in mind, this should not be too great a problem. Ideally, the actual performance numbers for your benchmarks should be easily derived from the accounting system.

For example, sales is a number every accounting system provides. There's no question when the actual year-to-date sales figures equate to the sales numbers in the implementation plan that were used as a benchmark. When the accounting system says you've hit the sales benchmark number, you have. Period.

We want our benchmark measurement to be both easy and reliable. Avoid selecting benchmarks that require complex computations based on assumptions. This only injects an element of doubt as to how the implementation plan is tracking.

Consignment sales is a good example. Book publishers sell on what amounts to a consignment contract. As with all consignment sales, book stores can return the books if they don't sell. Therefore, computation of sales figures requires guessing at the timing and percentage of returns for credit that the seller must bear. We really don't know for sure how many units have sold until expiration of the return period.

See what a problem such numbers become if they're used as benchmarks? It's much better to stick with concrete numbers that tell us how well our plan is being implemented.

SALES AND MARKETING

Benchmarks established for the sales department are among the most closely watched at small and medium-sized companies. Indicators of sales revenue guide other departments in executing their parts of the business plan.

The good news is that much of the sales data is easily reported and not subject to interpretation (unless you're a book publisher or other consignment seller). Most accounting systems can provide isolated sales revenue information all throughout the operating period if need be. Further, the sales staff seldom has trouble keeping track of its sales especially if this information is used to compute commissions.

Benchmarks

The most obvious benchmark in the sales and marketing group is revenue. Chances are the business plan tracks overall performance based on some sort of sales level.

Units Shipped
Equally valuable information can be gained by tracking units shipped. Depending on the firm's policies regarding income recognition, units shipped usually triggers an invoice. The invoice ordinarily generates recording of the sale in the accounting system.

Therefore, if a lag exists between shipment and invoice times (there shouldn't be for cash management purposes), tracking shipments gives an early indication of the all-important sales benchmark.

Advertising Expenses
Most companies keep a tight rein on advertising expenses. One good way is to make each advertising campaign a separate cost center. We do this by assigning a subaccount number in the general ledger to each advertising program. For example:

■ Advertising expenses is G/L account #400.

- Promotional expenses allocated to product X are coded into G/L account #410.
- Promotional expenses allocated to product Y are coded into G/L account #420, and so on.

The subaccounts are rolled up into the lead expense account #400. Advertising expenses still appear as one number on the income statement; however, *now* the sales and marketing department can track its programs separately simply by looking at the subaccounts.

Sales Per Advertising Dollars Spent   A useful benchmark establishes a cutoff for product and advertising campaign performance. For example, let's say our benchmark for product X is that sales revenue must be at least 100 times the advertising expenses paid for its promotion. Anything less means either the advertising campaign has failed or the product is just too costly to promote. At that point we consider either dropping product X or changing its promotion program.

Either way, the benchmark has served its purpose in alerting us to a deviation from our intended course.

Warranty Costs
Many firms charge warranty expenses to the sales and marketing department when they are part of a promotional campaign. These are a real cost of doing business. Further, they are an enticement to buy just as are price concessions.

When the promotional campaign was implemented there should have been estimates of the costs associated with making good on warranty promises. Those estimates often become benchmarks against which the actual performance is compared. If we begin experiencing repair costs beyond those originally anticipated in the benchmark, we've got a problem. Chances are there's nothing we can do about the units already sold. However, we certainly can alter terms of the warranty.

Sales Commissions
This is another useful benchmark in the sales and marketing department. We want to make sure that our commission program provides the right incentive to the sales force. We can compare the commissions paid against the specific products being sold. Additionally, we want to monitor the incentives we're giving against our experience with collection of accounts receivable for the customers to whom we are selling.

This may sound like a lot of analytical work. However, this particular benchmark keeps us from rewarding a sales effort that does not concentrate on our high profit margin products or on getting high-quality customers who pay their bills.

MANUFACTURING

The manufacturing department lends itself very well to establishing effective benchmarks. Much of manufacturing performance is quantitative in nature. Further, if your firm has a reliable cost accounting system, the results are already routinely reported.

Manufacturing benchmarks should emphasize specific targets of the business plan. Logic tells us the two most important parts of the manufacturing area are production and costs. Most likely both of these are featured somewhere in the business goals of the company. Additionally, without particular manufacturing benchmarks to guide them, neither the sales and marketing plans nor the financial plans can gauge the capacity to fill orders or fund obligations.

There are many manufacturing benchmarks used to guide implementation of the plan. Which ones to use depends on:

- What's important to successfully implement the plan
- Your firm's ability to generate the actual result numbers for comparison against the plan

Here are some ideas:

Cost of Goods Sold

Most companies carefully watch their manufacturing costs. This is usually close to the largest—if not *the* largest—cost of the firm. If your business plan stipulates profit targets, then the cost of goods sold (CGS) provides one of the benchmarks toward achieving them.

However, CGS can be a tricky number to nail down. Many different costs make up production numbers. Among them are:

- Purchases of raw materials
- Direct production costs, such as assembly line labor
- Indirect production costs, such as health insurance allocation
- Overhead allocation

Everyone must agree on *how* CGS is computed. Further, it must reconcile against the beginning and ending inventory balances (beginning inventory plus production costs less sales equals ending inventory). If everyone agrees on the computation, the danger of having an overly complex benchmark is reduced.

Production

Production benchmarks tell the sales department how much inventory is ready (or will be ready) to ship. These are often keyed on the anticipated sales from marketing campaigns. Production begins in advance of sales actually being booked. As launching of the campaign approaches, production benchmarks are taken more and more seriously. This is especially true of companies where intense competition exists and prompt delivery can mean the difference between making a sale or giving it away to a competitor.

Additionally, for companies that have a hard time building inventory reserves, production and sales benchmarks are used to guide this expansion. The controller watches it carefully so the product that is required becomes available without excess inventory eating up working capital.

Overtime

Production overtime is a benchmark often watched more closely in the manufacturing department than throughout the rest of the firm. A balance between production levels and costs needs to be struck. Some firms with heavy production level commitments make up for shortfalls by adding shifts and working overtime. This can raise the overall cost of goods to a point where profit plan implementation becomes endangered.

Therefore, overtime benchmarks are used to work in conjunction with the other manufacturing benchmarks. The manufacturing department identifies the overtime level in its action plan that is acceptable and that will still allow it to meet its commitments.

Machinery Uptime

Manufacturing levels usually depend on a specific level of machinery uptime. Additionally, the overall cost of goods sold is influenced by the proper production equipment being available so that idle labor costs and production rejects are kept within an acceptable range.

Machinery uptime is probably a benchmark used only by the manufacturing department in tracking its own departmental implementation plan.

Manufacturing Cost Variance

Most production departments track their manufacturing costs against some sort of standard. The standard costs were likely included in the business plan. Deviation from standard could present a problem in implementing the business plan. Therefore, production managers pay close attention to these types of variances:

Direct Labor Content of Production

As workers gain more experience or as more sophisticated production equipment is installed, the amount of direct labor costs that go into making each unit of production usually goes down. Effective labor cost benchmarks can verify this trend.

A variance that can throw off the labor content benchmark is labor price variance. This occurs when the cost of labor changes from what the plan had assumed it would cost. During periods of labor union negotiation or rising labor costs this can become a critical production benchmark.

Material Content of Production

Most products require specific quantities of raw material. Any more than that is a waste and creates a negative cost variance.

Material price variances can also occur, making it appear that more raw material is contained in each unit. During periods of rising prices this benchmark is watched carefully. Sometimes, actual steps to control material price variances are taken. Hedging raw materials prices is one such remedy.

Worker Idle Time

This is one of the most expensive negative cost variances. It can usually be seen when machinery is down for unscheduled repair or maintenance. Sometimes it occurs when production workers must wait for parts or tools before continuing with their work. Setup of new production runs can create worker idle time as well.

Quality Control Benchmarks

These are more often used within the manufacturing department to control production. QC provides very short-term (sometimes hourly) guidelines as to production performance. The most common QC benchmarks revolve around rejects from inspection of items coming off the production line. The manufacturing action plan probably assumes a standard number of rejects. Any more than that causes excessive rework costs and wastage.

However, too few rejects can also mean there's a problem. The production line may be running too slowly. The department must strike an acceptable balance between production flow and quality. The QC benchmarks help monitor that balance.

GROSS MARGIN

Using the gross margin percentage ([Sales − Cost of Goods Sold]/ Sales) as a benchmark combine results of both the sales and manufacturing efforts. Since gross margin has a significant bearing on the profitability of the firm, it provides a relevant guide to track implementation of the plan.

Many companies track the gross margin of each product separately. If any should fall below prespecified minimums a problem is recognized. Either the average sales price isn't up to what was planned or manufacturing cost overruns have occurred. Regardless, implementation of the business plan is in jeopardy and action needs to be taken.

INVENTORY

Inventory benchmarks are among the most important to companies that stock items for manufacturing, assembly, and sale. Too little inventory causes stock out costs along with possible stoppage of the production line. Too much inventory unnecessarily eats up working capital without returning the required profit. Additionally, too much inventory risks spoilage and obsolescence. Either way, it's an expensive mistake.

Benchmarks are set to strike the balance between manufacturing managers who want to build inventory for longer production runs and financial managers who insist on the bare minimum needed to keep the production line moving. The sales department usually comes down on the side of production. They don't want to risk having inadequate supplies to fill their customers' orders and thereby forgo potential commissions.

Inventory Levels

Establishing inventory levels can be tricky. They are a function of:

- Production requirements
- Vendor lead-time

- Ordering and safety stock requirements
- Pricing of purchases

Production Requirements

Certainly we want to stock enough inventory to meet production demands. This does not necessarily mean that we must have on hand the total amount needed for the entire production run. Indeed, a valid benchmark is often the number of production days of inventory held in stock. This is computed as:

Inventory on Hand/Daily Production Requirements = Production Days of Inventory

From a financial perspective the firm doesn't want such large investment in a single asset. Further, it takes up expensive warehouse space that could be better utilized. Many companies manage this conflict with several purchases of inventory items throughout the production cycle. Another alternative is to execute a single master purchase order for the goods needed but to have them delivered and invoiced over several increments.

Using either of these techniques, the days of production inventory on hand can be kept at the appropriate level. This also accelerates the inventory turnover, another benchmark used to measure inventory efficiency. Inventory turnover is computed as:

Cost of Goods Sold/Average Inventory Balance = Inventory Turnover

Both the days of production requirements in inventory and turnover are useful benchmarks. They are precise and easily calculated. Additionally, our use of both inventory turnover and gross margin provides another useful benchmark: gross margin per inventory turn. This is computed as:

Gross Margin/Number of Inventory Turns = Gross Margin per Inventory Turn

It makes no sense to have a benchmark (turnover) that doesn't deliver the required level of profit (gross margin). Therefore, we want to track this carefully. Here's an example where a company actually "improved" its inventory turnover, but reduced its gross margin with each turn:

TOBBY MANUFACTURING CORPORATION
Computation of Gross Margin Per Inventory Turnover
For the year ended December 31, 19X2

	19X1	19X2
Cost of goods sold	$10,000,000	$6,000,000
Average inventory of finished goods	1,000,000	500,000
Inventory turnover	10 times	12 times
Days of sales in inventory (360 days/turnover)	36 days	30 days
Gross margin	$3,500,000	$2,000,000
Gross margin per turnover	$350,000	$166,667

Inventory performance looks positive. The turnover has accelerated from 10 to 12 and the days of sales in inventory has fallen from 36 days to 30 days. Tobby's management appears headed in the right direction. But look at the gross margin per inventory turn. It has dropped by over 50 percent. Tobby has sacrificed profit for the sake of liquidity. The cause of this could have been a variety of things, perhaps an unplanned price discount, for example. In any case, by watching this benchmark, we could have identified the problem while there was time to correct it before the business plan was placed at risk.

Vendor Lead-Time

Both availability of inventory and the time it takes to get it are perpetual fears of production managers. Timing figures prominently in inventory balances. Production managers are concerned with having enough inventory on hand to cover delivery problems of new orders.

However, use of vendor lead-time as a benchmark runs into problems because it's not always reliable. By using some common sense, you can combine vendor lead-time with another benchmark— days of production in inventory.

> *Simply compare the supply of inventory on hand with what your purchasing manager says the lead-time is for a new order to arrive. If you have 30 days of an item on hand, yet the lead-time to get more is only 5 days, you're overstocked.*

Obsolete Inventory

Inventory can become obsolete if held too long. This is particularly true of computer components and other high-tech gadgetry. A useful benchmark is to track inventory that has been deemed obsolete. Many firms judge obsolete inventory by its turnover. Companies with obsolete inventory at the start of the planning period often include in their business plans reductions of this less valuable asset.

Keep in mind that we have both finite storage space as well as limited working capital to invest. We can't have either tied up in nonproducing assets such as obsolete inventory. Use obsolete inventory as a benchmark to guide the company toward acceptable levels.

EOQ and Safety Stock

In Chapter 4 we talked about economic order quantities (EOQ) and safety stock. The equations used to compute these two useful numbers are illustrated there. They can also be used as benchmarks. Both EOQ and targeted safety stock levels are inventory goals. They aren't absolutes. Achievement of these goals helps implementation of the business plan. They guide the management of inventory, which in turn contributes to working capital, interest expense, and the costs of allowing inventory to spoil or go obsolete.

Rework Due to Raw Material or Component Defects

Most manufacturing and assembly companies get some raw materials or components that are substandard when they arrive. If they aren't caught before they enter the production line they'll cause QC rejects.

By tracking the benchmark of rework due to raw material or component defects, we can take steps toward managing this cost of manufacturing.

HUMAN RESOURCES

Human resources benchmarks can be quantified just like any other planning target. We tend to measure HR benchmarks in terms of costs (in dollars) and in number of incidences. Depending on your company's business, some of these are more relevant than others.

Benchmarks

HR targets provide cost control guidelines more than anything else. The objectives are to keep not only the actual salaries, but all the ancillary costs associated with personnel within the parameters of the HR action plan. Let's take a look at some of the more common benchmarks.

Salary Expenses

Obviously salary expenses figure prominently in the HR action plan. They provide a useful benchmark to keep them under control.

Headcount

Be careful when using headcount as a benchmark; counting bodies is not really what we want. Instead, we count *full-time equivalents* (*FTEs*). Not all employees work a full day; some are part-timers.

The objective of a headcount is to guide the firm in the number of FTEs used to execute the plan.

Employee Turnover

This is easy to compute—just subtract W-2s between years. However, sometimes equally useful in this measurement are the *reasons* for turnover. It's expensive to loose a valued employee whom the company has trained. If it's because of the working conditions, benefits, or salary, then we want to know. The reasons, however, are usually more subjective and require interpretation. Often establishing the policy of exit interviews for all departing employees helps provide some answers.

Health Care

We want to track health care claims and work-related injuries, particularly stress cases. These are expensive and often precede litigation. To the extent the firm can identify problems before they become critical (such as a class action among a group of current and former employees who want their ticket out of a financial abyss to come from your company), we'll be that much better off.

Use of Outsiders

Many companies rely heavily on outside contractors, consultants, and temporary workers. These are expensive and aren't always the answer. By installing a benchmark that tracks use of these outsiders, we identify the cost versus the benefit. At some point of usage, it becomes more cost effective just to hire a person with the requisite skills than to keep on engaging an outsider.

Bonuses

Incentive bonus plans are provided to be paid out. The firm *hopes* its employees achieve the performance necessary to earn a bonus. This creates a win-win situation. A benchmark that tracks those employees receiving a bonus lets everyone know how the incentive plan is working toward achieving overall company goals.

Employee Profitability

Many firms measure the sales per employee or profit per employee. This is much like the return on invested capital. It may sound cold to measure an employee's worth simply by the sales or profits they generate. Yet, it does provide a useful *index* as to how productive the work force is in terms of meeting plan objectives.

Lawsuits

This is probably more relevant for larger companies than for smaller ones. Hopefully we can count all the lawsuits we're involved in on the fingers of one hand. We want to pay particular attention to suits for wrongful termination, stress, and job-related accidents.

Additionally, we need to have benchmarks for legal fees. These can get out of hand quickly. Often it makes more economic sense to just settle rather than go to court, even if it amounts to extortion on the part of a disgruntled employee being led on by a self-serving attorney.

PURCHASING

Purchasing contributes to implementation of the business plan in a variety of ways. Some of the benchmarks established for purchasing focus on price, others emphasize timeliness and terms.

Price Variances

A benchmark that helps track the material prices used in the manufacturing plan against what the buyers are actually able to obtain is called the *material price variance*. It simply means the difference between the "standard price" (that was planned for) and the actual price for which these things were purchased.

Negative price variances mean that the cost of goods will likely rise above that intended in the manufacturing plan.

When used as a benchmark, price variances can identify problems while there's still time to either correct them or compensate in other ways.

Timing

Some companies require critical materials in their manufacturing or assembly processes. If these become scarce or delivery isn't made during the time required, there's a risk to the production schedule.

For these crucial items, many companies use their delivery dates as benchmarks in monitoring plan performance. The benchmarks are established at specific points where decisions for alternate sources or other actions must be made.

Contract Terms

Some benchmarks used internally in the purchasing department revolve around contract terms. For example, a plan implementation item often found in the purchasing plan is purchases discounts. It's almost always a benefit to the company to pay a little early in order to receive a purchase discount. However, the buyers usually need to negotiate this part of the purchase order. It requires a conscious effort to accomplish.

Purchase Discounts

Many of the modern automated accounts payables systems provide for control over purchase discounts (ACCPAC and MAS 90 are two). They allow for entry of the discount percentage and automatically compute the dollars saved. Then they post this savings to the general ledger account that accumulates this savings. Further, they track the payment due date and remind you when it's time to pay in order to take advantage of the discount terms.

Some controllers avoid paying early, saying they can better use the cash than the vendor, despite the discount. Here's why such a policy *costs* the company money:

> *Let's assume you have a $10,000 invoice with terms of 2/10, Net 30. This means that if the invoice is paid within ten days, the buyer is entitled to a 2% discount. Otherwise the full amount is due within thirty days.*

> *Here's how to compute the value of this cash discount:*

$$(\text{Discount \%}/(\text{Due date} - \text{Discount date})) \times 365 \text{ days} = \text{Annualized interest income from taking advantage of the discount.}$$

> *The annualized interest income from taking advantage of the discount is 37% and was computed as follows:*

$$(.02/(30 - 10)) \times 365 = 37\%$$

> *As long as the company can borrow for less than 37% (and the cash is available), the discount should be taken. Taking this example one step further, let's compute the benefit in dollars and cents:*

> Invoice amount: $10,000
> Terms: 2/10, Net 30

Aggregate cost of funds rate: 10%
Discount yield (dollars): 100
Interest cost by taking the discount:
($10,000 × 10%)/365 × (30 days − 10 days) = 55
Net interest profit by taking discount: $45

Payment Due Date

Here's another benchmark often used by purchasing managers that can assist the controller in managing cash. Part of the combined purchasing and financial plans may be to increase the average payment due date on accounts payable to a preagreed level. That number is boiled into the cash flow plan.

The benchmark becomes important as the purchasing department negotiates contracts to acquire goods and services used by the company. If it's monitored every month, a good indication of the progress toward this goal can be obtained. Further, the benchmark is easily verified from the accounts payable system by taking the average aging of the whole A/P portfolio.

FINANCE

Financial benchmarks are probably seen most often by company management. Many business plan goals are financial in nature or at least their targets are measured in terms of dollars and cents. Further, the accounting department regularly puts out financial information that can be compared both against the plan and against prior periods. These two ingredients—commonly accepted definitions and accessibility of data—make financial benchmarks among the most useful.

The overall business plan probably has several financial benchmarks used to gauge the company's performance. The financial plan should identify these benchmarks in a separate section and compute how the plan stacks up against the standards already established. You should correct any situations in the financial plan that may breach the target benchmarks.

Every month management evaluates its progress toward implementation of the plan. Actual performance is measured against planned benchmarks. To the extent that these benchmarks were carefully chosen, they accurately identify implementation progress.

Ratios and Statistics

Many experienced financial planners take some of their opening financial benchmarks from the beginning balance sheet. That way, they have benchmarks against which to track changes as the financial plan spins out over the planning horizon. Some of these financial statistics were introduced earlier in Chapter 6.

Table 7–1 contains a summary of the most common financial benchmarks.

Table 7–1   Common Financial Benchmarks

Disposable cash:	Spendable cash after all expenses have been removed and current liabilities have been subtracted.
Cash capability:	Cash plus cash sources coming due such as A/R collections, maturity of short-term investments, available credit lines less cash requirements such as A/P and loan payments.
Loan balances and draws:	Compensating balances
Cash concentration system:	Speed with which cash inflows are turned into spendable cash
Working capital	
Interest expense:	Aggregate borrowing rate
Accounts receivable and payable:	Days of sales, turnover Average outstanding
Financial ratios:	Current ratio Quick ratio Debt/equity ratio times interest earned Proportion of long and short-term debt to assets financed Gross margin Inventory turnover

8

Delegate Authority and Responsibility

OVERVIEW

Chapter 8 identifies the principles employed to delegate responsibility for preparation of the plan and authority to make the decisions necessary for plan implementation. Delegating authority and responsibility involves all three areas of the business plan:

1. Design of the actual business plan
2. Implementation of the plan
3. Monitoring of the plan's performance

We usually designate a single person as being responsible for the success of each area. Generally it's best to give those with responsibility the authority to make whatever decisions are necessary to execute that responsibility.

At small and medium-sized businesses delegation is especially tricky, but no less important. Often the depth of management becomes shallow after the top few officers. That's why we see so many smaller companies run with an authoritarian management style. Even seemingly small decisions rest in the hands of just a few of the most senior people.

We see this authority being clutched in a death grip. Subordinates aren't trained by their superiors to make the decisions that more senior management would have made had they done it themselves. This wastes everyone's time: from the manager who has better things to do than make routine decisions to the subordinate who waits for the boss to get around to deciding what to do when the answer is already clear.

Designing and implementing a business plan provides the perfect opportunity to get away from decision-making restrictions often imposed by the corporate culture. Only by delegating both the

authority to make decisions and the *responsibility* for their success can
a company achieve its goals.

CHAIN OF COMMAND

With respect to business planning, the company's chain of command
usually goes something like this:

- Investors and/or shareholders of the company
- Board of directors
- Chief executive officer
- Leader of the planning team
- Individuals on the plan design team, implementation team,
  and monitoring team who are responsible for particular sec-
  tions of the plan

The investors of the company must be convinced that management has the vision (and capability to execute that vision) to reach an
expected level of investment return. The shareholders hold the board
of directors responsible by electing them at the annual meeting. The
directors hold the CEO responsible by employing at their discretion
the proper individual with this vision and management capability.
The same holds true for the leader of the planning effort and those on
each of the three teams. They report to the CEO and to the leader of
the planning effort. Their continued employment is at the discretion
of their boss.

Authority and responsibility *on the planning team* revolve around
a chain of command. There must be someone in charge who holds the
other team members responsible and accountable for their actions.
Without such authority, even the most committed planning teams
may wander from their mission.

The chain of command for the business plan involves the three
phases of planning:

1. Design of the plan
2. Implementation
3. Monitoring results and making mid-course corrections

Design of the Plan

The planning director designates a specific individual (or takes on
this responsibility himself) to oversee plan design. Here's how to
delegate the tasks for plan design:

Create Workunits
The plan design must be divided into the various components dealing with each department in the company. These are linked to the overall company goals of the business plan. For example, the sections of the business plan having to do with finance are separated from those having to do with marketing and manufacturing.

Assign Responsibilities
A single person should be made responsible for each section of the plan design. Very small companies may have one individual taking responsibility for several sections. No matter. Be sure that *someone* is held responsible for designing each section of the plan.

Identify the Expected Work Product
Each workunit requires a particular plan presentation so it can be incorporated into the overall business plan, then implemented and finally monitored as the plan is executed. The individual responsible must understand and agree on what the final design presentation for his or her section will look like.

Here are some of the characteristics of plan design coming from various sections:

- Specific identification of how the plan section fulfills the part(s) of the overall business plan to which it belongs
- Time frames for achievement of each milestone and benchmark
- Identification of which departments are responsible for meeting each benchmark
- Detailed description—using numbers—of how the plan targets will be achieved
- Indication of how the planning section meshes with requirements from other sections of the plan

This last characteristic is extremely important to the monitoring phase. We must know how the performance of other sections of the plan affects the one we're presently looking at, and vice versa. Conversely, we need to understand how benchmarks in a particular section affect other sections of the plan.

Authority Required
Authority delegation at the plan design stage is less critical than at the implementation phase. Still, there is usually some dimension of authority released to the plan section designers. An example would be the financial section that requires an increase in the working capital loan to bridge a cash shortfall resulting from increased credit sales.

Scheduling of such an increase in the firm's liabilities often requires board approval. Yet the plan designer needs the authority to schedule it in order to prepare the financial section. Of course, the board must eventually pass a resolution confirming the increase in company obligations once it accepts the business plan. Therefore, the release of authority is not without final review and approval.

The point is that the plan designers are constantly making decisions at the planning stage that exceed their normal limits of authority. That's fine. They are delegated the authority to put these decisions into the plan design *subject to* ratification by the normal chain of command.

Implementation of the Plan

The delegation of responsibility in the plan design phase includes those individuals responsible for implementing each section of the plan. It makes little sense to design a plan independently from those who'll be responsible for its success. Therefore, personnel on the plan design and plan implementation teams overlap to some extent. This should be true for at least one person in each section of the plan.

Benefits of this type of "grass roots" representation include the following:

- Commitment to the plan design is increased if those responsible for implementation have helped create the design.
- The design team should be as close to the real world as possible—that means the operational managers are included in the design phase.

Create Workunits
Just as we did in the design phase, the implementation phase is divided into component parts. These are normally along the lines of those already established in the design phase. Responsibility for implementation of the financial subplan, for example, is normally that of the chief financial officer. The CFO was probably also responsible for design of the financial plan.

Define Expected Results
Successful implementation of the plan requires specification of the results we want. Each section should define the results needed to fulfill that part of the plan. Particular individuals are assigned the responsibility for getting these results.

Delegate Authority
Those responsible for executing components of the business plan should be given the authority to do their jobs. Even if it means

increasing an individual's authority beyond that which is customarily granted, it should be done. After all, if a person is trusted enough to be held responsible for implementing a critical part of the plan, he or she should also be trusted enough with the tools necessary to do the job. Without such authority, management is saying that the individual is not really held responsible.

Coordinate Implementation

Once the actual implementation plan is established, the entire implementation team must agree on what will be done and when each result is scheduled for completion. This ensures coordination of those parts of the plan that are dependent on other sections being done first.

At this stage, the timing of each section's goals can be refined. If the job is done right, there will be very little loss of momentum in implementing the plan due to disjointed timing of critical steps.

Monitoring

The third step in delegating authority for execution of the business plan is monitoring the implementation. We're concerned with three things at this stage:

1. Data gathering
2. Comparison of actuals with plan
3. Interpretation of trends and action decisions for mid-course correction

Different companies approach responsibility for monitoring in various ways. Probably the best method is centralized management of the monitoring effort. This is done by giving one person (or department) the responsibility of monitoring the entire plan implementation performance. Larger companies often have a financial planning and control department consisting of several professional staffers. These people were involved in both the design and implementation phases of the plan as *staff assistants*. They're responsible for monitoring the implementation.

The job of plan monitoring is to keep a record of how each section of the implementation is proceeding. This includes scheduling performance benchmarks and seeing when they are actually hit. The monitors alert those responsible for implementation when there is a risk that benchmarks won't be hit. They also provide critical information on the *impact* of missed benchmarks in other departments.

Further, plan monitors are usually familiar with every part of the plan and departments in the company. Possible solutions for getting a wayward plan back on track are often apparent to the monitors. This is the value they bring to the table. With their overview of the entire plan as well as the performance of each department, they can provide a valuable staff function to the implementation team.

Keep in mind that we've emphasized the monitors' *staff* responsibilities. The monitors aren't given authority to make changes to the implementation schedule or targets of the plan. That's the job of the implementation team and overall plan manager. We want to keep this authority separate. However, the monitors *can* provide valuable information to assist the implementation team in doing its job.

Summary of the Chain of Command

Table 8–1 summarizes a possible chain of command used to control business planning effort. Note that all areas of the plan are not included. Nor are all of the responsibilities you may have in your own company. Nevertheless, a chain of command should look something like that shown below.

DELEGATE RESPONSIBILITY BUT *NEVER* ACCOUNTABILITY

Responsibility and accountability are flip sides of the same coin. Each member of the planning team must undertake the responsibility for achieving his or her part of the plan. Responsibility, then, is associated with an individual's work assigned for the good of the company. Accountability, on the other hand, includes not only responsibility for the work being done, but the *obligation* of hitting the planned targets as well.

For managers of departments with one or more workers, responsibility extends to actions of the staff. The same manager is accountable for the success or failure of the entire department. This includes all personnel and how they contribute to the overall plan. Managers can delegate their responsibilities. However, they can't delegate accountability for the results and actions of those whom they supervise.

Without seeming overbearing, the plan director must make every member of the team understand that they are both responsible and accountable for their performance in the plan. When they commit to hitting a target, everyone on the planning team must be able to rely on that goal being attained at the point in time required.

Attempting to share responsibility with others farther down the line doesn't work. It's time consuming and cumbersome. Further, there's too much room to shift the blame for failure.

Placing accountability and responsibility on the planning team members for the plan's success communicates the exact message we want to get across:

> *You are responsible for the plan's success. If you can't make that success happen, we'll get someone who can.*

Table 8–1   Summary of the Planning Team Chain of Command

Planning function	Responsibility	Authority needed
Plan design phase:		
Board of directors	Approval of a business plan that provides an acceptable return on investment consistent with company's objectives.	Board resolutions.
CEO	Formulation of a business plan in accordance with board requirements.	Ultimate executive authority to approve plan timing, expenditures, and targets.
Planning manager	Responsible for: ■ oversight of the entire planning effort including design, implementation, monitoring, and mid-course corrections ■ assembly of planning team ■ consistency of plan design with overall company objectives ■ target benchmarks ■ timing of benchmarks	Ultimate authority to make all planning decisions regarding planning team, timing, and mid-course corrections.

(continued)

Table 8–1 (*Continued*)

Planning function	Responsibility	Authority needed
Design components: ■ marketing ■ manufacturing ■ inventory ■ finance	Responsible for designing the detailed plans for each department listed to achieve overall business plan.	Authority to make all planning decisions within their planning component.
Plan implementation:		
Implementation manager	Reports to planning manager. Responsible for overall implementation of every department's plan. Oversees preparation of detailed departmental implementation plans.	Makes decisions regarding timing and nature of benchmarks. Changes implementation schedule as necessary.
Marketing implementation	Prepares and executes implementation plan for advertising, promotion, sales force, commission payout, warranty service, distribution of samples, contract terms, and development of new products.	Makes all marketing decisions relevant to implementation of the marketing business plan.
Manufacturing implementation	Prepares and executes implementation plan for manufacturing operation including production, inventory control, shipping, purchase of production related capital equipment, manufacturing labor, and production costs.	Authority to hire and fire production personnel, purchase equipment, control production facility layout, and purchase raw materials inventory.

(continued)

Table 8–1 (*Continued*)

Planning function	Responsibility	Authority needed
Finance implementation	Prepares and executes implementation plan for the financial department. This includes accounting, credit and collections, banking relations, borrowing, investor relations, and cash management.	Authority over banking relationships, borrowing (subject to board resolution and aproval), credit limits, tax issues, and accounting issues.
Plan monitoring:		
Head of monitoring	Establishes a monthly plan monitoring system, formats reports, gathers actual performance data, tracks actual performance against plan, and alerts implementation managers when their departments are moving out of the planning parameters.	Authorized to gather information and report to those responsible only. Has no decision-making authority to make mid-course changes in any department.

This may sound callous. However, small businesses can't afford anything less than a willingness to perform and be judged by that performance.

In a sense, the entire planning team holds *one another* accountable for their parts of the plan. This isn't as hard as you might think. The business plan evolves from much give-and-take between the company's key managers. The goals of the firm were agreed to by everyone. From that point, the more detailed objectives for each discipline involved in getting the company to the target were derived. If it is discovered the performance required of a particular group is impossible to meet, the tactics are revised, but not the ultimate goals. Most likely the required performance of other departments is adjusted to take up the slack.

The point is that *everyone* contributed to creation of the plan. Those responsible were committed to goals that *they* set. Given that level of involvement, there should be no reason for the planning process to fail. That's the type of blunt discipline among the planning team that successful implementation requires.

You'll find that by delegating planning responsibility, the group can be an unforgiving master. The planning team as a whole does not accept excuses from its members who were given every opportunity to refine and negotiate their individual targets before they committed to them. Additionally, such delegation of responsibility creates the type of teamwork required to make all components of the plan work together. The task of the plan director is to keep the criticism constructive and help the team work together. Disputes and disagreements are arbitrated. The leader acts as a *facilitator* rather than as an authority figure.

Keep in mind, however, the team must go in the direction consistent with the best interests of the company. This can become a problem if, for instance, the team has one or two very strong leaders. The plan bogs down if they are allowed to do things their own way (or worse, the way it was always done). Soon creativity is stifled and the team that should have been working together becomes the personal feifdom of a dictator.

Attributes of Planning Team Participants

The planning team is composed of just that—team players. We want people who put the good of the team and reaching its goals before their own agenda. Table 8–2 shows some of the things to look for in your planning team members.

Table 8–2 Planning Team Attributes

1. Commitment to fulfilling their responsibility to the planning organization and its goals to the best of their ability.
2. An ability and desire to work constructively with other members of the planning team.
3. Excellent communication skills.
4. Openness to new ideas; sensitivity to the effects actions in one area have on other areas within the firm.
5. Capacity to encourage and draw out the best in their team members.
6. Capability to think and reason beyond the obvious, and the skill to identify specific actions that further particular parts of the plan.
7. Enough humility to seek and evaluate the advice of specialists with knowledge greater than their own.
8. Orientation toward finding ways to make things work rather than identifying reasons why they will not.
9. Ability to identify and focus on the critical success factors of the business plan.
10. In-depth knowledge of their area of responsibility *and* how it relates to the overall goals of the company.

Performance Measurement

Performance measurement provides the cornerstone of every successful planning effort. The plan must have a reliable way to track its progress. Departures from your chosen path must be readily apparent and solutions to the problems must leap out at you.

At large companies they call the process we're about to describe *responsibility accounting*. Often there is an entire accounting subsystem that identifies the operating performance of every department involved in the plan. This system reports the actual performance for each department and compares it against the numbers they signed up for in the plan. The process tends to be even more complex when executives, themselves under the gun to hit their planning targets, require their department managers to write lengthy reports explaining what went wrong and detailing how it will never happen again.

Of course, entrepreneurs and the managers of small and medium-sized businesses have little patience for the overhead costs and time that a full-scale responsibility accounting system requires. However, with some finesse and common sense, we can create something that works almost as well with a tenth of the effort.

Responsibility Accounting

The objective of the responsibility accounting system is to:

- Identify the actual results for each of the departments critical to achieving the plan.
- Maintain an *accessible* record of the targets for each of these critical departments that were plugged into the plan and that everyone else is counting on.
- Compare the actual results against the planned results to identify departures.

We end up with a tracking and monitoring system that incorporates actual results with the plan and computes the differences. The comparison is done by the month and on a year-to-date basis. The entire process of monitoring the implementation effort is described in Chapter 10.

How Do We Implement a Responsibility Accounting System?

The most effective way to create what we want would be to revamp the entire accounting system. But wait! Before you climb the walls, this isn't necessary. Few businesses would be willing to change accounting systems just to accommodate their planning efforts.

To accumulate the necessary information that feeds into our responsibility accounting system, follow these steps:

■ Identify in the plan and in the departments critical to the plan all the variables we must manage in order to hit our targets. These targets should be selected so that when they are reached, the company also reaches its goals.

■ Match these details (sales revenue of a particular product, for example) appearing in the plan with a particular general ledger account number in the accounting system. This allows the ability to track actual performance against the plan, item by item (if necessary).

■ Generate monthly operating and performance statements *for each department that is critical to the plan.*

■ Generate monthly comparison statements showing the actual operating results against those that were planned.

A simple report flowing from the accounting system might look like the monthly operating statement shown in Table 8–3.

Table 8–3   Monthly Performance Report

	Monthly operating statement Product A		
	Month of June		
	Actual results	*Planned results*	*Act'l B(W) plan*
Gen'l ledger line item			
Sales revenue: Product A	$20,000	$18,000	$ 2,000
Less returns and allowances	2,000	1,500	500
Net sales: Product A	$18,000	$16,500	$ 1,500
Mftg. expenses: Product A			
Parts	5,000	4,500	−500
Labor	2,000	1,800	−200
Rejects	100	90	−10
Rework	500	450	−50
Mftg. overhead allocation	2,400	2,160	−240
Total manufacturing	$10,000	$ 9,000	$−1,000
Sales expenses	1,800	1,980	180
Total costs—Product A	$11,800	$10,980	$ −820
Net income—Product A	$ 6,200	$ 5,520	$ 680

A glance tells us that Product A is doing better than we had planned. However, check out sales expenses. Why would the sales expense for a product selling better than we had planned actually come in $180 *better* than the plan? Logic tells us that sales expense should be up as well, creating an unfavorable variance against the plan. Perhaps the sales manager initiated some sort of cost saving measures. If so, we should see the same favorable variance in the other products. Additionally, the plan should be updated to provide either a new standard to shoot for or a cushion in the event performance in other areas falls short.

This report should also include year-to-date columns for actual, plan, and the difference between the two for the same line items. This tells us how we're tracking for the year.

The point is that this type of report is easy to generate from most accounting systems and provides a quick comparison tool for busy managers. Problems as well as opportunities are highlighted. Each department critical to the plan is put into a similar reporting format. Suddenly, you have a fairly sophisticated responsibility accounting system that tracks the critical items necessary for successful plan implementation.

BEWARE OF THE AUTHORITY GAP

Identify the accountable person and his or her authority. It's best if each department manager is delegated the complete authority to do whatever is required within company policy to get the job done for which they are responsible. We don't want to create an *authority gap* where a manager is held responsible for achieving a particular goal, but lacks the authority to make decisions to get the job done. Nor do we want someone who is separated from the departmental goals having the authority to adversely influence achievement of those goals. This would allow leeway for failure and accountability for that failure to shift—not a desirable situation. If you are going to hold a manager responsible for a task, make sure he or she has all the tools necessary to succeed. Like anything else in life, if more than one person is responsible, then no one is responsible.

Absence of competent authority delegation is probably one of the biggest causes for failure of small businesses. Managers literally grow the company from their own sweat. They know more about every facet of the firm than anyone else. Without thinking about it, their *span of control* (the number of people who report to them and rely on them for decisions) soon explodes out of control. Eventually, key decisions grind to a halt while waiting for a single person to make a decision that someone closer to the situation should have made. Gradually the firm's ability to respond to market demand slows. Competition steps in to what was once your exclusive domain.

Owners unwilling to delegate authority often say they can't trust their employees to do the job the way they want it done. The answer is to either fire those who are not trustworthy or train them to do the job and hold them responsible for its results. Usually training is the best alternative. Further, the boss's way is not necessarily the best way. After all, that's one reason all those expensive employees were hired—for their background and creativity. If you don't let them exercise it, you're leaving half the value for which you are paying just lying on the table.

It's true: delegation of responsibility and authority to get the job done from start to finish is *that* important. Don't shortchange yourself or your company by refusing to delegate necessary authority.

CENTRALIZED VERSUS PARTICIPATIVE PLANNING AND CONTROL

Businesses mean different things to different people. However, regardless of the organizational structure, all companies are political in nature. We want the management framework to distribute power, authority, and responsibility appropriately. Those in need of specific authorities to execute their job responsibilities should have it without regard to political alliances.

These managers are held accountable to more senior management for their use of the powers granted them. Finally, the system of internal control monitors the use of authority and provides a mechanism for its review.

Certainly some central control over the plan, its implementation, and ongoing monitoring is required. Without control that adheres to the overall company goals, we run the risk of having a disjointed effort from the individual departments when they go to implement the plan.

The planning organization recognizes that specific people control various parts of the plan. That's where centralization comes in. Usually a single person carries responsibility for the overall design, implementation, and monitoring.

There's nothing wrong with centralizing overall responsibility. However, care must be taken not to allow those responsible for the centralized formation of the plan to work against those responsible for its execution. We don't want a power struggle between those who oversee the entire planning effort and those responsible for executing the plan. That's why centralization in the planning structure must quickly give way to a participative style. This is true both in power and authority granted to those responsible for execution of the plan. The trick is to create an environment where power can be exercised for achievement of the company's goals.

Management Style

The combination of a very small centralized management, supported by an open participative style, directs loyalty to the team and the product it's creating (the plan) rather than to a single authority figure (the boss). To do otherwise allows the potential for conflicts within the planning team.

The most successful planning structures emphasize open participation and constructive criticism. Selection of the planning director is important for just that reason. He must be aware of the influence that use of his authority has. People whose job it is telling others what to do are less inclined to ask people what they think. Yet such participation is vital to creating, implementing, and controlling a business plan.

Attitude Within the Planning Team

There are several ideas that members of the planning team should internalize. These help propel the team forward and maintain its momentum as well as its purpose.

Mission

There should be a sense of mission imparted from the top of the planning structure down to everyone else on the team. That mission includes the following concepts:

- The business plan is vital to the survival of the company.
- There are few things any member of the team can do that are more important than designing and executing the business plan.
- The planning team is composed of the company's best people.

Mistakes and Negative Attitude

We all make mistakes. However, when it comes to both the design and implementation of the business plan, the team must take the position that mistakes and negativism are unacceptable.

Quality Control

With the prudent delegation of authority, management can change its quality control philosophy. Many companies emphasize a QC concept that catches mistakes at the end of the line—before it's too late and the customer sees them.

A better philosophy often begun as part of the business planning goal is to stop paying workers to make mistakes or produce unacceptable products. Instead, exactness and quality are emphasized from the *beginning*. This improves the *process* rather than just the finished goods inspection.

Centralized Planning

One of the problems associated with centralized planning is the potential perception among line executives of management by fiat. Those who may not be involved in establishing goals are being dictated to by a small number of people more powerful than they.

If the plan is presented incorrectly or if the targets established for particular departments are seen as impossible, the pressure will be released somehow. An attitude of *us against them* begins to grow. The *us* becomes those being dictated to by *them*. If the problem gets severe enough, informal gripe groups within the company may sprout up. These groups vent some of the pressure by allowing people with similar concerns to know they aren't the only ones with a problem. Unless management fixes it, these groups may grow and begin more serious meetings. Soon a feeling of solidarity occurs and spokespersons emerge with a large support group. That's how unions gain entry into a company.

Operating unit heads who feel this pressure become reluctant to pass it down the line to their subordinates. They worry about fostering the same resentment toward themselves that they feel for their bosses. As a result, you may see supervisors blaming other departments for failure to meet their plan objectives. Much time is spent on finger-pointing. Efficiency of the entire organization drops. And it's all because the central planners didn't understand how to execute the operational implementation of the plan.

Participative Planning

People like to feel their input is valued. The operational planning effort is a great way to involve subordinates in the affairs of the firm. This is essential if they are to be held responsible for plan implementation.

The participative style emphasizes *leadership* rather than simply ordering people around or telling them what to do. Good leadership helps people do a better job that in turn allows the firm to hit its planned targets.

Care should be taken to delegate authority so that people that have it are aware of the impact of their decisions on other departments. We don't want goals in different departments conflicting with one another. Instead, the participative method emphasizes team-work.

Managers responsible for the operational plan need to *internalize* the plan as their own. The best way to gain this commitment is by asking those responsible for its execution to help design the operational plan. This forces groups within the company to interact with one another. The relationships and alliances that develop from this interaction later become crucial to actually carrying out the operational plan.

One caution exists, however. Never confuse participative management with weak leadership. Indeed, managers who promote the participative style are by necessity the strongest leaders. They have the muscle to open up an issue, debate it, hear what people up and down the line who will be affected by the decision have to say and then *jointly* resolve it.

Weak managers, on the other hand, are reluctant to share their power for fear of undermining their authority. They lack the self-confidence to listen to other people's ideas. As a result, their business plans are formulated in an autocratic setting. Goals are crammed down their managers' throats. Consequently, there is little commitment to the plan by those responsible for its execution. Such business plans constantly flirt with failure.

Interaction Between Participants' Goals and Company Goals
Individuals' goals within the company are shaped by their own needs and ambitions as well as those of the company with some external factors thrown in. When choosing participants for the planning team there should be conformity between individuals' goals and those of the firm.

By including line managers in the planning process, the company's goals—which the managers themselves helped create—become their own personal goals as well. A bonding between the plan and those responsible for its development and implementation forms.

Without going too deeply into the psychological aspects of goal interaction, Table 8–4 shows a schematic of how the individual goals are internalized.

Conflicting Objectives
Another skill required to effectively delegate authority and responsibility is to recognize the natural conflict between employees' objectives and those of the company. Certainly all members of the planning team place their own well-being over that of company profit. That's only natural. To expect anything different would be

Table 8–4 Formation of Individual Goals

Individual goals and goal internalization:

- Personal needs
- Personal ambitions
- Organizational goals influenced by:

  - organizational culture
  - organizational leadership

- Outside influences such as:

  - benchmarks and determination of goals being met
  - reward (or punishment) system

---

naive. Table 8–5 shows some of the conflicting objectives between employees and the firm.

False Participation

This is something to guard against. We've all seen managers who try to produce employee trust and commitment by making them *think* they are participating in key decisions when they are not. Such managers ask subordinates for their opinions, then try to persuade

Table 8–5 Conflicting Objectives

Employee	Company
Stable stream of income and job security.	Profits, stock price, net worth.
Authority to perform the job as required.	Control over employees acting in a manner consistent with management policy. Maintenance of established chain of command.
Job satisfaction.	Greater productivity, through improved efficiency.
Increased control over the job function.	Standardization of job functions, often through authority hierarchy, policies and procedures, or automation.
Participation in company profits.	Maintenance of return on investment. Control of labor costs.

them to see management's viewpoint. It quickly becomes obvious there's a right and a wrong answer. Operational plans force-fed in such a manner are seldom successful. The supervisor loses credibility and the confidence of subordinates. Senior management sees this supervisor as someone who lacks the ability to lead.

Participation is successful only when people believe that their information and assistance won't be abused. The point needs to be made clearly that decisions arising out of shared information and opinions are discussed jointly. Any problems or changes that arise are worked out together. Finally, the solidarity of the team is cemented by the understanding that success as well as failure is *jointly* shared.

Downside to Participative Planning

The big picture is not always shared with lower-level managers. As a result, they may have a more narrow point of view than more senior executives. Also, a manager responsible not only for creating the plan but for its execution may sandbag the targets so that she looks good by achieving a plan that is not ambitious. This can hurt other members of the planning team that had to unnecessarily take up the slack.

Another problem can be that lower-level managers are constrained by existing limits in their areas of specialty. An example might be the objections to particular sales targets by the manufacturing manager out of concern for capacity. Remember, creating a business plan *drives the company*, not the other way around.

Certainly concerns for the details of execution such as manufacturing capacity are valid. However, it requires vision to determine the action steps required to overcome routine obstacles such as capacity. It's that vision and a determination to beat existing constraints that we want on our planning, implementation, and monitoring teams.

Coordination of Centralized and Participative Planning

There's a place for both types of planning. Centralization of the plan typically takes place when the overall objectives of the company are formed. Top management and the planning team identifies the targets to be reached over the planning horizon. However, from this point, it doesn't make sense for this same group to dictate how the people responsible for implementing the operational steps get there. After all, the centralized planning group does not have line responsibility. To them, if the plan fails it's due to lack of execution at the operating level.

Once the plan transitions to an operational level, its style should become participative. The operating departments are closer to the situation and can better solve the problems as well as being more experienced in the technical aspects. Further, control of the operational plan and making sure it hits its benchmarks can be the responsibility only of the line departments who work with it every day.

Limitations to Decentralized Authority

Where does authority of decentralized plan control end? The best place is where a decision on the operating level could affect the outcome of the overall company plan. Prior to that point, however, the firm is paying for the line managers' creativity and resourcefulness—it should give them the authority to exercise the talent for which it is paying. Additionally, even on decisions at an operating level that could have global effects throughout the company, the line managers should be considered the authorities while the corporate staff is consulted only for its advice and to be kept informed.

9

Performance Incentives

OVERVIEW

Chapter 9 shows how to design and operate a performance incentive system to reward successful implementation of the business plan. We'll structure the incentive system so we get the most mileage from our incentive dollars. Using a proven framework, we'll identify the characteristics that make this reward system work. Something we *won't* do is try to give an old incentive plan a facelift. This leads to failure. People do what they are rewarded and reinforced for doing. Therefore, we want to be sure the right incentive exists to ensure success of the business plan implementation.

Additionally, Chapter 9 points out methods that may be counterproductive to the type of motivation that business plan implementation requires. Once warned, most managers avoid these like the plague.

Finally, we'll demonstrate how to employ the responsibility reporting system introduced in Chapter 8 to track progress toward incentives.

Effective incentives precisely focus on attaining specific business plan objectives. We're not using a shotgun approach that we hope provides motivation for our team to hit only the important targets. Instead, we create a rifle that accurately identifies the most advantageous administration of the incentive system. Those rewards, and the methods by which they are given, exactly match the needs of planning team members. The result is a business plan that's completely implemented according to the goals and timing already established.

We talked in Chapter 7 about the use of benchmarks. They're also used in the incentive compensation system. Choosing the appropriate benchmarks on which to base certain parts of the reward system can be crucial to keeping the plan moving forward.

Administration of an effective incentive strategy requires careful thought. The strategy behind this valuable motivational device encompasses:

- Establishing and communicating the performance on which rewards are based
- The most effective ways in which to fairly distribute rewards
- Types of rewards that are most likely to motivate achievement of the goals

OBJECTIVE OF THE INCENTIVE SYSTEM

Everyone works for some sort of incentive. That incentive is given in order to produce a particular result, often within a specific time frame. For our purposes, the objective result of an incentive system is full implementation of the company's business plan.

Managers who demonstrate they can implement their portion of the company plan should be rewarded. The enticement makes attaining plan goals that much more likely. Further, it gives the plan implementation team something solid to shoot for in a project that's extremely important to the company.

Indeed, the care taken with design and administration of the incentive program reflects the company's priority in implementing the business plan. Essentially, the plan defines the company's objectives. The incentive program channels performance in that direction.

Teamwork

One of the major objectives of the incentive system is to encourage teamwork. Each member of the planning team is vital to a successful effort. Further, they must all work together. This is particularly so in small and medium-sized companies where employee ranks are thin. Everyone usually has more than they can already do. Achievement of the business plan has to be made a priority. To do that everyone must help the cause.

The best way is to provide an incentive based on the team's overall results. This takes some of the motivational responsibility off management's shoulders. Instead, the team encourages its members through peer pressure. The team succeeds as a group and gets rewarded as a group.

Goals

The goals for our incentive system are several:

- Generate motivation to successfully implement the business plan.
- Create a structure that gives rewards to those responsible for meeting plan objectives.
- Identify progress toward meeting plan objectives.
- Establish short-term targets and rewards along the path toward full implementation.

The proper combination of motivation and feedback on progress toward the goal provides a powerful draw toward implementing the business plan. The incentive program says to the members of the planning team:

> *Implementation of the business plan is important. As a member of the planning team, you are special. Your contribution to this project is significant. The company wishes to recognize your effort in a way that is as special as both this project and your participation—in a way that no other group of people within the firm is recognized.*

Such exclusivity certainly promotes team spirit. It works as the glue that bonds the planning team together. Incentives properly administered help the team drive toward a common goal—one that helps the company.

STRUCTURE OF THE INCENTIVE SYSTEM

Most of us have worked before under some sort of incentive system. Few, however, are specifically designed for our purposes here. More often than not, corporate incentives are designed to please all of the people. As a consequence they end up pleasing none of the people.

Few companies can afford to fall short of their planning objectives. As a result, the incentive system must be structured to ensure successful implementation of the business plan.

Premise of the Incentive Plan

The first premise of the incentive plan is that we're not paying simply for the worker's time or effort—we're paying for *results*. The plan team is a group of intelligent risk takers. They understand the principles of reward for performance. Often such risk-takers will accept a portion of their income based on results. The net effect is that both the company and the planning team get more than they would have otherwise. Everyone wins.

Due to union contracts, such incentive plans are often difficult to implement for the rank and file. However, the planning team is usually made up of management types who may not be unionized. This type of reward system gets the benchmarks and implementation targets on everyone's minds and keeps them there.

By nature, planners are manipulators. That's not bad. They are adept at maneuvering a system to make it do what they want. They know that the system is indeed manipulating them. They expect to be paid based on their own performance.

Characteristics of the Business Plan Incentive System

We want to structure the simplest incentive plan possible. At the same time, we want to motivate our planning team to a degree sufficient to ensure the job gets done. Here are the characteristics we want in the plan:

Unambiguous Performance Requirements

Few things can shoot down an incentive plan faster than ambiguity. The team as well as management must understand exactly what is required in order to be considered successful. Imagine the damage to morale if the team thought it had succeeded in obtaining its goals and, therefore, the rewards, but management disagreed. Suddenly we've got a *dis*incentive plan—one that says, "We really don't think you did such a good job after all."

The best way to avoid such devastating misunderstandings is to present the performance requirements as quantitatively as possible. We'll be talking more about the incentive benchmarks used later. However, the entire plan must be structured around the *intent* that the team succeed as planned and be paid the incentive rewards as promised. That's the point. We want the team to succeed and get the rewards to which they're entitled.

Accomplishing that objective requires clear understanding of the required performance. There's no room for ambiguity.

Precise Rewards

As damaging as misunderstandings about required performance can be, so too are misconceptions about rewards. If that should happen, suddenly the planning team is placed in a position of distrusting mangement—and with just cause. After all, somehow they were led to believe that certain things would occur given a specified performance. The team did its part. Now everything they worked so hard for is being changed—taken away. How much credibility will management have the next time?

Disregard who is responsible for misunderstanding the reward structure. The point is that the people most important to the continued success of the company are unhappy. Management had the ability throughout the entire plan implementation to identify and correct this error. Instead, they chose to ignore it. Perhaps they wanted to deal with it once the plan was implemented. Maybe they were afraid of a confrontation halfway through plan implementation that could cause derailment. At the very least, management was at fault for not structuring the reward system in such a manner as to eliminate any misunderstandings.

Monitor Progress to the Targets

The incentive system should be structured to integrate with the benchmark monitoring system. Many companies take this so seriously that they provide progress incentives. These are given before full implementation of the plan. Generally they mark the achievement of a major milestone in the plan implementation.

Such reward milestones are chosen for:

Timing in the Plan Implementation Cycle   Interim rewards keep everyone interested. Further, it confirms that management is serious about its incentive program and can be trusted to perform as promised. From the planning team's point of view, interim rewards are a progress payment for work completed so far.

Timing can be used in several ways:

- In the form of an incentive, designed to maintain momentum of the implementation effort—strategically employed when enthusiasm is likely to be lowest
- In the form of a particularly important milestone that *must* be completed for other parts of the implementation to continue on schedule

Importance to the Plan   Milestones figuring in the interim rewards should be those on which further implementation hinges. Since we're emphasizing their importance by including a reward for completion, we may as well get the most bang for our buck.

ADMINISTRATION OF THE INCENTIVE SYSTEM

Keep in mind the kind of people we're working with: they are professional, smart, and among the top performers in the company.

We want to motivate them. They're doing an important job and should be rewarded in a significant way.

Administration of the incentive system is designed to get the most out of plan implementation efforts. There are many ways of administering an incentive system. Some work better than others.

Administration of the incentive system must be done professionally. When properly designed, it says to the planning team:

> *Your contribution will make the company more successful. You are invited to participate in that success. We will reward you in a manner consistent with the importance of this project.*

Value-Added Incentive System

This method of administering the incentive system combines both merit raises in salary with a bonus based on performance of the plan implementation effort. Here's how it works:

Salary Increase
Planning team members get annual salary reviews just like other employees. However, a part of their merit increase is based on competency and contribution to the planning effort. Sometimes, this determinate is judged by the planning team leader and used as input from the members' direct supervisor responsible for performance and salary review. This rewards the planning team members, for their *individual* contributions to the planning effort. It also recognizes the added responsibilities they have undertaken along with their regular jobs by working on the planning team.

Bonus
The team member is given a bonus based on the overall team's performance in implementing the business plan. Often the bonus comes in the form of a pool given by the firm to the team as a whole. Regardless of distribution method, the bonus pool recognizes the significant contribution made by the planning team to the company. Distribution of the shares is based on individual value and effort.

Benefits of the Value-Added Method
Using the value-added method does four things for us:

1. It enhances the firm's ability to reward based on how successfully the plan was implemented.
2. The company pays only for what was accomplished (implementation of the business plan).

3. It communicates to the team what's expected of them and how it affects their pay.
4. It rewards competitive performers who contribute to the firm's goals.

Value-added methods base the bonus on demonstrated competency, not behavioral traits or past accomplishments. The company does not pay for past accomplishments forever as it would through a straight merit increase.

Gain Sharing

A new and increasingly popular method of providing incentives is called *gain sharing*. This technique provides employees with a portion of the economic value they create. Gain sharing is accomplished by quantifying the benefit of reaching specific company planning goals, then giving back a portion of the resulting profit to those responsible for making it happen. Everyone wins.

Often an entire company can share in the plan implementation using gain sharing. This works like a giant bonus pool to be divided equally if the plan is achieved. PPG Industries successfully implemented this plan with its Blue Print Performance Award. The benchmark used to determine incentive payout was return on equity (ROE).

The gain sharing plan specified various levels of the incentive pool available for payout if certain ROE targets were met. Each employee had a stake in the firm's success. During its first year of gain sharing, PPG hit its 23 percent ROE target. As a result the share paid to each employee amounted to about $800.

Another spin-off of PPG's gain sharing plan was communication of the company's targets. Prior to the plan going into effect, few employees could say what ROE meant, much less what level their own company wanted to reach or how they could help it get there. After the plan most everyone understood not only the target and why it was important to the company but how their particular job contributed to attaining it. Of course, everyone carefully watched the firm's progress toward their goal—something the company made sure was always available. They also knew the likely amount of their gain share bonus when the target was reached.

Gain sharing creates a goal toward which everyone can contribute. When properly administered it can glue a team together and promote cooperation among employees that would have been more difficult otherwise.

There is a disadvantage to gain sharing, however. It doesn't reward peak performers for their special contributions. There's no individual incentive; everyone gets the same share. This can be particularly annoying to members of the business plan implementation team. As the firm's top performers, this group wants special recognition for their skills.

Spot Gain Sharing

A more focused approach is spot gain sharing, illustrated in Table 9–1. This emphasizes specific problems in particular departments during a stipulated period of time. Spot gain sharing can be used by the plan implementation team to help ensure particular goals are met in departments outside its control.

Here's an example of spot gain sharing in action:

A manufacturing firm needs to decrease wasted raw materials on its assembly line. They have determined that excess and unnecessary wastage accounts for a 5 percent increase in the cost of production, amounting to $250,000 per quarter. This falls right to the bottom line. The goal is to eliminate this excess waste. The gain sharing plan specifies that the 40 production department employees who control raw material usage receive a quarterly pool of $50,000 (20 percent) of the savings if this goal is reached. This potential annual $5,000 increase to each of the 40 production department employees represents a material increase in their income and a goal worth working for. The employees responsible for the improvement share in the profit gains made through their efforts.

Some of the benefits of spot gain sharing include:

- Increased morale
- Tangible sense of ownership of the problem and the results
- Sense of accomplishment

There's a downside, however, to spot gain sharing: It's more labor intensive to administer. There are often several gain sharing projects going on at the same time, each with different goals and time frames for completion. Still, the benefits of meeting the very important goals that these specific programs target are seen as being worth the extra effort.

Salary-at-Risk

Here's a method that has been tried at various companies. It has been successful in some and hasn't worked in others. Asking employees to

Table 9–1   Spot Gain Sharing Design

Use these considerations when designing a spot gain sharing plan:

1. *Choose the benchmark carefully.* Make certain the benchmark in the business plan:

   - Is important to achievement of implementation schedule timing

   - Creates a bottleneck for other departments if it isn't done according to the plan implementation schedule

   - Can be controlled by the employees for whom the spot plan is developed

2. *Explain details of the plan.* The spot plan participants must understand everything about the plan. Chances are they'll raise many questions about real or perceived problems associated with the plan. These must be thoroughly answered before the plan goes into effect.

   Additionally, one of the details that must be addressed is that fact that the spot plan is designed to solve a specific problem within a certain time frame. It's not a part of normal compensation and it will go away after the goal is accomplished.

3. *Identify participants.* Everyone who has an impact on the particular problem being addressed should be included in the spot plan. This includes line employees as well as support staff and supervisors.

4. *Specify success criteria.* Unless the plan clearly identifies the performance required for success it wastes everybody's time. If progress measurements are used, clearly designate *when* they will be taken and *what* the expected results should be at that point in time.

   The best success criteria are simple to calculate, readily available, and not subject to interpretation by people who are looking for a specific result.

5. *Emphasis on the team.* By definition the spot gain sharing plan pulls a team together for purposes of accomplishing a specific task. That's what is needed. It effectively uses peer pressure.

   Sometimes a spot plan provides for recognition of individual contributions as well. That's fine. However, the individual should not overshadow the team emphasis.

(continued)

Table 9–1 (*Continued*)

6. *Spot plan implementation.* The participants will have a greater responsibility to the program if they help in its development. Be sure that all operating issues of the plan are resolved and in place prior to start. The performance feedback mechanism is one such issue.

    Communicate all the details about the plan before it starts. These include such things as starting and ending dates, progress performance, and goals.

    Be sure that the promised rewards are paid out as specified in the plan when it succeeds.

    Set performance goals at attainable levels. If they're too high, the plan only promotes discouragement. If they are too low, the plan isn't achieving all it was capable of.

---

put up part of their salaries as being dependent on achievement of the firm's business plan requires a special type of work environment. Usually employees don't feel truly responsible for performance shortfalls. There are always myriad circumstances that can be blamed for failure. Nevertheless, good managers can usually find a way to compensate for the adverse conditions we all encounter every business day. The salary-at-risk plan helps overcome the inertia of blaming outside influences.

Salary-at-risk programs are best implemented at smaller companies. Here's how one method works:

Employees put up a percentage of their salary as a bet that the firm reaches or exceeds a specific plan benchmark. If 100% of the benchmark is hit, each employee gets the percentage they bet in the form of a bonus. Of course the firm boils into its profit projections the amount of this payout.

If performance exceeds the benchmark, a premium is paid. If the company falls short (this is the painful part) the salary percentage bet is *deducted* from the employee's salary.

Implementation Considerations
You've likely already thought of several potential pitfalls associated with a salary-at-risk program. It does require a unique company having a special relationship with its employees.

Labor Unions The most obvious problem is that of limitations arising from a union contract. Most don't allow for such a program.

1933 Securities Act Under the 1933 Securities Act, some salary-at-risk plans are viewed as an investment opportunity in the company.

That's logical, since a portion of compensation is dependent on the firm's profitability. Shareholders of the company's stock base their investment decisions on this same information.

As an investment opportunity, the firm may legally be required to disclose specific (and proprietary) financial information to participating employees. For large publicly held companies, this isn't a problem because most such information is public knowledge anyway. However, for partnerships or privately held firms, release of such information may not be desirable.

Du Pont Fibers tried to implement a salary-at-risk program. It was hailed as a new innovation in the field of incentive compensation. However, the SEC required them to divulge specific cost information to participating employees that management felt was proprietary and could place the firm at a competitive disadvantage. The plan was scrapped.

HOW DO WE GIVE REWARDS?

When it comes to incentives for implementation of the business plan small and medium-sized companies must get the most bang for the buck. The *way* in which incentive rewards are given has great influence on:

■ Perception of the individual's contribution toward achievement of business plan results
■ Importance of the incentive reward itself
■ Future motivation

Additionally, the plan implementation strategy must include some attention to the way in which rewards are structured. For instance, one type of reward system can succeed in emphasizing only short-term results and actually damage the longer-term capabilities of the company. Another structure may actually create animosity between departments that should be working together to achieve implementation of the business plan.

Short-Term Goals and Rewards

Everyone needs a series of small short-term targets. These give us positive feedback that our ultimate goals are indeed achievable and provide benchmarks toward our progress. They also make working toward the goal more fun.

Creating a business plan incentive program that includes these intermediate rewards is a little more complicated to administer. However, the benefits more than compensate for any added cost. Here are the two major benefits of using short-term goals:

Morale

Have you ever heard anyone say they didn't like being told they were doing a good job? Reinforcing positive behavior never hurts. The best way to stroke the business plan implementation team is through *action*.

By placing one or more intermediate incentive payouts in the path of plan implementation, we give ourselves the opportunity to say, "Good job." The team is told in definite terms:

- The sacrifices to get the plan to this point have been worthwhile.
- The company truly appreciates the team's accomplishment.
- The implementation team has upheld its part of the bargain and the company has demonstrated it is upholding its part.

Direction of the Plan

Like any good benchmark, an intermediate incentive payout helps control the plan implementation. The point at which the reward is given should be chosen because of its importance to the ultimate outcome. We want to be certain this point is hit because the rest of the implementation might hinge on getting to this point.

What better way to ensure this happens than emphasizing its importance by using an intermediate incentive reward? If the benchmark is missed and the incentive cannot be given, that says something too:

> *Management is serious about the incentive program. If the business plan targets aren't hit, the reward will not be forthcoming.*

Finally, everyone's attention gets focused on meeting the particular intermediate targets. Indeed, that's what we want.

Long-term Incentives

Don't structure the implementation reward system so that long-term objectives of the company suffer. There's usually a trade-off between short-term results and the long-range impact to the company. For instance, larger firms may cut the budget for research and development, management training, and equipment maintenance. This certainly helps the current-year bottom line.

However, eventually (usually sooner than later), the firm suffers. It begins to lag behind competitors who are developing new products in response to changing customer demand. Rather than the innovator it once was, the company becomes a copycat. Its once-aggressive marketing posture turns defensive. Getting talented employees who can grow with the firm becomes difficult since the management training budget was cut. The best and the brightest go to competitors and the firm is left with workers who couldn't find anything else. Lastly, product quality suffers because production equipment is not properly maintained. Cost of goods sold rises as a result of increasing equipment downtime.

Something we've probably all seen happen before is the short-term manager. This is the person who meets his short-term targets at the expense of long-term profitability. He gets promoted as a result of winning minor battles. No one realizes that he's lost the war until it's too late. After he leaves, things go into the tank. "Wasn't he a miracle worker?" they ask. No. Those who were supervising him and who designed the incentive system that rewarded such short-term performance were simply incompetent.

There must be a balance between attaining the short-term objectives in the business plan and the more far-reaching goals of senior management. Often the overall incentive package not only addresses the current year (which is still our topic) but also what will happen over the next five years. Even though such a comprehensive incentive strategy is beyond the scope of this book, be aware that decisions made for short-term purposes may affect what happens long into the future.

Team Rewards

An excellent way to give rewards to the plan implementation team is through a group incentive. After all, they function as a team. They cannot succeed without teamwork. Indeed, that's part of the objective in establishing the plan implementation incentive mechanism. Therefore, doesn't it make sense to reward the *team* for its success in working as intended? One of the best ways to accomplish this when the reward is easily divisible among team members (like money) is to give the team a money pool. The team then votes as to the shares each of its members should get. The vote of a senior executive on the team has no more clout than anyone else's.

Most companies conduct the balloting anonymously. After all, the *team* is the judge and jury of each member. Further, we want to maintain good relationships between members. Two major factors come into play when judging each member's contribution:

- The person's ability to hit targets for which he or she is responsible
- The team's view of the person's contribution in terms of group cohesion and teamwork in achieving overall team goals

These are the two factors we want to stress in the planning team. Some of the professional sports teams in the World Series and in the Super Bowl divided the money share given to their teams in this way. It's the same with our business planning team. They'll succeed as a team and should be rewarded as a team. It's no concern of someone not a member of that team how they choose to divide the incentive among themselves.

WHAT KINDS OF REWARDS?

Rewards communicate a lot about how seriously management takes implementation of the business plan. In the words of one planning executive, "Money talks and bullshit walks." It's true. The more the firm has to lose if the business plan isn't successfully implemented, the greater the incentives to make it happen.

However, money isn't the only incentive that works. Nor is it always the most productive in accomplishing our goals.

Properties of Rewards

Regardless of the physical incentive given for successfully implementing the business plan they all must have these characteristics:

Desirability of the Incentive
The people being motivated must want the reward and be willing to work for it. How hard would *you* work for something you did not perceive as being worth the effort to get it? Make sure the incentives are motivators for the work performed.

Achievability of the Targets
Don't forget, incentives motivate people to achieve something that *is* possible. It may be a stretch to achieve—hence the incentive—but success is possible. If goals are set so high that they are perceived as impossible, then no amount of incentive will be viewed as adequate. Consequently the effort won't be expended.

Some managers try to justify impossible targets, saying, "They'll try and fail, but what they produce will be that much more than they would have done otherwise." Nonesense. These managers are playing games with their employees' income.

A law of diminishing returns exists when dealing with the optimum stretch to achieve a goal. Beyond a certain point, higher objectives actually *reduce* motivation to attain the goal. For those mathematically inclined, it's a bell-shaped curve with productivity going up and stress going out.

Confidence That the Reward Will be Forthcoming

The incentive must be within the grantor's authority and ability to provide. More importantly, the implementation team members must *believe* that they will actually get the promised incentives if they do all these great things. Without this confidence, no incentive, regardless of its perceived value, will do the job.

An unfortunate example once occurred at a large money center bank in New York. Management came up with what they thought was a great incentive scheme. The bank would give 10 percent of the benefit derived from any idea suggested by the employees. In typical New York fashion, the incentive plan was promoted with much fanfare but little thought about the possible outcome.

A $30,000-a-year clerk named David came up with an idea that would prove to save the company over $3,000,000. His cut, $300,000, was more than the division president was paid. Unfortunately, it also exceeded the president's authorization level to bind the firm to any contract. David threatened to sue. The incentive plan was stopped.

Satisfiers

As most of us have learned, money is only the most obvious of a long list of things that satisfy employees. Often, rewards are tied to a combination of money and status within the organization.

Merit Increases

Merit increases deal with money. However, the *percentage* increase deals with status within the organization. There's a danger in giving merit increases for executing the business plan. First of all, the planning team is composed of the best and brightest performers of the firm. As such, they usually fall into the highest categories of the merit increase scale from the beginning. We want the planning team members to know the firm recognizes their special contribution. Therefore, their incentive compensation should be separated from the rest of the company. Merit increases don't accomplish this goal.

The planning team, just like everyone else, compares their percentage increases against those of their peers. The absolute value of the increase doesn't matter so much as how they did compared with everyone else. This can create problems.

For example, let's say the planning team was successful in implementing the business plan and that the firm meets its profit targets. The planning team is at the peak of the pay scale because its members are all stars. The incentive merit increases would have normally been only 7%, but the planning team gets 12% as their incentive. Now, how do you explain about the below-average performer elsewhere in the company who is given an 11% increase because he was at the very bottom of the pay scale and must be brought up to ensure equity with his peers?

The high-achievers who happen to be at the high end of the pay scale see their hard work being equated with someone who is deemed average at best. Suddenly the merit incentive becomes a disincentive.

Equally problematic is the fact that the merit increase used as an incentive is there forever. The company must pay the increased rates of the planning team next year even if performance falls short of the business plan targets.

The conclusion is that merit incentives for the planning team don't work. Stay away from them.

Onetime Bonus

A better solution for giving money incentives is a onetime bonus for hitting the targets. It doesn't affect long-term compensation so the firm doesn't continue to pay for performance it may not get in later years.

Recognition Rewards

Many motivated employees want rewards associated with quality of life, promotion, status, and recognition. These can be given to maximize the feeling of team spirit and recognition of the planning team's special contribution.

To foster team spirit the company may sponsor events to get the members talking and communicating with one another. These may be as simple as a planning retreat or sponsoring a softball team.

Some companies give gifts of recognition such as vacations, merchandise, special status offices, office furniture, parking slots, etc. This gives notification to the rest of the firm of the employee's achievement. However, they don't really foster a spirit of cooperation.

Don't forget, we're generally dealing with professionals on the planning team. These people don't want corny gifts or anything that might demean their professional status. Ball caps with the company logo on them, for instance, aren't the type of incentive rewards that motivate these people. First-class travel on business trips and company-paid mobile phones are more appropriate as rewards of recognition and status for these special people.

CHOOSING INCENTIVE BENCHMARKS

We've figured out *how* the incentive is to be given. We've also determined *what* the incentive is going to be. Now, we must choose the most appropriate benchmark at which to say, "You've done what you promised and you've earned the incentive."

This isn't as easy as you might think. Target benchmarks must be chosen carefully. They need to respect:

- The ultimate goal of the business plan implementation
- The potential for abuse of the system in order to reach the goal at the expense of something else

Attributes of Incentive Benchmarks

Just like the benchmarks we identified to track plan progress, the incentive benchmarks should be:

- Simple to understand
- Clearly discernible as to whether they were hit or not
- Timely in assessing progress and final outcome
- Able to produce the desired outcome
- Difficult to manipulate
- Able to promote the ultimate goal

Interim Targets

Choose important events along the implementation path as interim targets. These should give clear indication that the plan is proceeding on track. They should be visible in the sense that other departments can use this benchmark to perfect the timing of their own efforts.

An example of an interim target is getting the bank line of credit increased to fund working capital requirements generated by the sales targets. Once the LOC is raised, the rest of the business plan can go ahead. Without it, there won't be the money to fund increased accounts receivable and pay for the added inventory.

Another interim target might be a series of production cost levels that gradually drop during the course of the planning cycle. As it hits each benchmark, the production department draws that much closer to its final goal.

End Goals

Many targets are used to gauge the ultimate success of plan implementation. These are often a combination of things such as:

- Sales levels
- Revenues
- Profit margin
- Return on investment
- Return on capital employed
- Earnings per share

The best benchmark, however, is still that one number that says without a doubt that the business plan implementation was a success. Anything more than a single definitive benchmark can be confusing. For example, say we hit our sales targets but profits were off due to increased cost of goods sold. Which benchmark should we use to judge whether the incentive should be given—sales or CGS? In this case, neither. If the firm was really after net income, that's what should have been used in the first place.

Effects of Some Benchmarks

When choosing benchmarks, think about how they are likely to motivate your executives. For example, if earnings per share (EPS = Net income/number of shares outstanding) is used, how does it impact the firm's ability to grant shareholder dividends? The answer is that reduced dividends allow more money for reinvestment in the firm. Any return on this invested capital falls right to the bottom line and helps achieve the benchmark EPS. Is reduced shareholder dividends what senior management had in mind? Maybe not.

Alternatively, return on equity (ROE = Net income/owner's equity) ignores the impact of dividend payments. It encourages the most profitable investment of equity capital. But wait. There's a problem here too. Let's say the company plans on earning $200,000 on equity of $1,000,000. The ROE plan target was, therefore, 20% ($200,000/$1,000,000 = 20%). That's the incentive benchmark. The plan calls for $300,000 to invest in new production line equipment. The return will be 15%.

Where do we get the $300,000? If more stock was sold, the numerator in the ROE equation would rise $45,000 ($300,000 × 15% = $45,000). But the denominator (shareholder equity) would also rise from $1,000,000 to $1,300,000. Now ROE drops from 20% to 18.9% ($245,000/$1,300,000 = 18.9%). We're below the benchmark target and our incentive bonus is now at risk. If we are in a position to control the source of these funds, we'll think twice before selling stock, even though it may be the best solution.

Alternatively, the company could borrow the money at, say 10%. Now the return only rises $15,000 ($45,000 from the new equipment but less $30,000 in interest expense). The denominator stays the same because debt, not equity, was used to finance the purchase. ROE rises from 20% to 21.5% ($215,000/$1,000,000 = 21.5%).

If your incentive compensation was based on this benchmark, which alternative would you choose? The borrowing, of course, because it gets you to your targeted number. But the firm doesn't profit as much from this alternative.

The point is, pay close attention to the type of behavior you are encouraging when choosing a benchmark.

PLAYING GAMES WITH INCENTIVE PLANS

There's a danger in using business plan benchmarks to determine incentive payout. People—even members of the planning team—are human. Where are most people likely to set targets on which their incentive payouts are based? At points that can be easily reached.

Most of us have seen less-than-ambitious business plans that are certain to yield an incentive payout. To counteract this, senior management "doctors" the plan numbers, hoping to raise them to the correct point. Soon a vicious cycle emerges with one group trying to outguess the other. The business plan becomes more a negotiating tool than a management tool.

Careful Review of Incentive Targets

The targets coming out of the planning team on which incentives are based must be realistic. They have to get the company where it wants to be by year-end. Beyond that, the ways in which the business plan achieves these goals becomes less important.

Senior management reviews the incentive targets. They want to be sure of several things:

- The targets should reflect value for the amount of incentive compensation scheduled to be paid out when they are achieved.
- There should be enough stretch in the business plan that makes hitting the targets a challenge.

■ Plan targets shouldn't be so ambitious that they are viewed as being impossible to achieve.

Plan Objectives

A way to accomplish this is by making the incentive for achieving the business plan a significant part of the total compensation package. Enough flexibility should be built into the incentive plan so that superior performance enjoys an above-average compensation package. On the other end of the scale, there are no rewards for results that don't accomplish the firm's goals. Therefore, the unfortunate person's overall compensation will be lower than average.

This sends the appropriate signal:

> *Implement the business plan and you'll be rewarded.*
> *Miss it and you won't be.*

USING THE RESPONSIBILITY ACCOUNTING SYSTEM

Chapter 8 demonstrated how to establish and use the responsibility accounting system. It helps in establishing important benchmarks and tracking progress toward them. Another use of the responsibility accounting system is for the incentive system.

The plan implementation team is aware of the key benchmarks on which their interim and final incentives are based. The responsibility accounting system keeps them informed of their progress toward meeting these goals. If they are smart (better make sure they are) the team will construct a series of key indicators that tell them about progress toward meeting their incentive targets.

An example might be the sales and manufacturing departments jointly tracking sales and gross margin for every product against their planned numbers. If an interim incentive benchmark is company-wide gross margin, this responsibility tracking system tells:

■ How each product is doing compared with the plan
■ Who is responsible for each component on which the incentive payout is based
■ What changes need to be made and to what products in order to get the implementation plan back on track

Responsibility accounting establishes both the ground rules and the judging mechanism of the business plan incentive system. Additionally, incentives may be fairly distributed without question as to expected performance and actual results. These are constantly reported and updated by the responsibility reporting system.

PART III
KEEP THE PLAN
ON TRACK

10

Design a Monitoring Mechanism

OVERVIEW

The monitoring function is one of the most important aspects of a successful business plan implementation. When done properly it highlights deviations from the plan and points the way for corrective action. Chapter 10 demonstrates:

- Which information should be reported
- How often to present it
- Who should get plan monitoring information
- Reporting format

Monitoring implementation of a small businesss plan begins as soon as the plan has been formulated and approved. It continues through the end of the implementation process and into the next planning period.

CREATING THE PLAN MONITORING SYSTEM

The monitoring mechanisms found at small and medium-sized businesses are designed to identify departures from the plan in time to do something about them. Size and resources of the company determine the extent of the reporting system required. At smaller companies people to whom the monitoring system provides information are close to the daily operations. This eliminates the need for long detailed reports and explanations.

Larger firms, on the other hand, tend to remove senior executives from the real work of the firm. Consequently, these decision makers need detailed monthly performance reports hand-fed them by a staff of expensive MBAs. This *isn't* the type of monitoring mechanism we're designing here. Instead, we've trimmed the fat. We assume that our managers know what goes on in the firm at least on a daily basis (and more often than not, by the hour).

Additionally, our monitoring system assumes two other things:

- *No reports for distribution to regulatory bodies:* Companies in regulated industries must provide huge amounts of reporting to government regulators. This generally provides management no help in running the firm and takes inordinate amounts of time. Our plan monitoring system does not produce *any* of these regulatory reports.
- *No reports to owners and investors:* Often company reports that are distributed to the public require audit by an independent CPA firm. The general public does not help us implement our plan. Therefore, the monitoring system does not produce information intended for distribution to the general public. Monitoring system reports may not always follow generally accepted accounting principles and they certainly don't require attestation as to the fairness of presentation, compilation, or review by an independent CPA firm.

The emphasis is on *simplicity.* Here are the guidelines we'll use:

- The number of reports is kept small.
- Where possible, only exceptions are reported so the readers don't have to sift through reams of paper to spot deviations from the plan.
- The effort to produce the analysis is minimal.
- Progress toward key benchmarks is highlighted.
- The right people are given the information they need to monitor their role in plan implementation.
- Emphasis is placed on controlling progress toward the plan goals.

Structure of the System

Monitoring implementation of the plan needs a certain amount of structure. This structure, however, requires flexibility so that managers don't waste their time on things no longer critical to implementation. Priorities change, and so should information provided by the monitoring mechanism.

We want to structure the monitoring mechanism to include:

Monthly Financial Statements
Since many of the planning targets are financial in nature, it makes sense to produce a set of monthly financial statements. These are

easy to produce from most automated (or manual) accounting systems. The financial statements should include:

- Balance sheet
- Income statement
- Sources and uses of cash
- Schedule of compliance with lending covenants and restrictions

Usually, the financial statements and their sources of information serve as the basis from which the benchmarks and other progress monitoring is computed. At the very least, the information required to produce the financials is useful to the CFO as well as the senior planning executive(s) responsible for the bottom line.

Comparative Statements

We want to structure some sort of convenient reference point for the readers. The easiest way is to prepare our monitoring reports so they compare current actual numbers against a point of reference that tells us how we're doing.

Here are the most common points of reference used:

- Current month actual and current month plan
- Current month year-to-date actual and current month year-to-date plan
- Last month actual and last month plan
- Current month and this month last year
- This month year-to-date and this month last year, year-to-date

These comparisons account for deviations due to seasonality and particularly good (or bad) months. Occasionally firms find it useful to project year-to-date numbers to year-end using a method called *annualization*. This exercise answers the question, "If we continue for the rest of the year like we have so far, how will we do?"

Special Reports

Since we want to structure the monitoring system as simply as possible, special reports should be kept to a minimum. Generally, these additional reports are used to:

- Identify progress toward (and deviation from) designated benchmarks
- Mark progress toward performance incentives

For example, say one of the spot gain sharing programs for the collections group requires accounts receivable to fall $250,000 by

Example for Annualizing Performance Numbers:

Our sales for the first nine months total $4,500,000. Therefore, our annualized sales are $6.0 million. This was computed as follows:

$$\frac{\$4.5 \text{ million}}{9 \text{ months}} = \frac{X}{12 \text{ months}}$$

Solving for X, the annualized sales at the ninth month is $6.0 million. If our plan requires sales of $7.0 million by year-end, we've got some catching up to do in the fourth quarter.

June. One of the special reports used to track progress toward achieving this goal is the receivables aging report. This report marks progress toward the goal. Additionally, the controller probably wants other reports by which she can manage the collections effort.

Timeliness
One of the most important parts of any monitoring system structure is the *timeliness* of the reporting. The earlier the better. We want to produce the information needed to make the decisions necessary for the plan to stay on track. That can't be done if the numbers are late in getting to those who need them for decision-making purposes. Ideally, we'd like the prior month's reporting to be finished during the first week of the new month.

Accuracy
The monitoring structure should generate confidence in the numbers it produces. There should be a check of the monitoring reports by someone who understands them before they go to the users. We don't want to make decisions based on wrong information only to find out later that we should have done the opposite.

Further, credibility of the monitoring system suffers from even one incident of bad data. If it happens too often, no one believes the reports and they become a waste of time to produce.

Table 10–1 shows a few quick ways to tell at a glance whether financial statements coming from the monitoring system are accurate.

Reporting Exceptions
Exception reporting has long been a favorite topic of management analysts. The theory goes that only the problems need reporting. Therefore, the plan implementation monitoring system concentrates on results that have moved out of the planned range.

Conventional reports numbly provide a mass of figures on which management must spend time determining what's right and wrong. Exception reports, on the other hand, highlight the unusual and offer some explanation along with possible solutions to bring back areas that are going out of control.

There are two problems with exception reporting:

Emphasis on the Negative   Soon people begin to dread seeing exception reports because they always bring problems.

Neglect of Cause-and-Effect Relationships   By just reporting areas out of the planning range, the monitoring system neglects the cause-and-effect relationships. There are usually reasons why functions turn against the business plan. These causes are important for management to understand in order to fix them. Additionally, if one area is moving away from the plan, chances are it presents a problem elsewhere within the company.

FREQUENCY OF RUNNING THE MONITORING SYSTEM

Progress review of plan implementation provides one of the most valuable tools in the planning exercise. A somewhat structured

Table 10–1   Ten-Second Test of Financial Statements

■ Does the balance sheet balance? This means, do total assets equal total liabilities and equity on the balance sheet?

■ Does cash on the balance sheet equal the prior period ending cash balance *plus* the change in cash appearing on the Statement of Changes in Financial Condition or the Statement of Cash Flows?

■ Does the difference between retained earnings on the balance sheet between last period and this period equal net income or loss appearing on this period's Income Statement?

If the company is a partnership, there is no retained earnings account, however, the profit or loss should be used to adjust partner's capital balances.

■ Does accounts receivable on the balance sheet equal the balance in the accounts receivable subledger?

■ Does accounts payable on the balance sheet equal the balance in the accounts payable subledger?

If the answer to any one of these questions is no, your financial statements are *wrong*.

approach ensures regular assessment of progress along with analysis of particular areas of progress and problems. Mid-course corrections are made using results of the reviews. This procedure makes the plan a living tool—one that stays relevant because it is constantly being adjusted to take advantage of opportunities and to insulate the company from risk.

Most small and medium-sized companies run a monitoring system calendar like this:

- Monthly
- Quarterly
- Midyear
- Annual

The exceptions are for specific projects that need to be monitored throughout the month. An example might be how the receivables are being collected at companies with a borderline cash flow. In that case, collections are probably watched daily.

The most critical point is the midyear review. This is like half-time at a football game. It provides a time to assess what has been going on and where the firm stands midway through its plan implementation. Maybe the plan needs to be adjusted. Perhaps there are new opportunities to incorporate into the plan to ensure they are exploited the way management thinks they should be. Additionally, the planning team is beginning to gear up to prepare next year's plan.

The annual assessment is important from a review standpoint. Certainly by then there's nothing anyone can do about implementing that year's business plan—it's too late.

DISSEMINATION OF MONITORING INFORMATION

The most efficient performance monitoring systems draw a distinction between data and information. The object is *not* the production of as many numbers as possible in the hopes that there's something there the recipients can use. Rather, we want to give managers the exact information necessary to keep their areas of responsibility on track. This usually means providing different pieces of information to different managers.

Report Format

The monthly monitoring report format varies between individuals who get the information. Most companies avoid making performance and planning information available to just anyone. Therefore, monitoring information should be tailored to the specific needs of the recipients. Anything more than that runs the risk of putting out useless paper that diminishes the importance of the relevant information. Further, the less sensitive information floating around the company, the better.

Members of the plan implementation team probably should get all of the monitoring system reports. This information should be packaged as:

- Summary of monthly performance information
- Full set of comparative financial statements
- Information that shows progress toward particular milestones on the implementation schedule
- All the special reports prepared for particular individuals that track their areas of responsibility

A monthly reporting package that goes to the head of marketing, for example, might include the following:

- Summary of monthly performance—to provide a quick overview of how the entire firm is doing
- Comparative income statement
- Milestone chart showing sales by product compared against the plan for this month, year-to-date and this time last year, year-to-date—to provide the specific goals for which the marketing department is responsible
- Inflow and outflow of balances into the accounts receivable system—to show how well the target market pays its bills
- Summary of A/R aging—to show the impact to cash flow from customers to whom the marketing department is selling
- Analysis of gross margin [(sales − cost of goods sold)/sales] by product for plan versus this month and year-to-date—to demonstrate how product pricing ties in with manufacturing costs to hit the all important gross margin targets

Our goal is to implement a monitoring system that provides enough flexibility to give managers the exact information they need to hit their targets.

Table 10–2 shows a complete set of the reports that could be used by a marketing manager.

Table 10–2 Monthly Reporting Package

Purpose of this worksheet:
Demonstrates the monthly reporting package specifically tailored to the marketing department.

Table of contents

	Page
Summary of monthly performance	A
Comparative income statement	B
Accounts receivable flow	C
Summary of A/R aging	D
Gross margin analysis by product	E

MTH Corporation
Month of July 199X
Summary of company performance

	July actual	July plan	Act'l B(W) plan	Actual YTD	Plan YTD	YTD act'l B(W) plan	YTD act'l last year	Jly YTD B(W) last yr YTD
Revenue	$250,000	$240,000	$10,000	$1,250,000	$1,200,000	$50,000	$1,350,000	($100,000)
Cost of goods sold	100,000	110,000	10,000	500,000	550,000	50,000	750,000	250,000
Gross margin	$150,000	$130,000	$20,000	$750,000	$650,000	$100,000	$600,000	$150,000
Total expenses	105,000	100,000	(5,000)	639,500	609,500	(30,000)	636,500	(3,000)
Net income before tax	$45,000	$30,000	$15,000	$110,500	$40,500	$70,000	($36,500)	$147,000

MTH Corporation
Month of July 199X
Summary of company performance

	July actual	July plan	Act'l B(W) plan	Actual YTD	Plan YTD	YTD act'l B(W) plan	YTD act'l last year	Jly YTD B(W) last yr YTD
Dollars in inventory	$450,000	$455,000	$5,000	N/A	N/A	N/A	$500,000	$50,000
Units in inventory	15,000	14,000	(1,000)	N/A	N/A	N/A	30,000	15,000
Days of sales in inventory	15	20	5	N/A	N/A	N/A	22	7
Accounts receivable balance	$300,000	$275,000	($25,000)	N/A	N/A	N/A	$450,000	$150,000
Accounts receivable turnover	25	22	–3	N/A	N/A	N/A	36	11
Number of employees	26	28	2					
Direct labor costs	$25,000	$29,000	$4,000	$150,000	$174,000	$24,000	$180,000	$30,000
Total salary expenses	$32,000	$35,000	$3,000	$192,000	$210,000	$18,000	$250,000	$58,000
Cash balance	$50,000	$55,000	($5,000)	N/A	N/A	N/A	$40,000	$10,000
Available line of credit	$250,000	$250,000	$0	N/A	N/A	N/A	$200,000	$50,000

(continued)

Table 10–2 *(Continued)*

MTH Corporation
Month of July 199X
Comparative income statement

	July actual	July plan	Act'l B(W) plan	Actual YTD	Plan YTD	YTD act'l B(W) plan	YTD act'l last year	Jly YTD B(W) last yr YTD
Sales	$250,000	$240,000	$10,000	$1,250,000	$1,200,000	$50,000	$1,350,000	($100,000)
Cost of goods sold	100,000	110,000	10,000	500,000	550,000	50,000	750,000	250,000
Gross margin ($)	$150,000	$130,000	$20,000	$750,000	$650,000	$100,000	$600,000	$150,000
Gross margin (%)	60%	54%	0.06	60%	54%	0.06	44%	0.16
Advertising	5,000	4,000	(1,000)	30,000	24,000	(6,000)	36,000	6,000
Bad debt expense	12,000	9,000	(3,000)	72,000	54,000	(18,000)	80,000	8,000
Commission expense	29,000	25,000	(4,000)	174,000	150,000	(24,000)	142,000	(32,000)
Depreciation:								
Corporate offices	3,000	3,000	0	21,000	21,000	0	21,000	0
Machinery & equipment	4,000	4,000	0	28,000	28,000	0	28,000	0
Furniture & fixtures	1,000	1,000	0	7,000	7,000	0	7,000	0
Leasehold improvements	1,500	1,500	0	10,500	10,500	0	10,500	0
Insurance	3,000	4,000	1,000	18,000	24,000	6,000	23,000	5,000
Salaries & wages	32,000	35,000	3,000	192,000	210,000	18,000	183,000	(9,000)
Payroll taxes	7,000	8,000	1,000	42,000	48,000	6,000	46,000	4,000

MTH Corporation
Month of July 199X
Comparative income statement

	July actual	July plan	Act'l B(W) plan	Actual YTD	Plan YTD	YTD act'l B(W) plan	YTD act'l last year	Jly YTD B(W) last yr YTD
Utilities	5,000	4,000	(1,000)	30,000	24,000	(6,000)	41,000	11,000
Travel & entertainment	2,500	1,500	(1,000)	15,000	9,000	(6,000)	19,000	4,000
Total costs and expenses	$105,000	$100,000	($5,000)	$639,500	$609,500	($30,000)	$636,500	($3,000)
Net income before tax	$45,000	$30,000	$15,000	$110,500	$40,500	$70,000	($36,500)	$147,000
Tax accrual	17,000	13,000	(4,000)	44,200	16,200	(28,000)	(14,600)	(58,800)
Net income	28,000	17,000	$11,000	66,300	24,300	$42,000	(21,900)	$88,200

MTH Corporation
July 199X
Accounts receivable flow

Beginning A/R balance	$267,000
Increase to A/R:	
Credit sales < $100	25,000
Credit sales > $100 < $500	75,000
Credit sales > $500 < $1,000	90,000

(continued)

239

Table 10–2 (*Continued*)

MTH Corporation
July 199X
Accounts receivable flow

Credit sales > $1,000 < $5,000	47,000
Credit sales > $5,000	13,000
Total increase to A/R	$250,000
Collections on A/R balances:	
Current	80,000
30 days	50,000
60 days	40,000
90 days	33,000
120 days	8,000
Over 120 days	6,000
Total collections	$217,000
Ending A/R balance	$300,000

MTH Corporation
July 199X
Summary of A/R aging

	Current month	Last month	Current B(W) last
Current balance	$120,000	$100,000	($20,000)
30 days	50,000	66,000	16,000
60 days	30,000	40,000	10,000

MTH Corporation
July 199X
Summary of A/R aging

	Current month	Last month	Current B(W) last
90 days	60,000	20,000	(40,000)
120 days	15,000	18,000	3,000
Over 120 days	25,000	31,000	6,000
	$300,000	$275,000	($25,000)

MTH Corporation
Month of July 199X
Analysis of gross margin by product

	July actual	July plan	Act'l B(W) plan	Actual YTD	Plan YTD	YTD act'l B(W) plan	YTD act'l last year	Jly YTD B(W) last yr YTD
Margin analysis by product:								
Shower heads								
Gross revenue	$25,000	$23,000	$2,000	$150,000	$140,000	$10,000	$155,000	($5,000)
Cost of goods sold	6,500	6,000	(500)	32,500	28,500	(4,000)	70,900	38,400
Gross margin ($)	$18,500	$17,000	$1,500	$117,500	$111,500	$6,000	$84,100	$33,400
Gross margin (%)	74%	74%	0%	78%	80%	-1%	54%	24%
Bath faucets and knobs								
Gross revenue	$15,000	$13,500	$1,500	$70,000	$66,000	$4,000	$67,500	$2,500
Cost of goods sold	8,500	7,000	(1,500)	35,000	43,000	8,000	50,350	15,350
Gross margin ($)	$6,500	$6,500	$0	$35,000	$23,000	$12,000	$17,150	$17,850
Gross margin (%)	43%	48%	-5%	50%	35%	15%	25%	35%
Kitchen faucets and knobs								
Gross revenue	$65,000	$67,000	($2,000)	$410,000	$425,000	($15,000)	$483,000	($73,000)
Cost of goods sold	20,000	23,000	3,000	175,000	197,000	22,000	240,500	65,500

(continued)

241

Table 10–2 *(Continued)*

MTH Corporation
Month of July 199X
Analysis of gross margin by product

	July actual	July plan	Act'l B(W) plan	Actual YTD	Plan YTD	YTD act'l B(W) plan	YTD act'l last year	Jly YTD B(W) last yr YTD
Gross margin ($)	$45,000	$44,000	$1,000	$235,000	$228,000	$7,000	$242,500	($7,500)
Gross margin (%)	69%	66%	4%	57%	54%	4%	50%	7%
Pre-fab shower stalls								
Gross revenue	$21,000	$24,000	($3,000)	$80,000	$67,000	$13,000	$75,500	$4,500
Cost of goods sold	8,000	10,000	2,000	37,000	43,000	6,000	51,250	14,250
Gross margin ($)	$13,000	$14,000	($1,000)	$43,000	$24,000	$19,000	$24,250	$18,750
Gross margin (%)	62%	58%	4%	54%	36%	18%	32%	22%
Iron bath tubs								
Gross revenue	$33,000	$28,000	$5,000	$170,000	$186,000	($16,000)	$198,500	($28,500)
Cost of goods sold	18,500	16,000	(2,500)	75,000	88,000	13,000	120,250	45,250
Gross margin ($)	$14,500	$12,000	$2,500	$95,000	$98,000	($3,000)	$78,250	$16,750
Gross margin (%)	44%	43%	1%	56%	53%	3%	39%	16%
Fiberglass bath tubs								
Gross revenue	$45,000	$37,500	$7,500	$177,000	$160,000	$17,000	$175,000	$2,000
Cost of goods sold	20,000	25,250	5,250	75,000	78,000	3,000	110,000	35,000
Gross margin ($)	$25,000	$12,250	$12,750	$102,000	$82,000	$20,000	$65,000	$37,000
Gross margin (%)	56%	33%	23%	58%	51%	6%	37%	20%
Bath sinks								
Gross revenue	$37,000	$32,000	$5,000	$148,000	$120,000	$28,000	$135,000	$13,000
Cost of goods sold	15,000	12,000	(3,000)	60,000	57,000	(3,000)	75,250	15,250

MTH Corporation
Month of July 199X
Analysis of gross margin by product

	July actual	July plan	Act'l B(W) plan	Actual YTD	Plan YTD	YTD act'l B(W) plan	YTD act'l last year	Jly YTD B(W) last yr YTD
Gross margin ($)	$22,000	$20,000	$2,000	$88,000	$63,000	$25,000	$59,750	$28,250
Gross margin (%)	59%	63%	−3%	59%	53%	7%	44%	15%
Kitchen sinks								
Gross revenue	$9,000	$15,000	($6,000)	$45,000	$36,000	$9,000	$60,500	($15,500)
Cost of goods sold	3,500	10,750	7,250	10,500	15,500	5,000	31,500	21,000
Gross margin ($)	$5,500	$4,250	$1,250	$34,500	$20,500	$14,000	$29,000	$5,500
Gross margin (%)	61%	28%	33%	77%	57%	20%	48%	29%
Total revenue	$250,000	$240,000	$10,000	$1,250,000	$1,200,000	$50,000	$1,350,000	($100,000)
Less total cost of goods sold	100,000	110,000	10,000	500,000	550,000	50,000	750,000	250,000
Total Gross margin ($)	$150,000	$130,000	$20,000	$750,000	$650,000	$100,000	$600,000	$150,000
Total Gross margin (%)	60%	54%	6%	60%	54%	6%	44%	16%

MONITORING CONSIDERATIONS
DURING PLAN DESIGN

From the very beginning of the design stage, the planning team must be aware of monitoring system requirements. The plan should give consideration to tracking its implementation progress. This can't be done if, for example, the plan cites milestones whose progress numbers simply aren't available anywhere in the company.

This once occurred at a securities brokerage firm. Part of their businesss plan included steady increases in commodities trading commission income from Refco, the largest commodities house in the country. The plan called for specific income levels at particular points in time.

The problem was that the accounting system (neither the firm's nor Refco's) was unable to provide the trading room supervisor any midmonth progress reports on how they were doing toward meeting that month's target. They were always playing catchup in the current month, trying to replace shortfalls that occurred in the prior month *after* the performance reports finally appeared. In this case, when they were planning the milestones no one thought to consider availability of information.

Identify What Needs to be Tracked

Once the business plan has been established, our next step is to figure out how to make it happen. Part of this process determines which indicators need to be watched in order to control each phase of plan implementation.

This takes a lot of thought. We need to coordinate all the things that are being done throughout the company requiring a particular sequence. Therefore, the monitoring system must tell us at least three things:

Timing of Each Implementation Phase
Timing is important to many parts of the business plan. The monitoring system should tell us how the timing of each implementation phase is tracking against what the plan says it should be.

Impact of Changes in Timing
The implementation monitoring system needs to tell us not only where our timing has slipped, but what the effects are likely to be throughout the company. Probably the easiest way to accomplish this is through the use of an automated simulation model of the plan.

This may sound ominous, but it's not. The objective is simple: Simulate the effects of changes to the implementation plan. Analysis is focused on the key areas most likely to be adversely impacted.

Here's an example: Let's say the sales and marketing group is a month late in reaching their sales goals. Let's also say our business plan monitoring system has the ability to answer *what-if* questions so we can simulate the impact of this departure from plan. The first two critical areas of the company affected are accounts receivable and production. Let's take a look.

Accounts Receivable   Suddenly, receivables aren't at the level we expected. The accounting department hired and trained two additional collections people in anticipation of the added work resulting from projected sales increases. Now these people are taking salary and benefits with little productive work to keep them busy. But there's more.

The increased bank loan was granted on the condition that it be secured by accounts receivable. The bank understood that receivables would be growing and was counting on them reaching certain levels at certain times to provide collateral as the loan was drawn down. Now that schedule has been disrupted. The likelihood exists that the bank will curtail draws of the loan based on breach of the security agreement.

Inventory and Production   The production group made a certain number of products based on anticipated sales levels. Raw material inventory was purchased based on this number. Accounts payable was incurred for these items. Now, the sales level has fallen below that which can absorb this production. So it sits in the warehouse, taking up space and working capital. The company has to go out and rent additional space they hadn't planned on. Perhaps these goods may need to be deeply discounted just to move them to make way for more saleable products.

Monitoring systems with what-if capabilities are invaluable for use in assessing possible options to deviations in the plan.

Volume

By volume we mean both dollars and units. The monitoring system should be designed to provide information in the form that managers find most useful in tracking performance. For some items, such as finished goods inventory, the sales and production managers probably find units the most useful measure. Other performance indicators, such as 60-day-old receivables, are best measured in dollars.

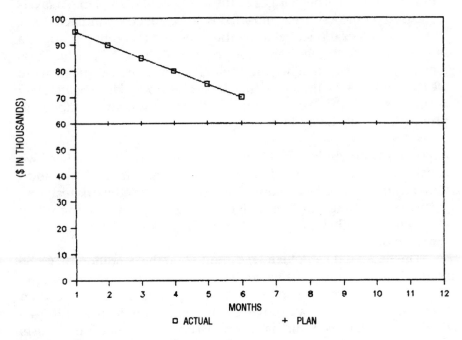

Figure 10–1   Actual sales vs. plan

Presentation

During the plan design stage, at the time you're thinking about how the implementation monitoring mechanism is going to work, also consider how this information should be presented. The bulk of the information is probably best presented in a tabular format. That way people can see what actually occurred and compare it against what should have happened. Tables are also good for illustrating the impact of deviations from the plan on other areas of the firm.

Graphs are also an excellent way to present information. For example, let's say that we're continuing to hit our sales objectives. Good!—except that the margin of error by which we're above the benchmarks each month is steadily decreasing. Shown as a downward sloping graph, the trend is obvious. The implication is equally obvious—shortly our sales level is going to fall below the benchmarks by greater and greater degrees. Figure 10–1 illustrates this situation.

Another effective method of presentation is the pie chart. If we wanted to illustrate the composition of our sales for the month, we could put it in a pie chart. The slices provide a visual depiction of the amount each product's sales represent of the whole. Even more effective is to have the percentage of total in each slice of the pie.

T-D-O PARTNERS, LTD.

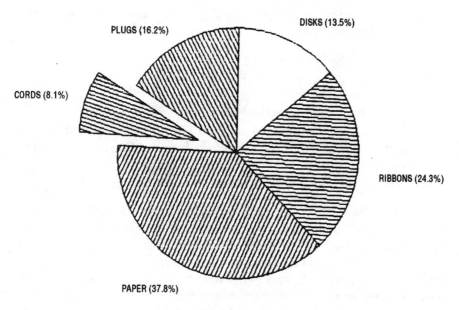

Figure 10–2   Sales Composition—March 199X

Figure 10–2 illustrates this point with the addition of highlighting T-D-O's highest margin product. Unfortunately, this item proportionately makes up its lowest sales volume.

CAPTURE OF MONITORING INFORMATION

Once we've designed the monitoring system, we need to begin capturing the information it requires. In some cases this data won't be readily available. Design of the monitoring system should have taken this into consideration. Still, many times the implementation team needs information that hasn't been developed by the company before.

At that point procedures are needed to capture the information, review it for accuracy, and put it into a format usable by the people who are to work with it. This task won't put you very high on the list of favorite people for those who do the data capture. It's usually viewed as more busy-work on top of what people already do at a small or medium-sized business. However, if the firm is serious about successfully implementing its business plan, when the reason for this information is presented forthrightly and the people agree with its importance, then the battle is won.

Techniques of Data Capture

We want several things from the data capture program that feeds the plan monitoring system:

- Data must be accurate and reliable.
- Format of the raw data must be easily convertible into useful *information*.
- It must be available within the time frame required.
- It should be captured as close to the source as possible so it doesn't run through too many hands and waste time as well as become subject to error or misinterpretation.
- Data must be verifiable by another party if necessary.

Ideally, the data is captured on the firm's computer (if it has one). It is then *translated* into useful information. One alternative to translating data into information is to move the raw data from a larger computer to a personal computer. The software on smaller computers is more user-friendly and better able to manipulate raw data into useful information.

Our orientation for business planning focuses on firms without a full complement of MBAs having nothing better to do than crunch numbers. Common sense dictates that *everyone* at a small or medium-sized business contribute to the bottom line.

Therefore, we emphasize efficiency. All the information we report must be used or it's discontinued. For example, let's say we need to track idle labor hours due to machinery downtime. If we're smart (and we are) the production department action plan calls for specific benchmark levels of such costs throughout the planning horizon. Some companies with more sophisticated cost accounting systems have a method that puts such idle labor costs into a special general ledger expense account for tracking purposes. If that type of resource is available, then the data capture is easy.

But what if it's not? How do we get the information? One solution would be to create a manual log of those employees who are idle due to machine downtime throughout the month. The log would be simple and could include:

- Date of downtime
- Name of employee
- Labor rate
- Number of hours idle
- Labor cost for the idle time

If there's a personal computer in the production department, the log could be kept on a simple automated spreadsheet. This most likely could be transferred to the computer on which the business plan monitoring system resides. The data would then be electronically incorporated into the performance monitoring system. The time such a procedure takes would be minimal for everyone.

Uses of Captured Data

Above all, we want to make sure the information captured by the monitoring system is relevant to those using it. A good way to be sure is to periodically talk with the managers who receive it. Find out what they do with it. Ask how it makes tracking their particular benchmarks more effective. Chances are, you'll be surprised at the answers you get. Often what you thought was useful information becomes marked up and further massaged to convert it into something that's really useful. Other times, the recipient just slides it under a pile of work without even looking at it.

Both instances are too expensive for small businesses to endure. If information is not used, then either make it useful or stop generating it. A good example is the idle labor costs we saw above. As machinery gets older, downtime increases with idle labor costs rising right along with it. Therefore, what the manager really needs is information on machinery downtime, *not* raw data on idle labor hours.

Notice how we focus on the probem source—poorly maintained or aging equipment—not the symptom, idle labor cost. This information provides some of the support necessary to make a decision on machinery purchases. However, it may not be something that should be generated for every incidence of downtime.

Therefore, by looking at the real use of the information and the types of decisions for which it will be utilized we can focus on just what's needed. Anything more than that is a waste of time and just serves to confuse already busy decision makers.

TECHNIQUES OF FINANCIAL ANALYSIS

Most business performance monitoring systems employ a kind of shorthand to determine how things are going. That shorthand is called *financial ratios*. It's simply a way of matching two independent performance numbers to arrive at a conclusion about a specific area of the company.

When the plan implementation monitoring system uses ratios to analyze the firm's performance, the actual number is usually less important than how it has *changed* from one period to another.

Additionally, if your company owns two or more different businesses, don't try to compare financial ratios. What may be an acceptable index for one company may not be for another.

Here are some of the ratios most commonly used when monitoring business performance:

Asset Ratios

Current Ratio

Current Ratio = Current Assets/Current Liabilities

We use this ratio to show the ability to meet payment obligations due within the operating period using assets that will convert to cash within that same operating period.

Quick Ratio

Quick Ratio = (Cash + Marketable Securities)/Current Liabilities

This measurement identifies the firm's ability to make payments due this month without cash generated from sales of inventory. Note that many analysts include either the current portion or the entire balance of accounts receivable in the dividend of this equation.

Often bank loan covenants carry specific benchmarks for asset ratios such as the current and quick ratios. If that's the case in your company, be sure to include them in the plan as well as in the monitoring system. You should know well ahead of time if these ratios are going to fall out of their specified ranges. If you can't do anything to fix it, then notify the bank. It's better to anticipate a problem and work with your banker to fix it than to appear surprised at bad news.

One last note. If your firm breaches a lending covenant or restriction and the bank waives whatever rights and remedies they inserted in the loan documents, then get the waiver in writing. Without a written waiver you run the risk of a capricious banker changing his mind.

Accounts Receivable

Accounts Receivable Turnover Rate

A/R Turnover = Annual Sales/Average A/R Balance

A/R turnover shows the speed with which a company collects its receivables. The faster receivables turn, the less cash is consumed by this component of working capital. The financial department should be most interested in the A/R turnover rate.

Average Collection Period

$$\text{Average Collection Period} = \text{Accounts Receivable Balance}/(\text{Annual Sales}/360)$$

Here's another measure of our collection efficiency. Average collection period tells us how many days of average sales we've got tied up in accounts receivable. Our objective is to have as few days of sales in receivables as possible.

Aging of Accounts Receivable

$$\text{Weighted Average Age of Accounts Receivable} = \text{Sum of}$$
$$(\text{Weighted Average \% of each aging bucket} \times \text{number of days in each aging bucket})$$

The weighted average age of receivables shows where in the aging distribution the company usually collects what it is owed. The lower the number of days receivables age, the less cash is invested in receivables. It also provides an indication of the receivables portfolio stability. For example, a 25-day aged portfolio has a higher probability of being collected than one with a 65-day weighted average aging.

Inventory

Average Investment Period of Inventory

$$\text{Average Investment Period of Inventory} = \text{Present Inventory Balance}/(\text{Annual Cost of Goods Sold}/360)$$

If part of your business plan calls for a lower drain on working capital, chances are at least a few of your performance benchmarks focus on inventory control. The smaller the investment in inventory—higher demand items, for example—the faster this asset can be turned into disposable cash.

Inventory Turnover Rate

$$\text{Inventory Turnover Rate} = \text{Annual Cost of Goods Sold}/\text{Average Inventory Balance}$$

Here's another way to determine the speed with which a firm's inventory investment converts into sales. The higher the turnover rate, the faster inventory flows out to customers and the less cash is tied up in low demand stock.

Accounts Payable

Aging of Accounts Payable

Weighted Average Age of Accounts Payable = Sum of (Weighted Average % of each aging bucket × number of days in each aging bucket)

The weighted average age of payables shows how fast the company pays its obligations. The higher the number of days payables age, the greater the leverage derived from the company's vendors. It's not usually a good policy to pay obligations before they're due. Indeed, during times of cash scarcity, many firms aggressively stretch their payables. This index helps manage that process. Further, by breaking down the A/P aging account by account, the controller can control the firm's payment policies even more precisely.

Average Payment Period

Average Payment Period = Accounts Payable Balance/(Annual Expenses/360)

Average payment period shows the days of average expenses vendors have invested in the firm's accounts payable. The higher the average payment period, the greater the company's use of trade credit. This is like a free loan—the company uses its vendor's credit policies to finance part of its working capital requirements.

Accounts Payable Turnover Rate

A/P Turnover = Annual Expenses/Average A/P Balance

Here's another way to identify the speed at which obligations are paid. The higher the A/P turnover rate, the more cash escapes from the firm and the greater the requirement for working capital.

For your convenience, Table 10–3 provides a series of worksheets that should make including these statistics in your own monitoring system a little easier.

Table 10–3   Computation of Financial Ratios

Company Name
Computation of Financial Ratios
30-Apr-92

Asset ratios	Current month

1. Current ratio:
   Equation: Current assets / current liabilities
   - Current assets $0
   - Current liabilities   0
   - Current ratio

2. Quick ratio:
   Equation: (cash + marketable securities + A/R) / current liabilities
   - Cash $0
   - Marketable securities   0
   - Accounts receivable   0
   - Current liabilities   0
   - Quick ratio

Accounts receivable ratios

1. Accounts receivable turnover rate
   Equation: annual sales / average A/R balances
   - Annual sales   0
   - Average A/R balances   0
   - A/R turnover rate

2. Average collection period
   Equation: accounts receivable / (annual sales / 360)
   - Accounts receivable $0
   - Annual sales   0

   Avg. collection period
   (days)

(continued)

Table 10–3 (*Continued*)

Company Name
Computation of Financial Ratios
30-Apr-92

Asset ratios	*Current month*

3. Aging of accounts receivable
    Equation: sum of (weighted average % of ea. aging bucket × # of days in each bucket)

		Weighting % in bucket	*Aging bucket weighting*	
A/R balances by aging bucket:				
Current	$0			Days
30 days	0			Days
60 days	0			Days
90 days	0			Days
120 days	0			Days
Total A/R	$0			Days

Inventory ratios

1. Average investment period of inventory
    Equation: present inventory balance / (annual cost of goods sold / 360)

Present inventory balance	$0
Annual cost of goods sold	0
Avg investment period of inventory (days)	

2. Inventory turnover rate
    Equation: annual cost of goods sold / average inventory balance

Annual cost of goods sold	$0
Average inventory balance	0
Inventory turnover rate (times per year)	

(*continued*)

Table 10–3   (*Continued*)

Company Name
Computation of Financial Ratios
30-Apr-92

Asset ratios	Current month

1. Aging of accounts payable
   Equation: sum of (weighted average % of ea. aging bucket × # of days in each bucket)

		Weighting % in bucket	*Aging bucket weighting*	
A/P balances by aging bucket:				
Current	$0			Days
30 days	0			Days
60 days	0			Days
90 days	0			Days
120 days	0			Days
Total A/P	$0			Days

2. Average payment period
   Equation: accounts payable balance / (annual expenses / 360)

Accounts payable balance	$0
Annual expenses	0
Average payment period (days)	

3. Accounts payable turnover rate
   Equation: annual expenses / average A/P balance

Annual expenses	$0
Average A/P balance	0
A/P turnover rate (times/year)	

11

Update the Plan

OVERVIEW

Updating small business plans is like using a compass to navigate. You'll miss your target unless you check progress frequently and make mid-course corrections. This a necessary step in the implementation process. Regular plan updates keep it relevant to the current issues confronting the company every business day. Obsolete business plans not only go stale for lack of implementation, but they are almost impossible to revive once enthusiasm has died.

Chapter 11 shows how to identify critical areas of the plan that must be reassessed frequently to be sure they are still consistent with company goals. Product demand provides an example. Most business plans target sales levels at particular points in time. However, consumer demand tends to be fickle. It makes little sense to keep pounding planned goals for products whose demand is clearly on its way down. Instead, smart managers update the plan to cut losses short and take advantage of new areas of opportunity.

WHEN TO UPDATE

There are two instances in which plans should be updated:

1. When business conditions change and require the firm to redirect its efforts
2. At regular intervals throughout the implementation process

Change in Business Conditions

The business climate changes over time. If the plan does not reflect the current business climate, then it's of little use. It won't get the company where it needs to go in order to achieve its goals.

Periodic Updating

Even if there is no "emergency" update required for implementation of the business plan, most companies do an update at some point during the year. Midyear seems to be the most common time. A routine update usually includes the company's responses to changes made as a reaction to business conditions, missed benchmarks, or goals of the overall business plan that have been altered.

Periodic updating provides these benefits:

Changes in Strategic Direction

Companies make major decisions throughout the year. These are done without regard to the planning calendar. Nevertheless, these resolutions can dramatically affect the current year's business plan. Further, most firms can't wait for the start of the new planning cycle to begin implementation. For these reasons, periodic updating of the plan provides a formalized time to implement these changes in strategic direction for the entire company and each of the departments affected.

Changes in Specific Parts of the Business Plan

Rarely does the subplan for any given department remain the same throughout the implementation cycle. The firm's goals and targets stay the same, but the ways in which individual groups hit their benchmarks often shift from they way things were planned.

For this reason the periodic update provides a structure for entire sections of the plan to be adjusted.

Departmental Changes

Separate departments reassess what they've done throughout the year to meet their implementation benchmarks. The changes they make usually affect other departments and need to be made known throughout the company. For this reason, the structure required of a midyear progress assessment lets everyone know what their co-workers are doing and how these new plans affect them.

WHAT PARTS OF THE PLAN TO UPDATE

Updating the plan usually doesn't require that every part be changed. The effect we want is one of looking at the new information we've obtained since the implementation was first begun for each department. Changes should be done only for parts of the plan that have strayed from their original course. To do otherwise would simply create busy-work and be unnecessary.

Parts of the plan most likely to require updating during the implementation include:

Sales Plan

For most companies, predicting sales is a difficult part of the plan implementation. So much depends on things outside the company, beyond management's control. The marketing strategy and mix of how firms spend their advertising dollars change constantly. With that, the impact on sales revenues and collections from movements in customer composition changes as well.

Plan updates serve to incorporate sales plan changes into the rest of the firm's business plan. It's important to have these changes conveyed to the rest of the company under the formalized structure of, say a quarterly or semiannual plan update. During this time, revised sales mix and customer compositions can be reviewed to determine how they impact the rest of the company's targets and benchmarks.

Production Schedules and Costs

The next part of the plan involved in the update is usually in the production area. Rarely do the costs of production and raw material purchases hit those that were planned. Along with changes in the sales price of these goods, the all-important gross margin target changes.

Gross margin is one of the most important determinates of overall profitability. As the gross margin components—sales price and cost of goods sold—change so does profitability. During the plan update the firm can control and adjust how it attacks problems with production schedules and costs. It can establish new targets to make up for deviations from the plan that occurred earlier in the year.

Overhead Expenses and Salaries

Overhead has a habit of slipping away from the planned course. There are usually some very good reasons. Nevertheless, expenses that were seen each month as only gradually creeping away from the plan come into sharp focus as a problem during the periodic plan update.

The best way to discover this deviation is to look at the year-to-date differences between actual overhead and salary expenditures compared with what was planned. Ask yourself these questions:

Which Overhead Items are Out of Range and Why?
Pay special attention to such things as:

- Bank charges
- Interest expense on the line of credit
- Bad debt expense from write-off of accounts receivable
- Travel and entertainment compared with what it bought you
- Postage, delivery, and messenger service

Within reason, each of these items is controllable. Taken separately, they shouldn't amount to significant money. However, for companies that operate on a thin margin, they're just more things to take away from an already overburdened bottom line.

Further, companies that don't follow their overhead cost plan often develop sloppy habits in management of the more important parts of the plan.

Where is Staff Salary and Labor Expense Out of Line?
It may sound coldhearted, but staff salaries and other non-revenue-producing employees must continuously be justified. This is especially true of small businesses. The only reason overhead salaries are incurred is to make those who actually generate revenue more productive. The secretary to the head of marketing is a good example. Without that person, the marketing department would be less efficient and sales would fall. If that isn't the case, then the person wasn't really needed after all.

If non-revenue-producing salaries are out of the planned range, find out what departments accounted for the overrun. Within each department, determine exactly which people (or overtime hours, temporary people, consultants, etc.) caused the problem. Ask the tough question:

Does the expense this person incurs justify the added profit her services bring the firm?

If not, then get rid of her. Alternatively, you might transfer her to another department that needs another revenue-generating person.

Where are the Offsetting Savings from Overhead Expenses?
Stop and think before you go wildly cutting out overhead costs that exceeded those planned. Often managers are willing to incur an expense in order to save more somewhere else or later on during the year. However, there's nothing wrong with pointing to a large overhead expense and asking for the rationale behind it.

If the business plan implementation team has been doing its job, overhead expenses that exceeded those planned were justified *before* they were made. Chances are, everyone associated with the transaction understands the reason for the overrun. Further, benefits of the expenditure (if it's ongoing) are watched to ensure they continue to meet expectations. If the return stops or falls below expectations, the expense is cut.

Should This Part of the Plan be Reworked?

Overhead is one part of the plan that can be affected by management control. Benefits of overhead expenses are more difficult to quantify. They don't usually have a direct effect on overall profitability of the company. Redirecting and reallocating parts of the administrative and overhead subplan can sometimes relieve pressure building up in the revenue producing departments. The effect can be that plan performance is once again brought back into line without a noticeable impact on company efficiency.

If the overhead plan is far enough out and reallocation of the expenses can help the revenue producing departments, then it may be a good idea to revamp this part of the plan.

Capital Expenditures

These are usually the largest and most carefully watched parts of the business plan. From both a cost and a timing standpoint a variety of departments are interested in tracking capital expenditures against the plan. Here are just three:

Operations

The operation department (also called production in some companies) is counting on the capital equipment to help them execute their part of the plan.

Purchasing

The purchasing department is interested in the seller meeting the deadlines specified in their contract.

Controller

The controller wants to know when the order was placed and when payment is expected.

If capital expenditures stray from the plan, it affects each of these departments (and probably some others as well). There's a good chance that at least some parts of each of these subplans will have to be updated to reflect impacts of the changes.

Nonroutine Events

During the course of a year you can count on the unexpected to happen. We lump these into the category of *nonroutine events*. Almost certainly, at least one of these occurrences will alter implementation of the business plan.

Many business plans contain contingency sections that provide for the unexpected. If you think about it, nonroutine events can be anticipated to a certain degree. Product liability suits offer a case in point. Some companies are well aware of their exposure. They accrue a certain amount each month against claims that will amost certainly be filed. It's treated like a reserve for bad debts.

Some of the nonroutine events you may encounter could include:

Litigation
Japan has just one lawyer for every 10,000 people. The state of California, on the other hand, has one lawyer for every *two hundred* people. With all these hired guns running around trying to earn a living, California is a lawyer's happy hunting ground and they've declared war on business.

Regardless of the merit of the case, it costs money to defend yourself. These funds were probably allocated to other more productive uses. If a big case comes up, the business plan should be updated, taking into consideration things such as:

■ Costs of fighting or settling the case
■ Costs and probability of losing the case
■ Estimated judgment against your firm in the event of a loss

If the suit is big enough, it could affect the entire business plan. At the very least, participating in litigation is time consuming to key members of the firm. It takes away from their normal revenue-producing activities.

New Opportunities
A nice problem to have is one where an unexpected opportunity occurs. If the company chooses to exploit it there will probably be reallocations of capital, management time, and other company resources. If the project is large enough, the business plan should be updated to include the resultant changes to timing of production, sales, and cash inflow and outflow, to name just a few. This is important so that we can monitor and control this new venture just as we do the other components of the plan.

Risk

As the environment changes, so does the risk undertaken by the company. An example is seen in the civil unrest prevalent in different parts of the world and in the United States. Political systems once thought to rule with an iron fist—such as the Communist party in the former Soviet Union—have been toppled.

During the plan update, risk should be evaluated. This includes the risk of loss from unanticipated events. Variables such as sales, interest rates, production capacity, and cost of materials all come into sharper focus as we get more experienced.

The periodic plan update is a good time to adjust and fine-tune the plan for the rest of the year using knowledge we've already gained. From this process often comes a task to some parts of the company and a realignment of objectives to other parts.

Of course, no one can predict the outcome of unknown events. However, you'll be surprised at how much you can insulate your firm from unknown risk just by *anticipating* what could happen and taking steps beforehand. A good example of just such a preemptive action is a company whose debt interest is tied to an interest rate index. Unless the firm is a bank, chances are management's profession is not that of predicting and speculating on interest rates. Therefore, they want to protect their bottom line as much as possible from rising interest rates that would cause interest expense to climb above that which was planned.

There are a variety of things this company could do to protect itself. One popular remedy is to purchase what is called an interest rate swap contract. This is an off-balance-sheet transaction where one company trades the cash inflow and outflow associated with their debt with another company having the opposite problem.

If the company is afraid of rising interest rates, they can swap (in other words, pay) another company (the *counterparty*) a fixed rate (specified on the swap contract) in exchange for receiving a variable rate payment from the counterparty. That way, if interest rates rise the company's interest expense stays the same and they actually make money on the spread between the variable rate they receive from the counterparty and the fixed rate they pay them.

Of course, in our swap example, as with many risk-reduction techniques, there's a downside. In this case, if rates fall instead of rise, the company is locked into paying a fixed rate that's now higher than what they would have paid had they stuck with their original variable rate loan. The counterparty is better off since their payment rate (the variable side) drops and they receive the higher fixed rate.

Nevertheless, the firm's overall risk has been diminished. They won't take as much advantage of changes in their favor, nor will they suffer as much from adversity. Insurance works like this. We buy insurance, hoping we'll never need it. If not, we're out the premi-um—so we're not as well off as if we never bought it in the first place and didn't need it. On the other hand, if we suffer an insurable loss, the policy will pay for at least part of the damage. In that case, we're better off by the reimbursement less the premiums.

Risk management is a tricky subject. The business plan should be updated as two things related to risk change:

1. The potential loss from a given risk
2. The probability of the loss occurring

Technological Innovation

Advances in modern technology occur without regard to the timing of our business plans. Yet smart companies watch for them, then implement them into their operations. Robotics is one such field. With the advances made in the interface between hardware and software, computer-controlled production equipment is rapidly en-tering the production line. Although the initial capital outlay can be stiff, the return from lower production costs, higher-quality prod-ucts, and less chance of employee lawsuits usually repays the investment quickly.

Companies who implement technological innovations into their processes must update the business plan to reflect the initial invest-ment in technology and the cost savings. We want to track the performance of each new program to make sure it is doing what we intended it to. Without the business plan being updated to account for improved performance, we've no way of telling if we made the right decision.

Table 11–1 illustrates key components of the business plan that should be updated periodically. Notice that most of these compo-nents are parts of subplans. In other words, they provide their departments a blueprint to execute *that part* of the business plan. Changing these components doesn't usually require a complete revision of the overall business plan.

KEEP THE PLAN RELEVANT

Small companies that have been operating for years without a business plan are used to flying by the seat of their pants. Chances are that somewhere along the line a plan was attempted. It was quickly scrapped when it became outdated and irrelevant to what was really happening in the firm.

Relevancy is especially important to companies implementing a business plan for the first time. It will be looked on with skepti-

Table 11–1 Business Plan Update Frequencies

Plan component	Monthly	Quarterly	Six months
Sales			
Units shipped	X		
Sales calls made	X	X	X
Commission paid	X	X	X
# of direct sales people			X
# of sales support staff		X	X
Sales overhead expense	X	X	X
Sales-related travel and entertainment expense	X	X	X
# of customers			X
Collections from customers	X		X
Gross margin by product	X	X	X
Product mix sold	X	X	X
Product prices			X
Advertising expenses	X	X	X
Production			
# of units produced	X	X	X
Cost of goods sold	X	X	X
Raw material purchase prices		X	X
Manufacturing labor expense	X	X	X
Machinery downtime	X	X	X
Machinery repair expense	X	X	X
Overhead expenses			
Administrative salaries		X	X
Temporary employees and consultants	X	X	X
Overhead travel and entertainment	X	X	X
Overhead advertising (corporate imaging)	X	X	
Charitable contributions			X
Bad debt expense	X	X	X
Capital expenditures			
Amount spent on each program		X	X
Timing of future expenditures	X	X	X
Equipment delivery dates	X	X	X
Payment dates	X	X	X
Deposits on purchases (amount and timing)	X	X	X

Plan component	Monthly	Quarterly	Six months
Nonroutine events			
Litigation: pending, newly filed, or just settled	X	X	X
New opportunities	X	X	X
Reserve for risk contingencies	X	X	X
Risk			
Probability of risk events occurring	X	X	X
Amount of potential loss from risk event occurring	X	X	X
Finance			
Interest expense	X	X	X
Accounts receivable and payable balances and other performance indicators	X	X	X
Cash on hand	X	X	X
Borrowing capacity		X	X
Financial ratios that determine creditworthiness	X	X	X
Liabilities such as taxes and their accruals	X	X	X

cism—as something else for the boss to use to exert his control over the workers. An excuse often used to explain why targets weren't hit is that the plan doesn't reflect the real world.

This complaint is usually correct. But the only way to ensure the plan remains relevant is to update it for changes that have occurred since it was first drafted. This doesn't mean that we change our original goals. After all, that's the point of making a business plan in the first place—to get the firm from point A to point B. The route we take *will* change and so will the interim results; but not the endpoint.

HOW TO AVOID CONFUSION

Larger companies have the resources to do several plan updates. This sometimes confuses those managers charged with the responsibility of executing the plan. They may begin to wonder, *which plan targets are we shooting for?* That's not something we wish to encounter. We want all our people singing from the same sheet of music.

The best way to avoid confusion is to keep the number of plan updates as small as possible—preferably just one update at midyear.

Hopefully, the underlying goals of the business plan won't be changed at that time. Subplans for the different departments are updated to reflect changes in strategy and timing.

Monthly progress reports on plan implementation compare actual performance against the plan. When the plan is updated, the new version becomes the standard against which progress is measured. The old plan is no longer used.

This means that the format of the updated business plan and the ways targets and benchmarks are computed must be identical. It becomes confusing when people have to go through a laborious reconciliation between performance indicators prepared for an existing plan and the ones for its new updated version (and maybe, God forbid, one more after that). Make no mistake, when a performance incentive is on the line people spend hours trying to reconcile two different plans. The point is just to make sure you can easily compare apples with apples.

Index

Business Plans to Manage Day-to-Day Operations

Real-Life Results for the Small Business Owners and Operators Disk Companion

Contents of This Disk:

README.BAT:	Prints this text.
FILE1.WK1:	Computes standard financial ratios.
FILE2.WK1:	Produces a sample month-end financial reporting package.
FILE3.WK1:	Computes the standard growth rate index of a business.
FILE4.WK1:	Compiles a sales forecast by product line.
FILE5.WK1:	Computes the financial ratios used for cash management purposes.
FILE6.WK1:	Produces a materials requirements plan.
FILE7.WK1:	Demonstration calculations for a sensitivity analysis.
FILE8.WK1:	Computes the expected dollar value of an event.
FILE9:WK1:	Computes the optimum safety stock in inventory under a variety of assumptions.
FILE10.WK1:	Produces a standard set of financial statements.
FILE11.WK1:	Prints a standard questionnaire for use in producing a manufacturing departmental business plan.

System Requirements:

This diskette requires an IBM PC or compatible computer with the following:

* DOS 3.1 or later
* 256K RAM
* Lotus 1-2-3 2.0 or higher

Instead of using Lotus 1-2-3, you may use any spreadsheet program that reads Lotus 1-2-3 version 2.0 files; for example, Excel or Quattro. All spreadsheet files are listed above with the extension WK1.

The spreadsheet files on this disk assume use of an Epson or Epson look-alike printer with compressed print mode capability. You are urged to consult your printer manual for compressed print set-up string commands. You can view and change the printer set-up string in Lotus 1-2-3 by pressing these keys: /POS The set-up string which is used for these spreadsheets is /015. If you are using another spreadsheet package, consult your manual for information on compressed printing.

Special Notes:

We strongly recommend that you make a backup copy of this disk immediately upon opening the sealed sleeve. Making a backup will guarantee that you do not accidentally copy over these files while you are working on them. Once you have made a backup copy using the DISKCOPY command in DOS, store the original in a safe place for future reference.

In each of the spreadsheet files on this disk, most of the individual cells are protected to avoid overwriting the formulas. The only unprotected cells in each spreadsheet are those that require data entry. Unprotected cells are usually shaded green (on some monitors, they may appear in a different color than the remainder of the text). You are encouraged to modify the spreadsheets to conform to your company's particular requirements. To do that, you must first disable the cell protect function. Consult your spreadsheet software manual for instructions how to disable the cell protect function.

Instructions:

Instructions for use of the spreadsheets appear at the top of each file. All files initially retrieve the instruction cells the first time they're accessed.

Macros:

Each of the spreadsheets on this disk have two standard macros:

ALT M   This macro moves the cursor to the macro menu.
ALT A   This macro prints the report. Before printing, be sure to calculate the spreadsheet using F9 and to save it!

How to Use This Disk:

Yo use this disk, follow these simple steps:

1. Copy all spreadsheet files to another floppy disk or your hard disk.
2. Load the Lotus 1-2-3 program or a spreadsheet software package that reads Lotus 1-2-3 files.
3. Retrieve the spreadsheet file you would like to work on. Using Lotus 1-2-3, you would press /FR and enter the location and name of the file.
4. Read and follow the instructions that appear on the top of the spreadsheet file.

For more information about using the functions for your particular spreadsheet package, consult your software manual. The original disk is a no-notch read only disk. You must make and use a backup copy of the disk in order to modify the files. You can get a 3½" disk if you send in your 5¼" disk.